WITHDRAWN BY THE
UNIVERSITY OF MICHIGAN

A Bridge Too Far?

A Bridge Too Far?

Commonalities and Differences between China and the United States

Edited by Robert Grafstein and Fan Wen

LEXINGTON BOOKS

A division of
ROWMAN & LITTLEFIELD PUBLISHERS, INC.
Lanham • Boulder • New York • Toronto • Plymouth, UK

LEXINGTON BOOKS

A division of Rowman & Littlefield Publishers, Inc.
A wholly owned subsidiary of The Rowman & Littlefield Publishing Group, Inc.
4501 Forbes Boulevard, Suite 200
Lanham, MD 20706

Estover Road
Plymouth PL6 7PY
United Kingdom

Copyright © 2009 by Lexington Books

All rights reserved. No part of this publication may be reproduced, stored in a retrieval system, or transmitted in any form or by any means, electronic, mechanical, photocopying, recording, or otherwise, without the prior permission of the publisher.

British Library Cataloguing in Publication Information Available

Library of Congress Cataloging-in-Publication Data

A bridge too far? : commonalities and differences between China and the United States / edited by Robert Grafstein and Fan Wen.
   p. cm.
Includes bibliographical references and index.
ISBN-13: 978-0-7391-2887-9 (cloth : alk. paper)
ISBN-10: 0-7391-2887-6 (cloth : alk. paper)
ISBN-13: 978-0-7391-3604-1 (electronic)
ISBN-10: 0-7391-3604-6 (electronic)
  1. China—Politics and government—21st century. 2. United States—Foreign relations—China. 3. China—Foreign relations—United States. I. Grafstein, Robert, 1948– II. Fan, Wen, 1956–
JQ1510.B75 2009
320.951—dc22   2008050919

Printed in the United States of America

∞™ The paper used in this publication meets the minimum requirements of American National Standard for Information Sciences—Permanence of Paper for Printed Library Materials, ANSI/NISO Z39.48-1992.

Contents

Note on Citation Styles   vii

Introduction   ix
    Robert Grafstein and Fan Wen

Part I: Democracy and Political Reform

1. Democracy in China? Go Figure   3
    Robert Grafstein

2. Public Administration Reform in China   35
    Fan Wen

3. Grassroots Democracy in China: A Comparative Study of Villagers' and Residents' Committees   51
    Jianfeng Wang

4. Hayek and the *Daodejing* on Order and Coercion   73
    Daniel Kapust

Part II: The Rule of Law

5. Legal Reform in China   97
    John Anthony Maltese

6. China's Intellectual Property Rights Protection and Sino-U.S. Relations   121
    Qingtang Kong

Part III: Interest Groups and the Policy Process

7 Interests, Groups, and Information Aggregation 137
   Scott H. Ainsworth and Ruoxi Li

8 China's Environmental Protection and Sino-U.S.
   Cooperation 161
   Shan Ningzhen

9 The Development of the Public Service in China 179
   Chen Xingbo

Part IV: International Relations

10 Reciprocity and Adaptation in Post–Cold War U.S.-China
   Foreign Policy Interactions 193
   Xiaojun Li

Index 219

About the Contributors 223

Note on Citation Styles

Readers will notice that the chapters written by Chinese-trained scholars tend not to use the form of endnotes and associated citations employed by those scholars trained in the United States. In this respect, these Chinese-trained scholars reflect a more traditional style of Chinese scholarship, which is marked by a general willingness to borrow and incorporate the ideas of others without attribution.[1] As chapter 6 details, China is slowly adopting the concepts of individual ownership and intellectual property rights. The Chinese academy is slowly reflecting this change as well.

NOTE

1. See, for example, Joel Bloch and Lan Chi, 1995, "A Comparison of the Use of Citations in Chinese and English Academic Discourse," in *Academic Writing in a Second Language*, ed. Diane Belcher and George Braine (Norwood, NJ: Ablex).

Introduction

Robert Grafstein and Fan Wen

The actions of great nations often provoke strong and dramatic reactions. When two such nations, China and the United States, occupy the world stage at the same time, an observer is apt to assume that their different policies and strategic positions reflect fundamental national differences. National differences often worry people. Moreover, since China and the United States pursue influence, natural resources, markets, and allies separately, not jointly, it is often assumed that a deep political, cultural, and social chasm must separate them. To many observers, this is even more troubling.

But we must be careful not to over-interpret the behavior of these important countries. Appearances can be deceptive. In international trade, for example, appearances suggest a deep strategic rivalry between China as an exporter and the United States as an importer. Basic economic theory, however, tells us that buyer and seller are in a cooperative relationship: it is either mutually beneficial or there is no exchange. Indeed when countries are the same in this arena there can be more tension than when countries are different.

So what are we to make of the differences separating China and the United States and the traits they share? All we know is that quick answers to this very important question are likely to be wrong. China and the United States are overlapping societies. They are not entirely different; certainly they are not the same. The purpose of this volume is to help sort out how they overlap and how they differ so we can begin a clear-eyed assessment of how China and the United States can prosper at the same time on the same planet.

Addressing Sino-American differences and commonalities takes more than assembling facts and data bearing on the two countries. The data are simply insufficiently articulate on their own. At some level of abstraction, everything points to commonalities between China and the United States. After all, (social) scientific generalization would be hopeless if different things could not be wrestled into a smaller set of descriptive boxes. At midlevel, China and the United States are a bundle of differences and commonalities. Finally, at some level of detail everything starts to look different. Ultimately, this would be true if one were comparing China in 2000 and in 2008 or comparing the United States in 2000 and in 2008.

The obvious conclusion is that, trite as it may seem and without intending any relativism about truth, comparisons depend heavily on perspective. This is one reason we believe the current volume has special value. Some of the scholars contributing to it are China specialists, others specialize in American politics, while others are political economists or political theorists who are not involved directly in area studies. Some are academically trained but work in the area of environmental regulation or are legal advisors for state-owned enterprises. All see commonalities beyond the obvious and deep differences between the two nations.

Although one section of this book focuses on Sino-American relations and foreign policy, the book is about the United States and China, not about foreign policy or international relations per se. Rather, the plan of attack is for scholars from outside China to examine Chinese politics and political theory in relation to United States through the lens of homegrown theories, and for Chinese scholars to offer their own more detailed examination of specific policy areas related to China, often with direct comparisons with the United States, and thereby confirm or contest the broader analysis offered by their outsider counterparts.

Put another way, the plan is not to bring together Chinese and American China specialists. This would be a perfectly reasonable thing to do and has often been done in the past. It could profitably reveal the different perspectives insiders and outsiders bring to their study of the same subject matter. However, this tack also may offer a less revealing or even jarring juxtaposition of views and approaches since both sets of scholars would have spent their professional lifetimes immersed in the study of the same subject matter, reading many of the same sources and primary materials.

The differences we care about in this book are not the product of differences of national or ethnic background among scholars in the same arena. Rather, we are interested in exploring the differences that emerge due to differences in analytical, theoretical, and philosophical approaches and perspectives regardless of actual national or ethnic identity. Accordingly, the outsiders are not defined by nationality but by their approach to the analysis of politics of any sort.

Specifically, the academic identities of the outsiders were forged not through the study of Chinese politics but through the modern political scientific and philosophical approaches, methodologies, theories, and models they bring to bear when they study politics of any kind. The hallmark of the approach each takes is that it was defined and developed independently of specific Chinese studies and therefore was formed outside the matrix of readings, panels, roundtables, and courses devoted to that one subject. This is a strength and, no doubt, also a weakness, but it offers a new possibility for discovering things.

By contrast, the insiders offer skills and techniques of scholarship as taught in China mostly about China. But what is also special is their insight and insider's knowledge of and concern about the actual policies, political developments, institutional changes, and challenges China has experienced. As readers will quickly discover, their analyses, however detailed, factual, and analytical the scholarship, offer a clear contrast with the more cold-eyed analytical approach of the outsiders. In addition to scholarly understanding, the insiders are also passionately interested in their country's prospects and achievements in a less than detached way. It also should be said that while they do not ignore China's weaknesses and policy failures, they are also interested in defending it against some of the criticisms made by American policymakers and both implicitly and explicitly in much U.S. scholarship.

This dialog in writing has followed face-to-face interactions between many of these American and Chinese scholars. The dialog began in 2003 when the American coeditor, who was spending a month in China as an exchange scholar funded by the U.S. Department of State, was giving a lecture in Beijing where he met Fan Wen. Fan had already been involved with the University of Georgia as part of a program to train Chinese administrators. During one of Grafstein's subsequent trips to China, which since 2003 have occurred at least once a year, he suggested collaboration on the present volume. Grafstein has met with the other Chinese participants and most of the American contributors have also had fairly lengthy stays in China.

Of special note, the background of the Chinese contributors alone makes their contributions worthy of attention. Fan Wen is a professor in the Department of Political Science at the China National School of Public Administration, a key think tank for the government. Indeed Wen has served as a consultant at the highest levels of government. Another Chinese contributor is a research fellow at Beijing University's School of Law, still another was assistant director of the Daning Environmental Protection Bureau in Shanxi, and one is the legal director at a major state-owned enterprise. Finally, Jiangfeng Wang is director of the China Governance and Development Program at the University of Georgia and has been involved with numerous training and exchange programs between the United States and China.

So the Chinese scholars participating in this project not only can claim insider knowledge in the nominal sense that they have live in China. They have participated in many of the government and state-connected sectors and reform efforts that students of China study. To an extent one can say that these contributors are academically trained examples of the types of people China scholars often seek to interview in their own research.

As soon as one broaches the possibility of a comparing China and the United States, political scientists will naturally think about democracy: the United States is democratic and China is not. But this is the short, not the long of it. Obviously, China is a complex of political arrangements, some of which have been changing in a democratic direction right before our eyes. As discussed in this book, China is developing a serious legal system. It is increasingly recognizing the importance of intellectual and other property rights (true, some of this is due to outside pressure, but it was China's decision to dramatically reverse its isolationist economic position, increase the role of markets, and to accept the conditions for accession into the World Trade Organization). Elections of village and residents' committees have become standard. The administration of government is changing and becoming more professional and rule-bound, and experts have an increasingly influential role. Western democratic theories and ideas embodied in books and articles are increasingly imported, translated into Chinese, and discussed in policy circles. The environment has been recognized as the pressing issue it is. There is growing consideration of ways to introduce intra-party democracy. And most dramatically and most notably, a large market-based economy creates the potential for a very real source of de facto power outside the ruling party, a potential stressed long ago by Milton Friedman in his *Capitalism and Freedom* but understood and sometimes feared by Chinese leaders.

This is not to say that the right way to see China is through rose-colored glasses, even if the right way to see China is no longer through red-colored glasses. China is not only authoritarian but there are many ways in which China has not moved toward democracy, even ways in which China has moved in recent years away from democracy. Indeed in his chapter, the American coeditor offers a fairly negative assessment of China's democratic prospects.

But the reverse mistake is to assess the Chinese political system against a democratic ideal-type. Avoiding this mistake is not only a matter of recognizing that no democracy is perfect and therefore no government moving in a democratic direction will be perfect. It also means recognizing that there may be fundamental ways in which democracies operate in practice that do not fit the ideal, not simply ways that provide interesting copy for journalists and unseat arrogant or greedy politicians.

Thus at the conclusion of Grafstein's chapter on China's democratic prospects he points out similarities between the United States in practice and China in practice that reflect the extent to which authoritarian governments react to pressure from outside the government thus functionally mirroring the reactions of democratic governments. Protests and even the threat of insurrection are blunt instruments for getting government to respond to felt needs, but in net effect these political weapons may produce the same policy responses. The main example given in the Grafstein chapter is social security, which is a particularly pressing problem in China due to its aging population and transition from state-owned enterprises. But social security is not the only example of functional parallels. To put the point more abstractly, some cross-national noninstitutional facts about policy may become obscured by an exclusive focus on institutions and elite selection mechanisms.

Some institutional facts may likewise transcend the form of government. As Ainsworth and Li's chapter details, special interest groups play a significant role in Chinese policymaking, which is true for the United States as the perennial animadversions of American politicians against the special interests suggest. The important issue here is not whether pressure groups violate the democratic ideal. The issue is whether serious and careful assessments of Chinese politics will recognize these commonalities when exploring how China's political system functions and how different it really is compared to democratic systems.

Accordingly, the first and a major section of this book is "Democracy and Political Reform." All chapters in this section are about China directly, with the United States entering as a point of comparison and a source of analytic material. Analysis ranges from the level of the political system as a whole, which highlights China as an authoritarian government whose rulers want to preserve their power if possible, down to the level of the peasant village at which elections and accountability are beginning to look normal.

Robert Grafstein explores the historical development of the Chinese political system and the prospects for political democracy in contemporary China. Noting important political continuities across China's long history, but eschewing cultural explanations for them, his analysis makes use of Daron Acemoglu and James A. Robinson's path-breaking work, *Economic Origins of Dictatorship and Democracy*. Oddly, although they apply their explanation for the rise of democracy and dictatorship to many different countries, China seems to evade their net. This is odd since China offers an excellent illustration of the power of their analysis.

In effect, Chinese governments with small exceptions seem to have entertained only two alternative strategies for dealing with citizens. One alternative to suppress, the other is to make policy concessions. But concessions that alter the fundamental distribution of resources, as Acemoglu and Robinson emphasize, are not credible if they are needed only to conciliate a transient eruption. The government would renege as soon as it was safe to do so. So if suppression were to become too costly, the government would be forced to appease the population by making credible concessions institutionalized in the form of democracy. Democracy arises, or would arise in China, when the cost of suppression exceeds the expected losses by the elite when democracy takes hold. This process, Acemoglu and Robinson suggest, accounts for the development of American democracy early in its history. The same calculation, Grafstein argues using Chinese history and contemporary circumstances, accounts for democracy's absence in China.

There is a core political logic to democratization, whether in China or the United States. In the second chapter Fan Wen argues that the institutionalization of concessions in China has progressed notwithstanding notable problems of corruption and its undeveloped system of law. China's governing theory has changed to support service to people and limited government. Greater transparency has been the byproduct of simplifying the organs of state. In the State Council, for example, there are twenty-nine units compared to ninety-three in 1993. In 2004 the Council explicitly committed itself to promoting the rule of law within a decade. Fan explores other ways in which creeping democracy is taking root, including further limits on "administrative licensing" to allow the resolution of problems by citizens and by enterprises and markets, and many other changes. Finally, in addition to the numerous administrative and political reforms Fan details, he emphasizes that the elite National School of Administration not only engages in exchanges of civil servants with the United States but also recognizes the important contributions Western political philosophy, with its focus on individualism, can make to Chinese political thought, both academic and practical.

While discussions of democratic development in China must confront the basic institutional structure of this large and important country, it is possible for the analysis to lose the trees for the forest, so to speak. Much of the genuine innovative democratic change taking place in China occurs at the local level. In his chapter, Jianfeng Wang notes that while there is serious dialog between the United States and China over trade, energy, international incidents, and related areas, constructive dialog over political values and practices has been difficult at best. Is there any common ground within this disputed terrain? The commonalities, Wang argues, can be found at the grassroots level. He focuses on the Villagers' Committees in the rural areas and the Residents' Committees in the cities. Both organizations provide a vehicle through which individuals can manage community affairs. These organizations are not technically part of the government, but the law explicitly requires that membership be determined democratically through local elections. Wang describes in detail the structure of these organizations and their mode of governance. His aim is to evaluate the progress of grassroots democracy through these organizations.

This evaluation is conducted against the background of China's rapid transition from a planned to a market economy, and from a totalitarian to an authoritarian form of government at the national level. The chapter concludes by comparing grassroots self-governance in the United States and China. Wang is particularly well-suited to make this comparison since he is a native of China who continues to work as an advisor, teacher, and consultant there, but is employed at the University of Georgia's Carl Vinson Institute of Government, which has a strong exchange and training program with China, yet its primary role is training and grassroots development in the state of Georgia.

Taking up a theme developed in Fan's chapter, Daniel J. Kapust focuses on the relation between Chinese and Western philosophy. Given the significant presence of both Confucian and Marxist ideas in Chinese thought, it is often assumed that a significant division exists between Chinese and American values. Whereas American political thought is viewed as both individualistic and marked by an emphasis on competition and pluralism, Chinese thought is viewed as collectivist and marked by an emphasis on cooperation and harmony. Because many view American democracy as rooted in the European Enlightenment values of individualism, competition, and pluralism, it is often held that "American values," such as individual rights, privacy, and government by consent, are alien to the Chinese tradition.

Yet one of the ironies of American political thought is that the leaders and writers of the America Revolutionary era looked to the past in their effort to create a new order. Themes of corruption, virtue, liberty, and tyranny, rooted in Greek and Roman history and political thought, played a powerful role in fomenting the Revolution. So, too, did distinctive English notions of liberty and constitutionalism, in particular Whig theories of politics and freedom. Given the powerful role played by classical thought and classically influenced writers in the development of American political thought, Kapust's chapter compares the classically informed intellectual currents of American political thought to classical Chinese thought (Confucianism, Daoism, and Legalism). In doing so, the chapter explores the relationship between American political thought and Chinese thought, with a particular emphasis on notions of legitimacy, happiness, and power.

The second section takes up "The Rule of Law." John Maltese addresses legal reform in China. He focuses on recent reforms of the Chinese legal system designed, in part, to implement the "rule of law." In many respects, this reform is extraordinary. As recently as 1978, China lacked any meaningful legal system: its existing constitution amounted to little more than a collection of political slogans, there was neither a comprehensive criminal code nor a system of civil law, and in a nation of nearly one billion people there were only about 2,000 lawyers. Economic reform initiated in 1979 spurred legal development in China as well. Deng Xiaoping recognized that a legal system was an essential component of economic reform, and in 1980 the National People's Congress enacted the Provisional Regulations on Lawyers with the specific goal of developing a legal profession. Given China's longstanding antipathy to law and lawyers (rooted, at least in part, in its Confucian tradition), this was a major step.

Today, less than thirty years later, China has a formal legal system with an extensive body of criminal, civil, and administrative law; its constitution explicitly embraces the rule of law and, at least in theory, protects such basic rights as freedom of expression and normal religious activity; and the legal profession is thriving, law schools have proliferated, and there are now over 150,000 lawyers. Maltese's chapter examines the reforms that have led to these dramatic changes.

Despite this remarkable progress, Maltese notes, significant obstacles still stand in the way of full implementation of the rule of law. With regard to the legal profession itself, shortages of lawyers continue to be a problem, many people in China cannot afford them, and—despite efforts to improve their training in the 1996 Lawyers Law—many lawyers remain underqualified. There are also broader systemic barriers that hinder the full implementation of the rule of law. These include the lack of judicial independence, corruption, and violations of procedural due process. Moreover, basic liberties (such as freedom of speech and religion) remain underdeveloped despite constitutional language to the contrary.

Can these and other obstacles be overcome? Can the rule of law take root in China without more sweeping reforms of the government itself? This chapter examines the progress made toward legal reform in China, assesses additional steps that need to be taken, and compares the Western conception of the rule of law with what exists in China today.

As a basic component of the modern rule of law, intellectual property rights loom large in China's future as a developing nation and, due to the stream of technical and product innovations emerging from the United States, the future of Sino-American relations. In his chapter Qingtang Kong reviews intellectual property protection in China during the last twenty years, including advances as well as serious weaknesses and their causes. He then turns to the history of disputes between the United States and China over intellectual property protection and the impact these disputes have had on the broader relationship between the two countries. The chapter concludes with a review of academic opinion in China concerning the necessity, possibility, and future of Sino-American cooperation on intellectual property. Throughout, Qingtang Kong relies on his extensive experience as the legal director for a large state-owned Chinese company.

Politics in China and the United States is more than institutional structure and law. The next section, therefore, focuses on "Interest Groups and the Policy Process." A crude way to characterize the need for this kind of analysis is to say that political scientists studying China and the United States study very different political systems but still study politics in both cases. But special interest lobbying is a feature of both countries, as groups both inside and outside government influence policy outside official channels (official nondemocratic channels in China, official electoral channels in the United States). We can see this in certain particular policy areas, such as China's policy response to its environmental problems, and contrast this response, in terms of substance and approach, with the United States. Similarly, one can ask whether China is adapting to these pressures by instituting specific administrative and official institutional changes pointing toward a more efficient and responsive government.

Scott Ainsworth and Ruoxi Li focus on the role of interest groups in China and the United States. There are considerable and obvious differences between the politics of China and the United States, the most obvious being the democratic electoral system that determines America's political leaders. However, one must distinguish between the process determining America's leaders and the process determining America's policies. For scholars have long noted the important role interest groups play in the United States and indeed Gary Becker has argued that elections are less influential in determining policy than are the pressure groups seeking help, benefits, and special treatment.

Moreover, the governing structures of the United States and China have certain characteristics in common. Particularly noteworthy are federalism in the United States and the structural forms *tiao*, *kuai*, and *tiao/kuai guanxi* in China. Perhaps the simplest definition of federalism is that it is a governing structure with at least two hierarchical levels with shared decision-making authority over the same geographic areas. Federalism in the United States creates a web of complex relationships that sometimes impedes coherent policy implementation. Policy implementation in China is similarly affected by vertical relations (*tiao*), horizontal relations (*kuai*), and the web or matrix of vertical and horizontal relations (*tiao/kuai guanxi*). In each country there is a clear formal hierarchy to maintain consistency and order, but there is also recognition that some issues might best be handled at the lower levels. Efficiency demands that lower levels have some autonomy, but fairness and consistency require that authority be established at the top of the hierarchy. When interest groups become political interest groups, they must navigate these complex institutional structures. Moreover, the history of both countries suggests that the relative authority of the levels changes over time, often in dramatic ways.

After introductory material establishing the rationale for comparing groups and group activity in China and the United States, Ainsworth and Li focus on basic topics. First, the chapter develops a theory of competing interest group demands based on the Madisonian view of factions. Second, they explore how political interest groups aggregate information. Every government relies on information related to the governed. Indeed information is widely considered a central problem for governments lacking democratic feedback. Yet all governments have other vital sources of information. To be sure, government bureaucracies can gather and aggregate information, but there are also nongovernmental sources.

The second section of this chapter examines the information aggregation characteristics of political interest groups, comparing and contrasting those characteristics with bureaucracies, elections, and markets. The third section of this chapter addresses the conduits for information. If the government seeks information from bureaucracies, elections, markets, or interest groups, then there must be established channels for the information flows. In any society, government officials typically have the upper hand in this regard because they are able to regulate the conduits for information. Channels for communication can be opened or closed. Of more interest is how a government can screen information, separating good information from bad: everyone recognizes that information from political interest groups, as well as bureaucracies, markets, and even elections, may be faulty or biased.

The final section explores the means by which government officials can screen information from political interest groups. To the extent the government can screen information communicated by these groups, interest groups become valuable entities for a state and its governance. This is a common challenge for China and the United States.

As noted above, one critical area where Chinese policy has collided with the influence of special interests is environmental protection. Shan Ningzhen focuses on this issue. She traces China's participation in international environmental institutions, including treaties. In a very candid discussion, she pays special attention to the substantial environmental problems China faces, including the problem of environmental justice. She argues that due to these problems cooperation with the United States is crucial. After detailing current Chinese environmental policy and practice—pollution control, ecologically sensitive agriculture, returning land to the farmers—and describing the important personalities involved in national and local environmental protection, she analyzes current Sino-American cooperation and the prospects for the future.

Chen Xingbo pursues the policy theme with a more detailed discussion of current forms of Sino-American cooperation related to poverty reduction, AIDS, sustainable development, healthcare, sanitation, and social security. Chen discusses up-to-date material from the central and provincial governments regarding these forms of cooperation.

While the main focus of this introduction has been Chinese domestic politics and domestic similarities and differences with the United States, it is impossible to ignore the international relations dimension, if only because key domestic developments, such as intellectual property rights law, apparently have been influenced by the United States both directly in the form of diplomatic and legal pressure, and indirectly as well to aid China's economic development through direct foreign investment and trade.

But it turns out that international relations specialists are not agreed, as a general theoretical proposition, on whether countries formulate their foreign policies based primarily on internal politics, in reaction to the foreign policies of other nations, or as a rational strategy based on national interests and rational expectations about the future policy of other nations. The final section of the book tackles Sino-American Relations with this concern in mind.

Thus for all the emphasis on changes in China and the need for a common analytic framework to assess the politics of China and the United States, it would be a mistake to focus on the two countries as though their histories unfolded in parallel isolation. Xiaojung Li uses advanced statistical time series techniques to analyze the subtle dynamics by which China and the United States have each influenced the other's foreign policy. He uses a large data set of international dyadic events involving the two nations over a long period to test different theories that have been proposed to explain dyadic relations in general, and draws some conclusions about international relations theories and about Sino-American relations in general. While Li finds some support for all three forces influencing policy the clearest confirmation is for the idea that for both countries internal bureaucratic political processes determine foreign policy. Note by the way that Li exemplifies the point made above that approach and perspective are not a simple matter of national or ethnic identity. Li is a native of Shanghai, but his contribution reflects much more of Palo Alto.

His interesting findings not only suggest important limitations on the ability of one nation's foreign policy to influence another's. They also remind us that our emphasis on domestic politics in this book is not as restrictive as it might first appear. It may be that understanding Chinese domestic politics, U.S. domestic politics, and their similarities and commonalities may offer the best way to understand Chinese-U.S. relations. In other words, a better understanding of both political systems may offer the best chance of understanding each political system. And an understanding of each political system may offer the best hope of understanding their international relations.

Indeed we hope this book and the collaboration it reflects also represent the first event in a scholarly time series involving dyadic relations between Chinese and American scholars. More broadly, we want this book to become part of its own subject matter by integrating the work of Chinese and American scholars, most of whom have interacted directly and some of whom personally bridge the U.S.-China divide. Without intentionally skimping on its theoretical or academic value, the book in the end is deeply concerned with promoting better understanding and cooperation.

As we have noted, some of the key contributors are academically trained but also major policy advisors to the Chinese government and practitioners in government and business. They understand their contributions not only as discussions of the United States and China in the abstract but as highly symbolic contributions to the furthering of Sino-American relations. We hope that students, academics, policymakers, and policy advisors, therefore, will all find value in this bridging of the academic and practical.

I
DEMOCRACY AND POLITICAL REFORM

1

Democracy in China? Go Figure

Robert Grafstein

Calculating whether China will ever become a democracy has become a popular pastime among policymakers, scholars, and ordinary citizens. The issue has become something of a Rorschach test, revealing the different perspectives different observers use in making their calculations. Economic determinists, of course, tend to be hopeful; students of Chinese history less so; philosophers are driven into the arms of their favorite western democratic theorists or Laozi and Confucius; taxonomists explore distinctions between one-party democracy and multiparty democracy; and so on. One thing is clear. Figuring out the prospects for Chinese democracy is not a purely empirical enterprise. It requires figuring out what conceptual or theoretical framework works best for addressing the issue.

And sometimes it requires more than disinterring a framework. As a value-laden idea, democracy often connotes the best politics has to offer and, accordingly, it has been adopted as a normative ideal by many Chinese intellectuals and reformers. To make matters even more complicated, the democratic normative ideal can serve as its own causal influence and therefore is also employed by scholars wanting to assess the empirical prospects for democracy in China. Thus in his attempt to explain the absence of democracy in China, Zhao (2000, 33–51) complains that one reason democracy has not gotten a solid foothold in China is that too often Chinese intellectuals have treated it not as a value in itself but as an "instrument" to further other goals like national strength and prosperity, an instrument they discarded when better political tools seemed more promising.

The analysis in this chapter likewise stands guilty of treating democracy purely as an instrument. If democracy comes to China, this chapter will argue, it will not arrive as a gift from government, a revelation, from the felt need to be philosophically consistent, out of belated recognition of the demands of justice, in response to popular demand, certainly not because the United States or the so-called international community will someday choose to apply unrelenting pressure on China to get it to democratize, or because China's leaders will become virtuous in ways their predecessors were not.[1] It will arrive, if it does, because the organized interests that matter at the time have decided that democracy as a means of settling disagreements is by their lights superior to all the alternative ways to advance their interests, including adherence to the status quo, repression, outright military assault, or resistance. If war is politics by other means, politics is also war by other means.

While I cannot canvass all competing explanations for the potential rise or future failure of democracy, my interest-based, instrumental approach stands in obvious contrast to a values-based one.[2] Values and culture, many argue, ultimately determine what kind of political system a country is likely to have. If ever a country begged for such an explanation, it is China (although see, e.g., de Bary 1983). With five thousand years of history and at best roughly two years of very tenuous democracy in the aftermath of the Nationalist Revolution of 1911, it is tempting to see the failure of Chinese democracy as rooted in a continuity of (Confucian) values underneath the continuity of Chinese history.[3]

A careful attention to the role of interests and rational actors within institutions was the hallmark of the American Founders' analysis, particularly Madison's cold-eyed assessment of democracy and the republican form of government. The same focus applies across borders. As I hope to show at the conclusion of this chapter, this approach will also indicate ways in which political convergence between the United States and China does not depend simply on whether China becomes a democracy. It will turn out that there is more than one significant way to converge.

CHINESE POLITICAL HISTORY

Imperial China saw peasant revolts, Mongol, Manchu, Western, and Japanese invasions, luminous dynasties and visionary emperors, and less luminous time-servers. Through it all, however, what emerged was inevitably an authoritarian ruler, often a powerful bureaucracy, and a large, economically desperate, and politically subservient peasant majority.

Why this continuity? To put the question simply, why in effect did society obey the emperor? To affirm its Confucian cultural values? The old joke—Why did the chicken cross the road?—is a joke (not all jokes are funny) because the punch line answer is so empty. While the typical values explanation for continuity is not as highly condensed and certainly is not meant to be a joke, it is close to being empirically empty as well. It also fails to account for the large number of peasant revolts and political disruptions in Chinese history. Moreover, its comfort with continuity becomes a burden when new circumstances arise or old alternatives disappear, both of which have occurred in China during the imperial period, after 1911, after 1949, and since 1978. These discontinuities are fatal to the cultural explanations. As the Nobel laureate Robert E. Lucas has remarked, habit will explain why you take the same route to work each day. But it will not explain or predict your course of action when your normal route is blocked.

I follow Barrington Moore's (1966) argument that the broad continuities of Chinese political-economic history are best explained by broad political-economic structural continuities. Although sometimes described as feudal (or semi-feudal if one includes later Chinese history; for an interesting discussion see Hozumi 1940), during much of the imperial period China's agricultural society in the substantially more productive south can be characterized as a capitalist form of tenancy with respect to land, familiar in the United States as share-cropping. In the north, fragmented, small farm ownership was the rule (Naughton 2007, 38). Under tenancy, peasants contracted for use of land in return for which they provided a portion of their output. They did not come attached to the land as with feudalism, and financial arrangements were explicitly or implicitly determined prior to the crop cycle. The result may be interpreted by some as exploitive. Certainly bargaining power was typically unequal. But the characteristic *individual* economic relation between peasant and landowner was not directly coercive in any ordinary sense.

In any case, even if there had been complete physical mobility of labor, which there was not, this structure would still exhibit a notable degree of stability. True, landlords in this system received payments simply by virtue of ownership, creating economic rents from their fixed asset. But this entailed unearned transfers of income rather than distortions in effort. Each peasant still had the incentive to maximize production since ownership of the crop is distinct from ownership of the land.[4]

This relative efficiency makes it difficult to argue that in the absence of authoritarian values the stability of the Chinese imperial system would have been particularly threatened by its economic performance during this period. Indeed according to most estimates China in the 1600s had a world-class economy, remembering of course the agricultural division in which all nations at the time competed. Naughton (2007, 35) describes the agricultural system as "highly productive" and notes that Chinese living standards remained close to the world average until the early 1800s.

China succeeded because its high relative performance within the agricultural division required only primitive technology. Given their limited technological options, the principal way for peasants to increase their marginal product was through increased labor. With no more than twenty-four working hours in the day, increased labor ultimately demanded an increased number of laborers. This influenced fertility decisions. As a result of these individual decisions, peasants found themselves facing a collective action problem in which fertility rates designed to maximize individual net income, particularly in old age, led to increased competition for land, which led to high rental prices. High rental prices encouraged high fertility. Thus reproducing peasants also reproduced the conditions of their own weak bargaining position and relative poverty

Still, children are produced, land is not. The long-run demand for land was somewhat elastic, while its supply was perfectly inelastic. Although conventional wisdom assumes that the burden of taxes needed to support the emperor and his government would fall on the weakest in society, the peasants, elementary economics suggests that the tax incidence fell on the inelastic factor, land, and therefore on its owners.[5] For landowners the way out of this economic logic was to derive income from the economy less directly.

In the imperial Chinese economy, agricultural rents were associated with ownership, not skills or labor. Landowners had the time and resources needed to pursue positions in the bureaucracy, although in principle appointments were made on merit and some non-landowners succeeded through the examination system. Ascension into the bureaucracy made a new form of rent available in the form of corruption, which could produce large multiples of a position's official salary. Political rents offset the more modest agricultural rents and burdens of taxation.

In this way landowner and bureaucrat became united in their support for a political-economic arrangement producing an ample supply of able bureaucrats who implemented the government's public works projects, provision of defense, protection of property, and tax collections.[6] Under these political-legal constraints, peasants were limited to making economic and demographic choices rather than decisions about the institutions under which they labored. Acting rationally within these constraints, peasants helped create the structural advantages of the landowners, who as bureaucrats helped solidify that advantage.

This portrait of the basic structure of imperial China is not meant to suggest it was a well-oiled machine in political-economic equilibrium. Political-economic reality, needless to say, was far messier and less stable, and the emperors and their governments differed in important ways. But this core structural insight, I believe, offers a useful antidote to the common view that in the absence of powerful traditional values, China would have been unstable. Put differently, it is unnecessary to appeal to the continuity of values to explain the continuity of China's political-economic system. This does not bode well for a values explanation of China's continuity. For redundancy, in this case, is not a virtue.

The system ultimately did collapse. As we all know, the proximate cause was the external shock of Western and Japanese imperialism. If the preceding analysis is correct, it may have been the deeper cause as well.[7] Seen as a proximate cause, the external shock apparently revealed China's existing structural weakness. It certainly revealed its relative technological weakness. Yet the shock of foreign intrusion actually created the structural weakness in this sense: if China had been left alone the imperial form might have continued for the indeterminate future. It was not inherently unstable, and certainly not inherently unstable simply for being undemocratic.

This is not to celebrate the strength of the late Qing Dynasty. The White Lotus Rebellion (1774–1804), the Taiping Rebellion (1850–1864), the Nian Rebellion (1853–1868), and the Southwest and Northwest Muslim Rebellions (1855–1873 and 1862–1878 respectively) are not the signs of a strong or efficient government. Tens of millions of Chinese died as result of these rebellions and at times the Qing lost control over a large amount of their territory. It is also true that the Qing Dynasty survived these onslaughts. Nor, given the nature of these movements and their leadership, is it clear that if one of them had been successful the government would changed its fundamental character.

Of course, autonomous economic development also could have led to fundamental political change. But not by economics alone. Somehow, individual actors would have to be prompted to make effective collective decisions about the constraints they faced instead of making decisions within those constraints. This involves politics, not just economics.

THE POLITICS OF DEMOCRATIC REVOLUTION

Values were not the real source of political-economic stability in imperial China, nor did they prevent challenges to stability. Chinese history records numerous peasant revolts, some of which were relatively successful although none until 1949 succeeded in altering basic structures. Landowners surmounted the economic constraints of the agricultural system. How were peasants able to challenge the political constraints maintaining the agricultural system? And why were they unable to surmount them decisively?

They did challenge their political constraints, but the episodic nature of peasant revolts provides an important clue about the peasants' ultimate political prospects. The peasants faced a political as well as a demographic collective action problem. Revolts were dangerous, uncertain, and economically costly to produce and sustain over the crop cycle. Each day away from the fields represented a potentially significant loss of income. By the same token, an individual's decision to endure these private costs would not contribute significantly to the likelihood of producing the public good of revolutionary success. I will summarize the vast literature devoted to the collective action problem of rational revolution by saying that in any society revolution is bound to be relatively rare and difficult to sustain (e.g., Lichbach 1995). The geographic isolation of Chinese peasant communities, their poor communication technology, their meager military resources, and a subsistence economy compounded these universal constraints.

In general, the circumstances under which peasants revolted had to be extreme. Natural calamities—cyclones, floods, typhoons, and drought—made peasants desperate and greatly reduced the opportunity costs of abandoning their fields. But extreme conditions are subject to regression to the mean: weather returns to normal, floods subside, the storm season passes, and even emperors are replaced. Peasant revolts could be triggered by particularly harsh natural circumstances and the failure of publicly funded flood control and granary stores to prevent or alleviate the damage adequately.[8] Revolts occurred but the clock was always ticking.

The episodic and transitory nature of revolts put pressure on any peasant movement. Paradoxically, the nature of peasant revolts also placed constraints on the emperor. For promises of reform or economic relief are not particularly credible if the pressure for reform cannot be sustained. Peasants know that once the pressure subsides, the emperor's reforms will subside as well.

So like all dictators under pressure, emperors lacked an obvious means to respond to revolts except through suppression. This is the central insight of Daron Acemoglu and James Robinson's important book, *Economic Origins of Dictatorship and Democracy* (2006). Dictatorships, they argue, may repress but they cannot credibly commit to reform, which ultimately means greater sharing of wealth. Their only alternative to repression is to institutionalize their commitment to reform by creating a democracy. Democracy represents a ceding of discretionary power and therefore a ceding of the power to renege on commitments.

It is surprising that China makes no appearance among the numerous case studies Acemoglu and Robinson (2006) use to illustrate their formal analysis. China's absence probably reflects their own historical knowledge, but unfortunately this lacuna encourages the notion that Asian values or Chinese culture place the emperors and post-imperial governments beyond the realm of standard empirical democratic theory. As already noted, I think this would be a serious mistake. In the remainder of this section, I want to connect Acemoglu and Robinson's analysis to the analytic history already reviewed.

As we have seen, "public order" in China included property and agricultural relations that were economically self-sustaining. This does not mean that these relations could not be transcended or that peasants had no interest in transcending them. Rather, under normal circumstances there was no direct economic mechanism pushing this structure to the breaking point. On the other hand, political pressure from the peasants tended to be relatively temporary and therefore any peasant movement faced the pressure of time and resources. If Acemoglu and Robinson's analysis is correct, both parties to the (potential) political conflict—rulers and ruled—would understand the pressures they and their adversaries were under.

First consider the strategic situation of the peasants. They can accept the status quo or decided to revolt. Choosing to accept the status quo means getting the status quo. The emperor would have no incentive to alter course. The decision to revolt, we have seen, was no simple decision. But under certain extreme circumstances it becomes a live option despite collective action problems. Choosing to revolt presents the emperor with three alternatives. One, he can suppress. In their formal analysis Acemoglu and Robinson assume that suppression always succeeds (although see Acemoglu and Robinson 2006, 215–18). However, it succeeds at great economic cost. Therefore the emperors' nonmilitary alternatives are also real options.

Promising reform to produce economic relief is one nonmilitary option. If chosen, peasants, in turn, can respond to the offer by ending their revolt or continuing. Continuing would reinstate the original situation, effectively negating the reform option. If, on the other hand, the peasants end their insurgency the emperor would now face two new alternatives: continue to implement reform or renege on the promise. Since the insurgency would have ended, the emperor would no longer have any motivation to implement reform and he would renege, or at least renege at the first favorable opportunity. So reform in this simple model is not a credible option.

This analysis, of course, assumes that peasants are as strategically adept as the emperor. They recognize that acceptance of reform produces the status quo ante, not fundamental change. Their effective options reduce to revolt and quiescence. Yet the emperor also appreciates the strategic problem the peasants face. Promises of reform have no impact on the peasants' calculations. From the emperor's perspective, this means that his only effective alternative to suppression is to produce a commitment device that makes his own reneging much more costly if not impossible. Democracy is such a device.

According to this analysis, democratization represents a dramatic political change primarily serving an economic purpose. Economically speaking, democracy is redistributive. Or to use the disparaging language of the American Founders, democracy has leveling tendencies. In particular, since the majority of people in imperial China, as in every contemporary society for which we have data, had below-average incomes, even the most radical redistribution scheme—taxing all income and rebating the revenue in equal lump-sum amounts—would secure popular support. In short, when the elites accede to democracy they flirt with financial disaster. Note that this disaster is larger, the greater the existing degree of inequality. When the elites have farther to fall as a result of redistribution, their resistance to democracy will be greater.

Extending the theme of redistribution, Boix (2003) notes that a fixed asset—specifically, property in land—is more vulnerable to redistribution than a mobile asset like capital. Accordingly, countries dominated by landowning elites are less likely to become democratic than are countries dominated by industrial and particularly financial interests. At the very least, democratization is more likely to be painful. When assets are mobile, the threat of capital flight will deter extensive redistribution and therefore the prospect of democracy will be easier for the elites to bear.

In all cases, the emperor would accede to democracy only if the alternative were worse. As noted above, Acemoglu and Robinson simplify their model by assuming that suppression is always possible, but only at some large, fixed cost. It is more realistic to assume that uncertainty about the outcome of suppression may make the economic losses associated with democracy potentially less threatening than defeat on the battlefield. The balance of military force induces political compromise.

Acemoglu and Robinson characterize this compromise as the institutionalization of democracy. It is difficult to know exactly what this means. The compromise is as strong and persistent as the interests and calculations creating and sustaining it. The parties to the compromise determine the institution. The institution does not determine them.[9]

Put another way, the rules of democratic behavior do not constrain the parties simply by virtue of their being rules, or even because they are the rules on which the parties agreed.[10] They characterize political behavior in democracies insofar as they reasonably well describe the behavior of the parties in democracies.[11] Of course, there are often enormous transactions costs to breeching the compromise and accepting the uncertainty of renewed bargaining and struggle (Shepsle 1989). But as Goldberg (1985) argues, this makes the transactions costs standing in the way of institutional change no different than the costs facing anyone comparing more uncertain and less uncertain alternatives. Institutions do not become special forces in the environment (Grafstein 1992).

Much of the political science literature, of course, is inclined to see a values or cultural consensus as the glue maintaining institutions and their rules. However, citing studies by Almond and Verba (1965); Inglehart (1990); and Granato, Inglehart, and Leblang (1996) that attempt to use democratic values to explain the stability of democracies, Przeworski (2006) counters that "there is not a shred of evidence that the answers [to questions about democratic attitudes] have anything to do with the actual survival of democracy."

I should say parenthetically that the values perspective, nonetheless, is hard to resist. Przeworski's (2006, 316) own analysis of democracy, based on Przeworski (2005) and Benhabib and Przeworski (2006), assumes that "even if we allow that the losers in the conflict over dictatorship may suffer more, we also allow that everyone may dislike dictatorship to some extent" because at a sufficiently high level of income "the additional gain that would accrue from being able to dictate redistribution becomes too small to overcome the loss of freedom."

But it is not clear in what sense dictators lose *their* freedom or whether someone who aspires to dictatorship possibly relishes freedom in some broader egalitarian sense. It is much more plausible to think of aspiring dictators as restrained by the prospect of operating in a political framework in which political losses in the future make them subject to dictatorship.

Consider Qín Shǐ Huáng, who established his leadership of the first unified empire of China in 211 B.C. During his reign, all of China became governed by the Qin system of private landowning and a uniform system of laws and taxation. He began construction on the precursor to the Great Wall and numerous road and canal projects. In a further effort to insure stability, he ordered the burning of philosophical works and histories from other states. But in addition to the extraordinary toll on the peasants these public works and other projects exacted, the emperor reportedly ordered killed all 700,000 workers who built his famed tomb in Xi'an to keep the tomb a secret. It is doubtful that this emperor valued the freedom of others or labored under some residual cultural concern for freedom. If he did not, it is unclear when the transition to a different kind of emperor took place.

Similarly, public works and imposed ideological uniformity did not adequately compensate for the demands the emperor placed on the peasants. In order to the forestall unrest arising from any sign of weakening government capacity, the emperor's foreign minister felt it necessary to cover up his death until the imperial court had returned to the capital. Even so, by 206 B.C. the Qin Dynasty had crumbled. Reischauer and Fairbank (1960, 91) write, "The sudden collapse of the Ch'in should not be attributed solely to a failure of leadership. A more basic reason was that the new empire lacked the support of the vast majority of the people over which it ruled with such severe rigidity." But the issue, they note, was not a simple loss of legitimacy, a failure to mesh existing values with the new form of government. "The constant drafting of men for campaigns abroad and construction work at home made the new imperial order seem less desirable than the old inter-state anarchy." In this respect, the Qin Dynasty created the basis for a new institutional form, but in the process made itself functionally equivalent to a natural disaster.

CHINESE REVOLUTIONS

China's dynastic history came to an end in 1912. The Nationalist Revolution, however, did not produce democracy. If the analysis in the preceding sections is correct, what doomed democracy was not so much the strength of those defending the old order but their weakness. If the Qing Dynasty had been in a position to suppress the rebels at relatively small cost or with a fair degree of certainty, it would have. If suppression were possible but too costly or too uncertain it would have been induced to compromise, perhaps by creating a democracy "institutionalizing" its loss of power. Too weak to put up real resistance *or* to interest its opponents in anything less than total victory, the Qing Dynasty could not win and could not compromise. It collapsed.

The Qing Dynasty could not compromise; most of those attempting to pick up the post-revolution pieces would not. Without going into the maneuvering of the various Nationalist factions that eventually emerged, the so-called warlords, and the attempt by Yuan Shikai to reconstitute the imperial system, we can summarize the entire tragic period by noting another external shock, duly provided by the Japanese, leading to the overthrow of the post-dynastic order and the total victory of the communist revolution in 1949 (see, e.g., Eastman 2001).

Mancur Olson's (1982) explanation of why major socioeconomic change, although rare, can occur suggests one reason why this second revolution in 1949 was so thorough. The incursion by the Western powers and Japan, the fall of the Qing Dynasty, and the internecine Nationalist conflicts dramatically changed Chinese politics. But the Japanese invasion uprooted basic socioeconomic institutions and the elites rooted in them. The Japanese cleared the society of many of the encrusted interest groups and institutional arrangements that simultaneously held China together and hobbled its political-economic development. And like nature, Olson argues, society abhors a vacuum. Hence the communist revolution could have and did have a massive impact.

China under Chairman Mao underwent three noteworthy systemic changes. One was the collectivization of agriculture in the 1950s and the nationalization of China's key manufacturing and extractive industries. Another was the Great Leap Forward, an attempt from 1958 to 1960 to exploit the government's control over the economy to produce industrial gains beyond what could be produced by any market system hampered by the need to provide ordinary material incentives to workers and producers. The last was the Cultural Revolution.

The Great Leap Forward revealed in extreme form the inherent weaknesses of political control of the economy and planning when feedback mechanisms, let alone anything like democratic accountability, were weak or nonexistent.[12] Under the Great Leap Forward, production was based on top-down plans, whether central or provincial, and the arbitrary scoring of production success, instead of leaving the definition of value to the intended consumers. The predictable result was the overproduction of shoddy, even useless goods and the crippling diversion of agricultural resources, including labor, to pseudo-industrial production. Agriculture suffered, but in the absence of market forces there was nothing approximating price signals to restore balance to investment decisions. In a word, the result was economic catastrophe and, in 1959–1961, arguably the worst famine in human history.[13]

These extreme conditions did not produce a revolution. Generalized discontent, the loss of legitimacy, and manifest economic failure were not sufficient to prompt revolution without a means to organize the resulting inchoate dissatisfaction into rebellion. Indeed when the possibility of change emerged in 1978, it appears that the enthusiasm with which provinces embraced rural reform reflected not so much the depredations of the recent Cultural Revolution but the degree to which the famine more than fifteen years earlier had affected the particular province (Yang 1996a).

Yet, as we have seen, catastrophe can episodically produce revolts, so the possibility was real, notwithstanding China's continuity of values or, alternatively, the active post-1949 inculcation of socialist values of sacrifice and subordination. At least the possibility evidently was real to leaders in the 1960s who feared the implications for their hold on power of continuing the Great Leap Forward.[14] As early as the 1959 Lushan Conference, Chairman Mao was pressured to reorganize the Great Leap Forward and, more significantly for our purposes, urged to become more open to other views if China were to avoid what from these realistic leaders' point of view would have been a great political leap backward. Politics trumped reality and the effort of Great Leap Forward was intensified (see MacFarquhar 1983).

The power struggle resumed a few years later with a revolution against the revolutionary party leadership that had put reality above politics, or at least had the bad fortune of acting as the messenger with the bad news. The Cultural Revolution initiated in 1966 was, in a sense, the political counterpart of the Great Leap Forward, asserting the reality of pure political power in one case against economic reality, in the other against the reflection of economic reality in politics.[15]

The politics of the Cultural Revolution did not come to an end until the death of Chairman Mao in 1976. After his death, the same pragmatic economic pressures that pushed the leadership against Mao in 1962 now pushed with even greater force in the aftermath of what the Communist Party of China now calls a "catastrophe." The country's social institutions and norms had been turned upside down. The economy was paralyzed. Meanwhile, China's Asian neighbors had not been standing still. Japan,

Hong Kong, Taiwan, South Korea, and Singapore—the Asian Tigers—had, from the perspective of China's leaders and people, reversed the natural economic order, which clearly required their country's dominance.

Like the Great Leap Forward, its polar opposite, the change initiated by Deng Xiaoping was largely from the top down, albeit in light of perceived potential international and domestic pressures.[16] And the change in course was decidedly political, not in any economic sense inevitable. Indeed Deng had to contend with strong political forces pushing for a revitalized form of centralized planning after the enormous economic decentralization under Mao (e.g., Shirk 1993, 33–37). While not democratization, the ensuing liberalization was tantamount to a careful and initially very selective releasing of the heavy hand of government on the *economy*. In fact, until the post-1989 period, creating a market economy was not the party's explicit aim (Naughton 1995). In any case, if democracy is to be understood as a political state of affairs, this initially unintended enhancing of individual freedom was not democratization.[17]

Granted, there are other, more socioeconomic conceptions of democracy that might well equate the expansion of the market with democratization. But ultimately there is little point to debating alternative definitions. The key consideration is that democracy, as understood here, is an institutional arrangement reflecting a balance of power. It arises because the key participants assess it to be better than the alternative ways of resolving conflicts of interest. Democracy, to say it again, is instrumental. The reform was not a form of democratization.

To put the point another way, it is clear that the economic liberalization initiated by Deng was also instrumental. His goal, however, was the preservation of the party's political power, and developing the national economic and military strength needed to preserve that power and make it worth having (see, e.g., MacFarquhar and Schoenhals 2006).

In the end, economic liberalization may have unleashed forces that will someday lead to democracy. Yet is difficult to call the process leading to it "democratization" when democracy, should it develop, will be an unintended consequence of the original reform. Indeed, democratization of the former Soviet Union in the 1990s posed a warning to the later Chinese leadership that democracy is a fate actively to be avoided. And so far, the familial continuity of the political-economic elite before and after the reform indicates the elite bet correctly (see Li 2001). One might also add that the fate of democracy in Russia since then poses a warning to observers of China who assume that steps that can be interpreted as democratization necessarily lead to democracy.

Another heralded sign of incipient democratization is the growing rule of law in China (perhaps more accurately characterized so far as rule by law). This noteworthy development is covered extensively in another chapter of this volume. As for its role in democratization, one can measure the relevant impact of this development by the extent to which a system of law serves to control the discretionary power of authorities (there has been no problem historically in using law to control the potentially rebellious behavior of Chinese citizens). Thus in his address to the Sixteenth Party Congress in 2002, outgoing General Secretary Jiang Zemin advocated reforming the "socialist legal system" (not producing the rule of law) to assure that "all people are equal before the law," which means that the party needs to "tighten supervision over law enforcement."[18]

Whatever its potential, the point of the reform is twofold. One, market relations thrive best under clear expectations about ownership and rights. In a major step, the Seventeenth National People's Congress in 2007 legalized property rights. These rights, of course, are only as good as their means of enforcement. An independent legal system has been the historic tool to promote property systems. A legal system is also valuable in a society that still needs considerable foreign direct investment. It is particularly valuable when about one-fourth of the labor force is in state-owned enterprises (SOEs), and SOEs include key industries such as utilities, energy, steel production, air and ocean transportation, military industry, and finance.[19] Without rule of law, disputes with these powerhouses are a lost cause and this consideration must temper any investment decisions involving them. Another chapter in this volume covers the very special important problem of intellectual property rights.

Two, the market economy and China's rapid transformation into it have created extraordinary social and economic dislocations. In addressing these problems, the legal system can serve as a *substitute* for democracy (see deLisle 2008). Along with legal petitions, it can provide feedback about policy and market failures.[20] When the rule of law is operating, the system can also deliver a reasonably equitable resolution of small problems and discontents before they become major and widespread. One encouraging sign of rule by law is the growing number of lawsuits charging the government with abuse of authority and, more impressive, their relatively high success rate (see Pei 2003), although the rate may have declined since its peak in 2001 (Pei 2006, 68).

It is no accident, as Marxists say, that in his report to the Sixteenth Party Congress cited above, General Secretary Jiang described stability "as a principle of overriding importance" and as "a prerequisite for reform and development."[21] The emergence of the rule of law is a means to insure the stability of the political order. A better test of the law's democratic potential, therefore, is the extent to which legal challenges with overt political content are successful. These include challenges related to government corruption (although reducing this is an official goal of the government) and violations of political rights guaranteed by the Chinese Constitution (rights always explicitly balanced by reference to social order or stability). So far, the record of success is mixed at best.[22]

Finally, a more explicit democratic development is the use of elections to select village and urban residents' committees and some local people's congresses at the township and county levels. A separate chapter in this volume addresses local governance. Here, it is worth stressing that this development, like the development of law, points in two different directions. Under a more optimistic interpretation, one direction is a growing experiment with democracy designed to move the society toward more encompassing democratic institutions as elections move up the administrative ladder. Moreover, it can be argued that even if elections are not intended as a true trial run for democracy, they may wind up playing the role of the camel that got its nose under the tent.

Village elections also point in the direction of pseudo-democracy (see Pei 2006, 72–80, for a mixed assessment). To a large extent, after all, they remain essentially one-party elections involving candidates who are "acceptable" to those above. Also, village civic organizations are not officially part of the government. In any case, like the legal system, these elections may have no greater significance than any instrument for providing useful feedback, removal of unpopular lower-level leaders, and conflict resolution, all through procedures the central government can manage and at a scale the central government can absorb. In this sense, local elections serve one function of democracy, but not the decentralization of power crucial to its institutionalization.

Were China to become a democracy, historians would no doubt point to the development of markets, the rule of law, and local elections as the early signs of this political revolution. If democracy fails to develop, they will explain how the political elite successfully held the political ramifications of these developments in check. In any case, signs of democratization are not causes. These developments serve the purposes of the central government and, in general, one can say at most that they are not responses to the expressed will of the people but are anticipated reactions to a will the leaders did not want to see expressed.

Law and elections, in other words, are not autonomous forces leading somewhere, unknown to those in the present, but vouchsafed to history. Whether they are harbingers of democracy depends on the "correlation of forces" developing pari passu with China's economy. Whether they will be wrested from the central government as instruments of democratization is not a fact inherent in these instruments but depends on those who can gain control over them. In the next section, we turn to this political question and its relation to economic growth.

CHINESE DEMOCRACY?

In this section, I refocus on the application of Acemoglu and Robinson's (2006) model of democracy to contemporary China. First, given China's extraordinary economic growth, it is important to consider the issue of economic determinism as an explanation of democracy. The classic theory of modernization (Lipset 1959) hypothesizes two logically independent political roles for economic growth. One, higher economic development can make democracy more likely to develop (endogenous democratization). Two, once democracy develops, higher economic development can make it more stable. Put crudely, under either or both hypotheses does economic growth preempt exogenous political influences?

The answer depends on the hypothesized mechanism according to which economic development gives birth to democracy. Przeworski (2006), for example, argues that the higher elite incomes are, the less relative increases or decreases will matter to them.[23] When incomes are higher, therefore, elites should be less tenacious in defending their privileges against democratic revolutions.

Whether this is a satisfactory explanation depends, in part, on the rest of the story. *Ceteris paribus*, the higher relative elite incomes are, the more drastic the impact of income or wealth equalization will be. Put another way, inequality, which will become important to the discussion later, may increase the tenacity of elite resistance.[24] At high income levels, in other words, *marginal* reductions may matter less, but large discrete reductions can still matter a great deal. Moreover, the circumstances under which increases in income produce diminishing increases in marginal utility are the circumstances under which income losses produce increasing losses of marginal utility.

What is important for now is that according to this extended version of the modernization story, it is true that economic development is statistically associated with democracy, but the actual link is effected through the rational calculations of the various economic players. This is not quite economic determinism.

In any case, Przeworski (2006) cites considerable empirical support for the existence of a threshold level of per capita income necessary for the success of democracy (Boix and Stokes 2003; Przeworski, Alvarez, Cheibub, and Limongi 2000; Barro 1999). More broadly, as Acemoglu, Johnson, Robinson, and Yared (2008, 808) remark, "One of the most notable empirical regularities in political economy is the relationship between income per capita and democracy." Unfortunately, in their own, methodologically sophisticated analysis they find no such link, or better put, no such causal mechanism. They do not dispute the statistical relation; they claim it is spurious. Some deeper historical factors, they argue, account for the divergent paths of typically poorer nondemocracies and richer democracies.

"These results shed considerable doubt on the conventional wisdom both in the academic literature and in the popular press that income per capita is a key determinant of democracy and that a general increase in income per capita will bring improvements in institutions" (Acemoglu, Johnson, Robinson, and Yared 2008, 836, also 2007; but cf. Gundlach and Paldam 2008). This form of economic determinism may be incorrect.

Rather than looking at a country's economic level, it may be more promising to look at its economic structure: the starkly unequal distribution of resources in modern China.[25] This inequality takes many forms. The distribution of environmentally degraded soil and water is highly unequal; the distribution of public works such as roads and transportation generally is highly unequal; the distribution of education is highly unequal; and what I will take as representative of all of these, the distribution of income is highly unequal. I do not include political power on this list, although its distribution is similarly unequal, since the empirical question is to what extent those seeking to address economic inequalities target the distribution of political power.

Using their model, Acemoglu and Robinson (2006, 189–201) conclude that when inequality is low enough, potential revolutionaries do not have a sufficient incentive to revolt and the elites survive without additional effort on their part.[26] As inequality increases, the rewards to revolution increase, but so do the rewards to repression.

The key conclusion is that democratization occurs when the loss of productive resources from revolution is sufficiently low, repression is relatively costly, and democratization would produce enough redistribution to satisfy the poor. "Cost of repression" is a label for the usual resource demands placed on a repressive government, including the availability of appropriate technology in the age of the Internet. But the critical resource threshold above which the governing elite throws in the towel is higher the greater the degree of pre-revolutionary inequality, that is, the greater the economic distance the elite has to fall. On the other hand, when repression is relatively costly but a revolution's threat to productive assets is sufficiently large, the poor can be bought off, at least temporarily. The elites redistribute income to ward off democratic revolution.

So Acemoglu and Robinson's (2006) analysis qualifies the conventional wisdom that the growth of inequality in China inherently threatens regime stability. Lower levels of inequality undercut the economic rationale for revolution. At intermediate levels, democracy is more likely: revolution is sufficiently rewarding, but not so rewarding that the government is willing to shoulder the cost of repression. Finally, at high levels of inequality, no feasible level of redistribution would satisfy the potential revolutionaries. Yet redistribution is too costly to the elites, so they choose to repress.[27]

With respect to repression, it is interesting to note that Lieberthal (2004, 164), citing a Chinese report, indicates that the number of party and government cadres grew by an average 3 percent per annum from 1966 to 1979, but contrary to the central government's expressed desire the rate of growth increased to an annual average of 7.7 percent between 1979 to 1989, and by almost 9 percent during the last five years of the latter period. This occurred during a period of reduced government supervision of the economy and low population growth.

Of course, one reason for this growth in personnel might have been the need to absorb individuals who in the pre-Deng period would have worked in a SOE, not to mention the need to assuage ministries threatened by economic reform and bring in more pro-reform bureaucrats (Shirk 1993, 136–37). However, it may also reflect the increasing need for management and control in other sectors when the economy is less subject to direct control, not to mention the increased revenues a growing economy provides (e.g., Pei 2007). In particular, the roughly 400,000 public security system police reportedly employed in 1978, when China launched its major reform, doubled by 1994, while an additional 600,000 were in the People's Armed Police, the armed wing of the civilian security forces (Lieberthal 2004, 234). Then too, China's efforts at repression include subtler methods such as control of media of all kinds, entertainment, and education (see, e.g., Brady 2007; cf. Baum 2008).

Evidently, in contemporary China the state's repressive apparatus is growing alongside growing inequality. Again, if much conventional wisdom is correct, this repression serves only as a holding action while the political system continues to accommodate itself to the inevitable. If, on the other hand, Acemoglu and Robinson (2006) are correct to argue that the relation between democracy and inequality is curvilinear, then the holding action may work to the advantage of government and party elites. If leaders have the stomach for it, and the population is held in check during the period of intermediate inequality, inequality may increase to a level at which democratization is actually thwarted.

At this point, it is worth reemphasizing the strategic nature of the calculations this analysis imputes to both the elites and the citizenry. Consider the hypothesized curvilinear relation between inequality and democracy. This hypothesis is certainly counterintuitive. After all, if those with lower incomes do not like inequality, one might reason, they surely will like greater inequality even less. So following the conventional wisdom, growing inequality should represent a growing threat to the regime. This plausible line of reasoning, however, overlooks the impact of growing inequality on both sides of the divide.

Although growing inequality motivates revolutionaries, it also strengthens the will of the regime's defenders.[28] The defenders have more to lose. Moreover, since growing inequality in China is, in part, a byproduct of a growing economy and therefore a growing tax base, the repressive resources available to the elites grow as well.[29] In short, when the two strategic players, the elites and the potential revolutionaries, calculate their options, they consider not only their own preferences and assets but also the likely reactions of the other side to each of their strategy choices. This is the strategic reality behind the rather abstract description of Acemoglu and Robinson's (2006) findings given above. That vanilla description disguises the complex calculations anchoring the equilibrium alignment of forces produced by a chain of contemplated reactions to reactions to reactions.

This is not to say that economic development necessarily inhibits China's long-run democratic prospects, directly insofar as it increases income and indirectly insofar as it increases inequality beyond the tipping point. As a contrary consideration, as noted above, Boix (2003) and Acemoglu and Robinson (2006, 287–312) argue that industrial economies, with their greater capital intensity in production, are more likely to democratize than agricultural economies. Once again the explanation lies in the calculation of the elites. With fixed assets in land, the elites know that there is little to inhibit the redistribution or high taxation attending democracy. For in a market agricultural economy, as we have seen, land is inelastically supplied whether or not the political system is democratic.[30] Capital, however, is elastically supplied. Indeed when redistribution is threatened, capital can flee across borders along with its original owners.[31]

Democratic governments, therefore, are much less constrained in redistributing land or taxing income derived from it than they are in taxing capital or the income derived from it. Democracy is much less threatening to owners of capital. As a consequence, they are less likely to be willing to pay a given cost of repression. For this reason, economic development in China has produced growing inequality, which can temper revolution, but likewise a relatively declining agricultural sector, which can temper elite resistance to democratization.

China's economic development has also produced a growing middle class (the exact size of which is difficult to determine even if one picks one of the variety of definitions). This class figured prominently in Europe's democratization and in Latin American politics. In its particular business incarnation as the bourgeoisie, it also figures in Moore's (1966) classic analysis of why some societies become democracies. It is natural to wonder whether it might fulfill the same role in China.

The middle class in China lacks direct political power, but it can exert increasing economic power, at least through its individual members. Historically, the middle position of the middle class has allowed it to pivot toward the lower classes, here workers and peasants, or toward the ruling elites. The latter possibility takes two different forms. One is for the middle class to join the elites through partial democracy: the elites develop democratic forms, including elections, but deny the lower classes the franchise.

The distinction between co-optation and partial democratization becomes less sharp if the CPC democratizes internally but governs society in its traditionally authoritative fashion. As Bueno de Mesquita, Smith, Siverson, and Morrow (2003) argue, the group capable of determining the rulers, a group they call the selectorate, is a variable cutting across many of the somewhat arbitrary distinctions coalescing around a given definition of democracy.[32]

A second way in which middle class aligns with existing political elites is through co-optation: the middle class can be incorporated into the elite. The downside for the hosting elites is that rents and power must be distributed more widely (see Pei 2006, 96–131). Further, the economic interests of the middle class make them less receptive to a policy of maximizing rents (consistent with social order), whether garnered through corruption or not, when those rents reduce profits (see Pei 2006, 95). Thus co-opting the middle class is a double-edged sword. It brings a powerful and potentially threatening group into the tent; but once the middle class is inside it can exert internal constraints on the use of its own wealth as a source of revenue.

In any case, the doctrine of the Three Represents adopted at the Sixteenth Party Congress in November 2002 signaled the CPC's openness to this kind of corporatism. In General Secretary Jiang Zemin's words:

> Our Party must always represent the development trend of China's advanced productive forces, the orientation of China's advanced culture and the fundamental interests of the overwhelming majority of the Chinese people. They are the inexorable requirements for maintaining and developing socialism and the logical conclusion our Party has reached through hard exploration and great practice. . . . Emerging in the process of social changes, entrepreneurs and technical personnel employed by non-public scientific and technological enterprises, managerial and technical staff employed by overseas-funded enterprises, the self-employed, private entrepreneurs, employees in intermediaries, free-lance professionals and members of other social strata are all builders of socialism with Chinese characteristics. (english.people.com.cn/200211/18/eng20021118_106983.shtml)

However obscure the doctrine, clearly this report signaled the party's willingness to bring the middle class into the political fold.

It may be, as some argue, that the Three Represents has had little practical effect, serving mainly Jiang Zemin's desire to burnish his reputation. Yet at the very least the doctrine puts a name on the party's very real and delicate problem of designing a policy toward the middle class. This problem may be insoluble: the middle class may contain the seeds of Chinese democracy. For now, one can note, again, that these problems are strategically two-sided. The middle class's own political difficulties make its future revolutionary role far from secure.

Ironically, sensitivity to these difficulties is as old as Marxism itself. In the *Communist Manifesto*, Marx and Engels (1988, 57) famously proclaimed, "The executive of the modern State is but a committee for managing the common affairs of the whole bourgeoisie." Translating to the new terminology, the middle class needs the state and uses the state but does not occupy the state, possibly because it needs institutions capable of transcending the class's own internal division of interests.

Thus one way the middle class can resolve its paradoxical political position—the need to surrender power in order to increase its power—is by allowing itself to be represented by the state instead of participating qua class in it. In its own interest the middle class deliberately refrains from exercising direct political power, an idea Elster (1985, 411–22) calls the abdication theory of the state. For his part, Marx focused on the French bourgeoisie's abdication to Napoleon III. Today, he might focus on the political impotence of the rising middle class in China, which at the same time is increasingly intertwining with the elite.

Both theoretically and historically speaking, then, there is nothing necessarily unnatural about the failure or even reluctance of the middle class to exercise direct political power. It may simply choose and so far has chosen to abdicate in favor of political elites that are willing to create conditions favorable to economic growth and provide appropriate financing, contracts, and other economic support to those who are sufficiently loyal. In many respects, there has indeed been a merging of interests into a system of "crony communism" (see Dickson 2008).

Nor, for the same reason, does the middle class have a necessary affinity with democracy. Marx himself initially saw Napoleon III as a high-wire act destined for a quick fall. Instead it was Louis Napoleon's political tenacity that forced Marx to grapple with the abdication theory and tested his conviction that political forces invariably represent classes.

Nevertheless, the middle class can also place a fundamental wager that its interests will be protected under democratic rule. This scenario, however, is best understood not in terms of a process by which the middle class directly forms a democratic coalition with the workers and peasants. It is difficult to imagine the middle class trading rule by the CPC for rule by the more numerous peasants or workers, with the potential for a Mao II playing the role of Napoleon III. Indeed Marxists and others have long puzzled over why, historically, the bourgeoisie would ever have willingly encouraged a political process in which power is determined by numbers, which they lack.

Based on the European model the answer seems to be that the middle class's role in creating democracy occurs through the intermediate path of partial democratization. The middle class forms a coalition with the ruling elite, or better, the middle class is invited into the halls of power when the alternative coalition threatens to form, as it arguably did in 1989 during the Tiananmen Square period. The issue then becomes whether the middle class, once in power, will push partial into full democratization.

Acemoglu and Robinson (2006, 255–86) explore two scenarios for this transition. In one, the ruling coalition, now including the middle class, fractures over internal divisions of interest (see also Collier 1999). In the case of China these potential divisions have already been discussed. The divisions cause the coalition to fracture, as one component, here the middle class, attempts to bolster its position by gaining new allies through the extension of the franchise or, in other terms, by redefining the selectorate.

Gilley's (2004) optimistic predictions about democracy in China rest on something akin to this scenario. He writes (2004, 118), "Broadly speaking, there are two exit routes for a CCP [Chinese Community Party] faced with popular protests it can neither repress nor embrace: it can be overthrown by protest leaders riding the wave of unrest; or it can be 'extricated' from office by reformers within its own ranks." Gilley (2004, 120) looks to the latter: "all evidence suggests that the state remains powerful enough to force revolutionary change to take place on the inside rather than the outside. While the strength of society has grown manifold, it is not enough to overthrow the state." Democracy will emerge when the moderate elites, standing between the democrats and the conservatives, shift toward the democratic faction.

"The key for a successful extrication," Gilley (2004, 126) concludes, "is for democrats to be stronger than conservatives and for them to gain the complicity, if not outright support, of the moderates." But to say the democrats are "stronger" may give the misleading impression that democratic values will lead China to democracy. Rather, Gilley (2004, 129) acknowledges the relative weakness of a normative belief in democracy as the real driving force. Instead, democracy is seen by reformers as "the only solution to the political crisis." The relevant statement is worth quoting at length (2004, 129–30):

> In the face of popular pressure and a breakdown of internal consensus, the "selectorate" . . . confronts alternatives to autocracy. It may consider broadening the franchise to more groups within the regime to make it into an oligarchy. . . . Or it may decide to throw the doors open completely to create a democracy. . . . China will likely follow this path. The only system [members of the elite] can all agree on that will ensure they are not trodden by others is democracy.

Gilley (2004, 131) nonetheless insists that democratic values constitute the necessary background for this compromise. China has seen the rest of the world embracing full democracy. "While we focus here on the elites, it is these 'background' conditions that push them to embrace democracy. . . . [T]he looming presence of mobilized society, whether it's workers on the streets or intellectuals in advisory positions, makes it harder to embrace anything short of full democracy."

Acemoglu and Robinson's (2006) analysis raises doubts about the likelihood that democracy will emerge from an expansion of the franchise motivated by middle-class defection. The key to understanding the strategic situation of the relevant players is to look beyond the creation of democracy and try to predict its material consequences for its prospective supporters. Thinking in terms of three classes, poor, middle class, and political elite, there are two possibilities. If the poor are in the majority and inequality is sufficiently advanced, in particular if the poor have substantially below-average income, then the middle class will likely find itself hurt by any procedure using full majority rule to determine their effective tax rate.[33] The distribution of income in China may already be sufficiently unequal to constrain intra-elite competition in this way. If, on the other hand, the middle class becomes the decisive voting group under full democracy, it is more plausible that they would be willing to extend the franchise. Unfortunately, the historical evidence for this scenario is weak (Acemoglu and Robinson 2006, 269–70). The uncoerced dilution of power's perquisites is unlikely.

The more likely scenario, then, is for full democratization to occur under the threat of revolution. Here my analysis tracks the pessimistic two-class model already discussed. Yet the revolutionary threat will be even weaker in this context insofar as the middle-class component of the elite coalition is willing, within its partial democracy, to support redistribution involving net transfers from the rich to itself *and* the poor.[34] From the standpoint of democratization, it is striking that the adoption of this "democratic" policy of redistribution under President Hu Jintao has been "top-down and nondemocratic" (Naughton 2008, 155). Under this redistribution, of course, the revolutionary incentive of the poor is diminished.

Put another way, partial democracy is more stable when the income of the middle class is relatively close to the poor, which means the redistribution plan selected by the regime is not too far from what the poor themselves would choose. Conversely, as the middle class gains wealth, they become more distant from the poor and closer to the rich. Here, the logic of the two-class model holds full sway, with the caveat that insofar as a relatively rich middle class extracts transfers from its rich coalition partners, full democratization may not be as materially threatening to the rich as a revolution in the absence of a middle class. By the same token, a relatively well-off middle class is not inclined to tax anywhere near the rate threatened by the poor. If so, the rich in conjunction with the middle class will continue to favor repression.

In sum, this analysis suggests considerable caution about any prediction of full democracy for China, with or without an active middle class. To repeat, in no way is this meant to downplay the enormous challenges China's rulers face (e.g., Pei 2006, 167–205): continuing the successful management of the economy which has necessitated an increased decentralization of power, environmental degradation far exceeding that experienced by the

West during its comparable period of industrialization, pervasive corruption, resource constraints, increased communications capabilities among ordinary citizens, and restive members of the Moslem and Tibetan minorities, working class, and peasantry.

Democrats, however, also face challenges. There is a huge gap between discontent, even widespread discontent, and revolution. Revolutions do not always lead to democracy, nor are successful democratic revolutions necessarily successfully consolidated.

Moreover, it is not clear that democracy, prospectively in the calculations of a possible revolutionary public or in practice, is capable of addressing these challenges any more successfully than are authoritarian governments.[35] Some problems are technically hard to solve, period. Others are politically hard to solve, period. Still others are harder to solve politically when a majority of the population must be persuaded by a proposed solution and the dissenting minority's power must be overcome.

CONCLUSION

The conclusion of the last section questioned the prospects for Chinese democracy. Accordingly, should this chapter conclusion question the prospects for political convergence between the United States and China? Of course, but with two important caveats.

One, the United States is a democracy but it cannot be realistically described by the simple majority-rule voting model anchoring much of the preceding analysis of China's democratic potential. At the beginning of this chapter I characterized democracy as the instrumental product of groups seeking the best institution to advance their interests. In such a democracy, voting is an essential part of the arrangement, but only part. Groups continue to advance their interests in other ways. In particular, it is striking how much a sophisticated interest-group analysis of U.S. politics (e.g., Grossman and Helpman 2001) is able either to ignore the role of voters or to treat them as passively affirming the deals worked out behind the scenes. As the chapter on lobbying in this volume shows, special interest groups in both China and the United States play a powerful role in determining public policy (see also Shirk 1993; Kennedy 2005).[36] Indeed intra-party factions participating in "inner-party democracy" are widely touted as China's natural path toward full democratization (e.g., He 2005).[37]

Two, there is an important distinction between political structure and policy outcomes. Not only may policies converge when political structure does not. This convergence may tell us that political institutions, even democratic institutions, are not as important in determining policy as one might think (see, e.g., Mulligan, Gil, and Sala-i-Martin 2004). Consider social security policy. Mulligan and Sala-i-Martin (2004) have documented the pervasiveness of key program characteristics independent of government type. Of course, this commonality could reflect imitation. However, Grafstein and Li (2008) argue that an economic logic transcending countries dictates China's adoption of some of these key features. More important, they provide evidence that labor disorder serves a political role in determining the sustainability of this program in ways that are functionally analogous to the role of electoral pressure in democracies such as the United States. Specifically, China's government, like any government developing a typical social security program, faces a serious commitment problem. So far social security is effectively funded on a pay-as-you-go (PAYG) basis. Therefore current workers must rely on the government's *future* willingness to produce sufficient revenues to support their retirement and to spend those revenues on their pensions.[38] There is now a large literature explaining why PAYG is politically sustainable in democracies. Crudely stated, the voters will punish the government's failure to honor the commitment. In the case of China, Grafstein and Li (2008) argue, the threat is civil unrest.

What is their evidence? The standard theory of consumer behavior holds that individuals save for two reasons. One is to smooth their lifetime consumption by shifting income from higher-income periods to periods expected to be less productive. The other, more relevant motivation is precautionary: even when their expected income is constant, individuals will save when they are uncertain about it. Insofar as unrest creates uncertainty, presumably it would induce consumers in China to increase their savings. However, Grafstein and Li (2008) find that labor unrest is associated with a different kind of response: the more labor unrest there is, the more Chinese in aggregate *reduce* their savings in response to higher social security taxes. The interpretation is that savings are less necessary when the government's promise to provide pensions is more credible. And the government's promise is more credible, in turn, when workers exhibit the capacity to organize and protect their interests.

In short, democracy is an institution many value for the dignity and respect it accords citizens. It also has instrumental uses and arises, I have argued, for instrumental reasons. Ironically, it may turn out that a democratic United States and a nondemocratic China may converge in their capacity to fulfill many of the goals for which democracy is instrumentally established.

NOTES

1. See Bueno de Mesquita, Smith, Siverson, and Morrow (2003) for a skeptical assessment of the wisdom of using personality or culture to explain the difference between autocratic and democratic leaders.

2. Although see the chapter on Chinese and western philosophy for a philosophical analysis of an instrumental view of democracy and a democratic reading of Daoism.

3. For a fairly recent example of this view, see Mosher (1998). There was a similar argument about China's resistance to modern economic life (e.g., Fairbank 1969). See Nathan (1993) for a skeptical assessment of the distinctiveness of Chinese culture and He (1996, 157–74) for skepticism about the culture argument in particular. For what it is worth, then, Nathan (2008) reports little real support among influential political leaders and public intellectuals for full democracy in China. For a different view, see Yu (2008). Finally, considering one important alleged economic component of culture—different attitudes of Americans and Chinese toward thrift and risk-taking as an explanation for differences in savings rates—Modigliani and Cao (2004, 166) conclude from an extensive empirical analysis that "that type of explanation is fundamentally baseless."

4. Naughton (2007, 37) describes the pre-1949 Chinese economy as characterized by "Competitive and efficient markets for land and labor."

5. The actual system, which included complex land taxes, ownership arrangements, and labor service requirements, is too complex to describe here, but over time it induced complicated and illegal attempts to circumvent and shift taxes, which led to the "single-whip" reform, in the sixteenth and early seventeenth centuries.

6. Wickham (2005) notes that Rome and China were unique in the pre-industrial world in having this civilian elite.

7. There is an ongoing debate over whether the Chinese economy in the nineteenth and early twentieth centuries had failed, which is the conventional view, or whether it exhibited reasonable growth (for a review of the debate, see Richardson 1999).

8. There was a serious decline in public granaries and large-scale irrigation maintenance during the late-Qing period (Naughton 2007, 39).

9. Assertions like these pass over very large and complex issues. For my own assessment of these issues, see Grafstein (1992).

10. Przeworski (2006) points out that two parties may undertake a democratic compromise that one party agrees to support unconditionally and the other agrees to support so long as it wins the subsequent elections.

11. Weingast (1997) and Hardin (2003) argue that written constitutions do serve one "normative" purpose: they are signaling devices allowing the coordination of participants when their rational strategies are consistent with multiple equilibria.

12. It is worth noting that China never became a fully command economy controlled from the center in the manner of the Soviet Union, and in many respects the Great Leap Forward entailed the decentralization of economic control (e.g., Naughton 2007).

13. For balance, one might cite the usual additional causes such as drought but, as Sen (1999) argues, famine seems to be a hallmark of nondemocratic societies. In other words, the famine primarily represents a political failure.

14. In fairness, ethical qualms about the torments being inflicted on the country may have played a role, as even the very negative assessment of Mao by Chang and Halliday (2005) allows.

15. Harding (1997, 242–45) notes that more than 50 percent of the members of the Politburo prior to the Cultural Revolution were removed by 1969.

16. Agricultural reform initially occurred at the provincial level and spread somewhat spontaneously (see, e.g., Shirk 1993, 38–39).

17. There is an interesting theoretical issue here. Contrasting Gorbachev's political reform in the Soviet Union with China's economically oriented reform, Shirk (1993, 9) argues that the former "accords with our views of communism better than Deng's strategy": "We usually expect communist party and government officials to defend their vested interests in the command economy by blocking market reforms." My more instrumental view is that we more expect government officials of any stripe to defend their political position since without it command of the economy is not *their* command of the economy.

18. See english.people.com.cn/200211/18/eng20021118_106984.shtml.

19. See Naughton (2008, 148). Technically, the 25 percent figure (actually 27 percent) includes state-held enterprises as well as SOEs (see the 2007 Chinese Statistical Yearbook).

20. Since the 1950s *xinfang* offices for hearing citizen complaints have offered a substitute for the legal system's safety value function. These offices can be found in many parts of the government and party bureaucracy, including the people's congresses, judiciary, and police. They too serve a key feedback and monitoring function (Huang 1995). In 2005 the government passed new regulations to make the system more responsive.

21. See english.peopledaily.com.cn/200211/18/eng20021118_106983.shtml.

22. For a skeptical assessment of Chinese legal reform, see Pei (2006, 65–72).

23. This result follows from the assumption that individuals, including elites, are risk averse with increasing concave utility functions (i.e., utility increases with income but at a decreasing rate). Accordingly, utility increments from equal-sized increases in income are smaller the larger the base level of income. Of course, barring interpersonal comparisons of utility, this argument holds, strictly speaking, only when comparing different income bases of a given member of the elite. Even the inference in the latter case requires a constant utility function over the periods being compared.

24. Boix (2003) argues that economic growth tends to decrease inequality, which, in turn, means that elites are less threatened by democracy. Obviously this relation between growth and inequality has not yet materialized in China.

25. Despite an enormous literature devoted to the topic, it is no clearer that a country's economic rate of economic growth is any more connected to democracy than is its economic level (Acemoglu, Johnson, Robinson, and Yared 2008).

26. As a technical aside, their formal analysis gives both comparative statics and dynamic results. The former includes a misstep (see p. 191). They argue that $p[\tau^p(\theta^*)(\theta - \delta) - (1 - \delta)C[\tau^p(\theta^*)]] > 0$ implies that $\theta^* > \mu$. Substantively, this important conclusion says, crudely speaking, that the prospective reduction in inequality from a revolution outweighs the prospective destruction of productive assets resulting from that revolution. But dividing through by $p > 0$ and noting, from p. 188, that $\tau^p(\theta^*) > C[\tau^p(\theta^*)]$, the implication holds only if $\theta - \delta > 1 - \delta$ and therefore only if $\theta > 1$. But by assumption, $\theta < 1$ (since this parameter represents the share of income going to the rich, the assumed inequality is very realistic).

27. An important consideration for elites is the extent to which the failure to repress signals weakness. When the distinction between strong and weak governments is modeled, the result is a "pooling equilibrium" in which both types choose to repress to avoid sending the wrong signal (see Acemoglu and Robinson 2000).

28. For now I assume that China's political elites prosper along with the economic elites who therefore have little reason to rock the boat. Later I explicitly consider the role of the middle class.

29. See Pei (2006, 19–20), although he sees this as a short-term benefit.

30. There may be a practical difference in the consequences of redistributing land and redistributing income through taxation. In the former case, owners of land may also have specific managerial skills that are lost with a change of ownership.

31. Although China generally receives poor ratings on the usual political indices measuring democracy, corruption, and rule of law, the risk of debt repudiation and asset expropriation is considered to be very small (Pei 2006, 5).

32. See Shirk (1993) for an application of the selectorate concept to China and Yang (1996b) for a critique.

33. Some estimates put the middle class at about 5 percent of the population, others closer to 20 percent with a projection of 38 percent by 2020 (Solinger 2008, 258–59). Ignoring complications like turnout rates and other factors, these figures suggest that this class is unlikely to constitute the pivot voters in a full democracy for the foreseeable future.

34. The agriculture tax was abolished in 2006 and, more generally, there has been greater regional redistribution and an emphasis on rural development (e.g., Naughton 2008). Of course, within the coalition the middle class may target or preserve transfers to itself alone but this makes the ruling coalition less stable. More broadly, self-targeted transfers increase the economic stakes associated with political dominance and therefore threaten to undermine political stability (Acemoglu and Robinson 2006, 246–47).

35. There is little convincing evidence, for example, of a link between democratic forms of government and greater economic growth (e.g., Przeworski, Alvarez, Cheibub, and Limongi 2000).

36. Strictly speaking, within China only one official interest organization can be devoted to one issue or group in any one locale and nongovernmental organizations cannot span locales (Lieberthal 2004, 300) but the number is extraordinarily high (see Cheng 2008, 10–11). But unofficially, of course, there are many unregistered NGOs and also factions and different interests within the party, such as the PLA, the financial bureaucracy, and so on.

37. See Lieberthal (2004, 242) for an insider's discussion of expanding elections for the government and the party.

38. Even if the program is prefunded with a trust fund, workers must believe the fund will not be raided or diverted to other government expenditures.

REFERENCES

Acemoglu, Daron, Simon Johnson, James A. Robinson, and Pierre Yared. 2007. "Re-evaluating the Modernization Hypothesis." econ-www.mit.edu/files/1372.

———. 2008. "Income and Democracy." *American Economic Review* 98 (June): 808–42.
Acemoglu, Daron, and James A. Robinson. 2000. "Repression or Democratization?" *European Economic Review* 44 (May): 683–93.
———. 2006. *Economic Origins of Dictatorship and Democracy*. Cambridge: Cambridge University Press.
Almond, Gabriel A., and Sidney Verba. 1965. *The Civic Culture: Political Attitudes and Democracy in Five Nations*. Boston: Little, Brown.
Barro, Robert J. 1999. "Determinants of Democracy." *Journal of Political Economy* 107 (December): S158–83.
Baum, Richard. 2008. "Political Implications of China's Information Revolution: The Media, the Minders, and the Their Message." In *China's Changing Political Landscape*, ed. Cheng Li. Washington, DC: Brookings Institution Press.
Benhabib, Jesse, and Adam Przeworski. 2006. "The Political Economy of Redistribution under Democracy." *Economic Theory* 29 (October): 271–90.
Boix, Carles. 2003. *Democracy and Redistribution*. Cambridge: Cambridge University Press.
Boix, Carles, and Susan C. Stokes. 2003. "Endogenous Democratization." *World Politics* 55 (July): 517–49.
Brady, Anne-Marie. 2007. *Marketing Dictatorship: Propaganda and Thought Work in Contemporary China*. Lanham, MD: Rowman & Littlefield.
Bueno de Mesquita, Bruce, Alastair Smith, Randolph M. Siverson, and James D. Morrow. 2003. *The Logic of Political Survival*. Cambridge, MA: MIT Press.
Chang, Jung, and Jon Halliday. 2005. *Mao*. New York: Knopf.
Collier, Ruth Berins. 1999. *Paths toward Democracy: The Working Class and Elites in Western Europe and South America*. New York: Cambridge University Press.
de Bary, William Theodore. 1983. *The Liberal Tradition in China*. New York: Columbia University Press.
deLisle, Jacques. 2008. "Legalization without Democratization in China under Hu Jintao." In *China's Changing Political Landscape*, ed. Cheng Li. Washington, DC: Brookings Institution Press.
Dickson, Bruce. 2008. *Wealth Into Power*. Cambridge: Cambridge University Press.
Eastman, Lloyd E. 2001. *The Nationalist Era in China 1927–1949*. New York: Cambridge University of Press.
Elster, Jon. 1985. *Making Sense of Marx*. Cambridge: Cambridge University Press.
Fairbank, John K. 1969. *Trade and Diplomacy on the China Coast*. Stanford, CA: Stanford University Press.
Gilley, Bruce. 2004. *China's Democratic Future*. New York: Columbia University Press.
Goldberg, Victor P. 1985. "Production Functions, Transactions Costs and the New Institutionalism." In *Issues in Contemporary Microeconomics and Welfare*, ed. George R. Feiwel. Albany: State University of New York Press.
Grafstein, Robert. 1992. *Institutional Realism*. New Haven, CT: Yale University Press.
Grafstein, Robert, and Li Ruoxi. 2008. "The Politics of Social Security in China." Paper presented at the Annual Meeting of the Midwest Political Science Association.

Granato, James, Ronald Inglehart, and David Leblang. 1996. "Cultural Values, Stable Democracy, and Development: A Reply." *American Journal of Political Science* 40: 680–96.

Grossman, Gene M., and Elhanan Helpman. 2001. *Special Interest Politics*. Cambridge: MIT Press.

Gundlach, Erich, and Martin Paldam. 2008. "A Farewell to Critical Junctures: Sorting out Long-Run Causality of Income and Democracy." Kiel Working Paper No. 1410.

Hardin, Russell. 2003. *Liberalism, Constitutionalism, and Democracy*. New York: Oxford University Press.

Harding, Harry. 1997. "The Chinese State in Crisis, 1966–69." In *The Politics of China: The Eras of Mao and Deng*, ed. Roderick MacFarquhar. Cambridge: Cambridge University Press.

He, Baogang. 1996. *The Democratization of China*. London: Routledge.

———. 2005. "Intra-Party Democracy: A Revisionist Perspective from Below." In *The Chinese Communist Party in a New Era: Renewal and Reform*, ed. Kjeld Erik Broedsgaard and Yongnian Zheng. London: Routledge.

Hozumi, Fumio. 1940. "A Study of the Character of Current Chinese Economy." *Kyoto Economic Review* 15: 41–66.

Huang, Yasheng. 1995. "Administrative Monitoring in China." *China Quarterly* 143: 828–48.

Inglehart, Ronald F. 1990. *Culture Shift in Advanced Industrial Society*. Princeton, NJ: Princeton University Press.

Kennedy, Scott. 2005. *The Business of Lobbying in China*. Cambridge, MA: Harvard University Press.

Li, Cheng. 2001. *China's Leaders: The New Generation*. Lanham, MD: Rowman & Littlefield.

———. 2008. "Introduction: Assessing China's Political Development." In *China's Changing Political Landscape*, ed. Cheng Li. Washington, DC: Brookings Institution Press.

Lichbach, Mark Irving. 1995. *The Rebel's Dilemma*. Ann Arbor: University of Michigan Press.

Liberthal, Kenneth. 2004. *Governing China*. New York: Norton.

Lipset, Seymour Martin. 1959. "Some Social Requisites of Democracy: Economic Development and Political Legitimacy." *American Political Science Review* 53 (March): 69–105.

MacFarquhar, Roderick. 1983. *The Origins of the Cultural Revolution 2: The Great Leap Forward 1958–1960*. New York: Columbia University Press.

MacFarquhar, Roderick, and Michael Schoenhals. 2006. *Mao's Last Revolution*. Cambridge, MA: Harvard University Press.

Marx, Karl. 1988. *The Communist Manifesto*. New York: Norton.

Modigliani, Franco, and Shi Larry Cao. 2004. "The Chinese Saving Puzzle and the Life-Cycle Hypothesis." *Journal of Economic Literature* 42 (March): 145–70.

Moore, Barrington, Jr. 1966. *Social Origins of Dictatorship and Democracy*. Boston: Beacon Press.

Mosher, Steven W. 1998. "Are the Chinese Ready for Liberty and Self-Government?" *The American Enterprise* 9 (July–August): 50–53.

Mulligan, Casey B., Ricard Gil, and Xavier Sala-i-Martin. 2004. "Do Democracies Have Different Public Policies than Nondemocracies?" *Journal of Economic Perspectives* 18 (Winter): 51–74.

Mulligan, Casey B., and Xavier Sala-i-Martin. 2004. "Internationally Common Features of Public Old-Age Pensions, and Their Implications for Models of the Public Sector." *Advances in Economic Analysis & Policy* 4 (1): 1–54.

Nathan, Andrew J. 1993. "Is Chinese Culture Distinctive?" *Journal of Asian Studies* 52 (November): 923–36.

———. 2008. "China's Political Trajectory: What Are the Chinese Saying?" In *China's Changing Political Landscape*, ed. Cheng Li. Washington, DC: Brookings Institution Press.

Naughton, Barry. 1995. *Growing Out of the Plan: Chinese Economic Reform, 1978–1993*. Cambridge: Cambridge University Press.

———. 2007. *The Chinese Economy*. Cambridge, MA: MIT Press.

———. 2008. "China's Left Tilt: Pendulum Swing or Midcourse Correction?" In *China's Changing Political Landscape*, ed. Cheng Li. Washington, DC: Brookings Institution Press.

Olson, Mancur, Jr. 1982. *The Rise and Decline of Nations*. New Haven, CT: Yale University Press.

Pei, Minxin. 2003. "Rights and Resistance: The Changing Contexts of the Dissident Movement." In *Chinese Society: Change, Conflict and Resistance*, ed. Elizabeth J. Perry and Mark Selden. London: Routledge.

———. 2006. *China's Trapped Transition*. Cambridge, MA: Harvard University Press.

———. 2007. "How Will China Democratize?" *Journal of Democracy* 18 (July): 53–57.

Przeworski, Adam. 2005. "Democracy as an Equilibrium." *Public Choice* 123: 253–73.

———. 2006. "Self-Enforcing Democracy." In *Handbook of Political Economy*, ed. Barry R. Weingast and Donald Wittman. Oxford: Oxford University Press.

Przeworski, Adam, Michael Alvarez, José A. Cheibub, and Fernando Limongi. 2000. *Democracy and Development*. Cambridge: Cambridge University Press.

Reischauer, Edwin O., and John K. Fairbank. 1960. *East Asia: The Great Tradition*. Boston: Houghton Mifflin.

Richardson, Philip. 1999. *Economic Change in China, c. 1800–1950*. Cambridge: Cambridge University Press.

Sen, Amartya. 1999. *Development as Freedom*. New York: Knopf.

Shepsle, Kenneth A. 1989. "Studying Institutions: Some Lessons from the Rational Choice Approach." *Journal of Theoretical Politics* 1 (January): 131–47.

Shirk, Susan L. 1993. *The Political Logic of Economic Reform in China*. Berkeley: University of California Press.

Solinger, Dorothy J. 2008. "The Political Implications of China's Social Future: Complacency, Scorn, and the Forlorn." In *China's Changing Political Landscape*, ed. Cheng Li. Washington, DC: Brookings Institution Press.

Weingast, Barry R. 1997. "Political Foundations of Democracy and the Rule of Law." *American Political Science Review* 91: 245–63.

Wickham, Chris. 2005. *Framing the Early Middle Ages: Europe and the Mediterranean, 400–800*. Oxford: Oxford University Press.

Yang, Dali L. 1996a. *Calamity and Reform in China: State, Rural Society, and Institutional Change Since the Great Leap Famine.* Stanford, CA: Stanford University Press.

———. 1996b. "Governing China's Transition to the Market: Institutional Incentives, Politicians' Choices, and Unintended Outcomes." *World Politics* 48 (April): 424–52.

Yu, Keping. 2008. "Ideological Change and Incremental Democracy in Reform-Era China." In *China's Changing Political Landscape*, ed. Cheng Li. Washington, DC: Brookings Institution Press.

Zhao, Suisheng. 2000. "A Tragedy of History: China's Search for Democracy in the Twentieth Century." In *China and Democracy: Reconsidering the Prospects for a Democratic China*, ed. Suisheng Zhao. London: Routledge.

2

Public Administration Reform in China

Fan Wen

China started the Reform and Opening Policy in 1978.[1] Significant economic and social progress has been achieved over the past three decades. During the same period, the Chinese public administration system has also experienced six reforms, and is gradually shifting from a "controlling government" to a "service-oriented government," from "totalitarianism" to "limited government," and from "rule by ruler" to "rule of law."[2] The public administration reform in China follows the real situation of China, and it also borrows some elements from the public administration reforms in the United States and other countries. Along with the increase of exchange and cooperation in public administration reform, Chinese diplomatic philosophy has also witnessed new changes. "Harmonious world" has replaced "revolution and war" as a new idea of Chinese foreign diplomacy. Although disputes still exist, the Sino-U.S. relationship has gradually developed into a new era in general.

HISTORY OF PUBLIC ADMINISTRATION REFORM IN CHINA

Since the Reform and Opening Policy in 1978, China had made important economic and social progress. For example, the GDP was 362.41 billion Yuan in 1978 but by 2007 it was 24.66 trillion Yuan. The average annual growth rate is above 9.6 percent. China has already become the fourth largest economy in the world, and will soon move up to the third. The period from 1978 to 2008 marks a thirty-year period of economic growth, reform, and opening. The public administration system also experienced a series of reforms along with economic reform. There were six major administrative reforms in the past thirty years. Those reforms set the targets for adapting to a market economy and promoting the rule of law, and focused on changing government functions. They also established the principles of efficiency, unity, and efficacy, and combining the streamlining of administrative policy and personnel with improvement of the governmental structure through organizational reform. This organizational reform was tied to civil servant reform to improve the quality of the government employees. Those reforms were carried out under unified leadership and stratified responsibilities in a gradual process.

Reform in 1982

This round of reform was aimed at improving government efficiency and reducing the average age of civil servants. There were three major steps: the first was to abolish the tenure of senior leadership; the second was to reduce the size of leading units at each level; and the third was to reduce the age of civil servants. After this reform, the total number of the senior leaders at the cabinet level was reduced, and also the average age of the ministers and their deputies was reduced from sixty-four to sixty, and that of the bureau chiefs from fifty-eight to fifty.

Reform in 1988

This round of reform was instituted to promote political reform and deepen the reform of the economic system. The focus of the reform was to change the relation between government and business enterprises. The historical contribution of this round reform was to set up the theme for future reforms, that is, it was understood that "changing government functions is the key to structural reform." The State Council made good progress in adjusting and reducing industrial and other economic management organizations. In addition, the beginning of a new civil servant system was instituted.

Reform in 1993

The historical contribution of this round of reform was to adapt administrative reform to the needs of the market economy. Business management power was given back to individual enterprises, and government was no longer directly managing their activities. In addition, the reform also increased administrative oversight inside the government.

Reform in 1998

This round of reform ended the old practice by which economic management units inside government directly controlled individual enterprises.

After this reform, the government function has been greatly changed. Almost all industrial and other economic management organizations were abolished, changing the structural base of the combination of government and enterprise.

Reform in 2003

This round of reform happened when China joined the World Trade Organization (WTO). The goal of the reform was to adjust for the trend of globalization, further change government functioning, reform management methods, promote e-government, improve administrative efficiency, and to lower administrative costs. The administrative system was expected to behave legally, operate coordinately, justly and transparently, and cleanly and efficiently. Several specific reforms were carried out, including reform in state-owned assets, the macro-management system, the financial oversight system, transportation and logistics, food security, and assuring a safe working environment oversight. This round of reform grasped the major problems of social and economic development at that time, and furthered changes in government functions.

Reform in 2007

This round of reform is called "Grand Ministry Reform." The goal was to increase comprehensive management and coordination in governmental affairs. Following the principle of balance and coordination among decision-making, implementation, and supervision, this reform combined some ministries with similar or overlapping functions to form so-called super-ministries. The number of the ministries was reduced accordingly to ease coordination among different ministries and to make government operations more efficient. This reform allowed government to set its role as macro-manager of the economy to help establish a public service–oriented government.

SPECIFIC MEASURES IN CHINA'S PUBLIC ADMINISTRATION REFORM

Change Government Functions

The most salient feature of China's public administration reform is the positive change in governmental functions. The government has dramatically reduced its intervention in the micro-economy and has basically established the indirect approach as the major means for macro-management. A market system has been created. The government plays a role of facilitation, standardization, and oversight, and starts to emphasize social management and public service. This represented a great change in economic management by government. The traditional management approach based on administrative examination has been greatly scaled back, and foreign-related economic management is now closer to international conventions. The government's ability to sustain social and economic coordination has also been improved.

Promote Structural Change

The cabinet started to be reduced in 1982. The number of ministries was reduced from forty-five to forty-one, agencies directly under the State Council from twenty-two to nineteen, and ad-hoc organizations from seventy-five to forty-four in the 1988 reform. Total personnel were reduced by 9,700. The number of ministries was further reduced to twenty-nine in 1993. The internal agencies were reduced by a quarter. About 200 functions were transferred to enterprises, local organizations, social intermediates, and self-regulating associations, which resulted in a 50 percent reduction in personnel. Meanwhile, four ministries were created, including the Commission for National Defense Science, Technology, and Industry; the Ministry of Information Industry; the Ministry of Labor and Social Security; and the Ministry of Land and Resources. The personnel cut at the provincial level followed the State Council's example with a 50 percent cut. Lower-level governments, including cities, counties, and townships, assessed their personnel on the basis of jurisdiction, population, and social and economic development level. Provincial-level governments were responsible for drafting the plan and its implementation. After four and a half years of structural reform, the total personnel cut in all levels of government reached 1.15 million by June of 2002.

The 2003 reform created several new ministries, including the State-Owned Assets Supervision and Administration Commission, the China Banking Regulatory Commission, the Ministry of Commerce, the State Food and Drug Administration, and the Bureau of Safety Supervision. The previous National Development and Planning Commission was converted into the National Development and Reform Commission. The total number of ministries was now twenty-eight. The 2007 reform further reduced it to twenty-seven, including the adjustment to fifteen ministries and organizations. The ministry-level organizations were reduced by four.

Gradually Promote Administration by Law

To establish a nation ruled by law, China began construction of a legal system, and promoted administration law at all levels of government.

China issued several important laws in the 1990s, which served important roles in supervising the operation of administration, standardizing the behavior of government, and protecting the rights of citizens and other legal entities. Those laws included Administrative Procedure Law, State Compensation Law, Administrative Reconsideration Law, and Administrative Penalty Law. The Administrative License Law, which was published on July 1, 2004, further requests that the Chinese government implement a system of administration by law, reform the administrative examination system, and also promote a market economy. The Civil Servant Law of January 1, 2006, replaced the twelve-year-old National Civil Servants Temporary Rule. It has great significance in building a civil service system that suits the Chinese reality as well as borrowing from successful foreign experience.

It also helped to improve the quality of civil servants and governmental efficacy. In November 1999 and March 2004, the State Council issued two important documents to implement administration by law and build a nation ruled by law: "The Decision to Comprehensively Promote Administration by Law" and "The Implementation Summary to Comprehensively Promote Administration by Law." The second document promises the accomplishment of administration by law in the next ten years. The general office of the State Council issued "Several Ideas about Implementing Administrative Legal Responsibility" in 2005, stating that it wished to establish an administrative system that has clear legal responsibilities, has standardized operations, maintains effective oversight, and provides strong legal protections. In recent years, some problems emerged, such as rural land taken over by the state, population relocation into cities, enterprise bankruptcies, and weak environmental protection. Some citizens sued the government in the court for violating laws. On one hand, these incidents show that problems with the government remain; on the other hand, they also indicate that citizens have increased their awareness of rule of law and rights protection, which helps the progress of administration by law.

Promote Administrative Decision-Making

The promotion of scientific and democratic decision-making processes is an important task for administrative reform. Some governments have started experimenting in this area.

The first experiment was a decision-making process that combines civic participation, expert consultation, and collective decision-making.

Based on investigation and research, some governments began to listen to different interest groups to limit the government's blindness, capriciousness, and the leaders' arbitrariness in making some major decisions related to social and economic development, the making of appointments and the dismissal of important civil servants, key projects, and to a large amount of the budget allocation. Those decisions directly related to citizens' interests had to be publicized and hearings held in order for decision-makers to listen to their opinions. For those decisions with strong technical elements, experts must be consulted. Expert consultation is standardized to guarantee the objectivity, rationality, and feasibility of the decisions. Some governments also promote and perfect a system of responsibility, requiring resignations for incorrect decisions, and penalties based on the determination of responsibility. An error-correction system was also established to prevent or reduce bad decisions. Emphasis was given to scientific and democratic decision-making. The State Council and local governments are experimenting with collective decision-making procedures, expert consultation systems, policy publication systems, and systems of assigning clear responsibility for decision-making. For example, there are public hearings before the decision to increase the price of water, natural gas, and railroad tickets.

The second is to reform the administrative license system.

Since the Administrative License Law, the State Council alone has reduced more than 1,800 licensing items. All local governments have also implemented reforms in this area to dramatically reduce government licensing power. Some governments even started their second or third round of reduction. The licensing reform also included innovation and reform in licensing procedures. Many governments established a licensing center, promoting rapid and even online processes. The licensing procedures were also greatly simplified. The total number of licensing items was cut by 50.1 percent in the State Council, and by a similar amount in different local governments.

Reform on Administrative Implementation

This reform is designed to improve the government's implementation capacity, and enhance administrative law enforcement.

Enhancing Administrative Implementation Capacity

In his government report of March 5, 2006, Premier Wen Jiabao clearly mentioned the need to establish an administrative responsibility system and improve government's implementation capacity and public trust. This is the first time implementation capacity is written into a government report, signifying that it is formally included in the state's governing structure. On March 5, 2007, Premier Wen outlined the tasks for administrative reform, including changing government functions, standardizing administrative power, adjusting and improving government structure and the division of labor, reforming government management and service, greatly promoting governing publicity, promoting e-government and governmental websites, improving the quality of civil servants, increasing administrative efficacy, and enhancing administrative implementation capacity and public trust.

Increasing Administrative Law Enforcement

The legal construction over the past three decades created a good environment for administrative law enforcement, and rectified the absence of administrative laws. Central and local governments have created legal departments and trained a large number of administrative law enforcement officers. The government also recruited many officers from the public. It enhanced legal inspection over administrative activities, legal protections, and the efficacy of administration implementation.

Reform on Administrative Oversight

Progress has been made in this area. First, on April 17, 2002, the Hong Kong Special Administrative Region developed an accountability system for its legislative branch. It became law on July 1, 2002. Influenced by this reform, the Chinese government dismissed several senior officers during the SARS crisis in 2003. This is the first time that senior officers were held accountable during a natural disaster. The accountability system further developed following a series of natural and man-made incidents. Many major cities have created regulations on accountability. Many government documents also give clear direction in favor of accountability, such as the government report on March 5, 2004, "The Temporary Regulation on Resignation by Senior Civil Servants"; and in April 2004, "The Implementation Summary to Promote Comprehensive Administration by Law" issued by the State Council. "The Civil Servants Law" further legalized and standardized accountability, legitimating the implementation of an accountability system, and providing legal protection for its implementation. Premier Wen further emphasized this issue in his government report in 2006 and in a teleconference on September 4, 2006.

A second reform promoted the principle of publicity regarding governmental affairs. The central government decided to promote this policy in rural village management in June 1998. The general office of the State Council issued "A Notice to Promote Publicity in Township Governments" in December 2000 and "An Idea to Further Publicity in Governmental Affairs" in March 2005. The principle of publicity is this: except for national security and business secrets and privacy, all other administrative affairs need to be open to the public. The emphasis is on the following issues: those administrative activities with easy potential for corruption, and public service organizations that are directly related to the public interest, such as requiring schools and hospitals to publicize their fees and schedules.

This publicity policy is an important measure to protect citizens' right to know, to participate, and to exert oversight. There are many problems in government procurement and investment, such as corruption. For example, some officials waste public money for high public relations projects in order to get promoted. Others embezzle public funds. Now the publicity policy makes public project decisions accountable, imposes "sunshine" procurement, and promotes a public bid system.

Reform on Public Management

This includes two areas. One area is performance measurement in government. China started experimenting with this reform in the 1990s based on China's experience as well as the experience of western countries. The Ministry of Personnel also designated Hunan, Liaoning, the Langpu District of Shanghai, Nantong City of Jiangsu, and Jingyang County of Shaanxi as the experimental sites. China proposed this idea of scientific development, emphasized correct job performance, and established public service–oriented government in October 2003. This gave concrete direction to performance measurement. The China Government Performance Measurement Project Team under the Ministry of Personnel designed a system of performance measurement for local governments (thirty-three parameters) in August 2004. The system is based upon other performance-measurement systems and underwent a thorough investigation.

In its 2005 statement of major tasks the State Council stated that the government needed to set up performance-measurement content and parameters. The measurement procedure was to combine international assessment, public assessment, and expert evaluation. The goal was to promote performance evaluation compatible with the idea of scientific development. All levels of government started to experiment with performance measurement in 2006. Premier Wen requested the establishment of this measurement system in his government reports in 2006, 2007, and 2008, as well as the teleconference on September 4, 2006. According to the Ministry of Personnel, about one-third of the governments in China have experimented with performance measurement and have accumulated a certain degree of experience with it.

A second area of reform is the promotion of e-government. It is a major undertaking in reforming public management. The "Government Online Project" was proposed by China Telecom, the Information Center at the National Economic and Trade Commission, and forty other organizations in January 1999. The National Information Leading Group issued "The Plan for National Economic and Social Information" and "Suggestion to Construct E-Government in China" in July 2002. Those documents played positive roles promoting information technology in government, helping government accomplish its tasks, increase government transparency, improve efficiency and service quality, and change public management methods. Today, the central government and more than 73 percent of local governments (province, city, county) have their own websites; 93 percent of cabinet-level ministries and organizations have open websites. Websites in Beijing, Shanghai, and Qingdao have reached a high level of public service.

Reform in Public Finance

Tax adjustment gained emphasis after the reform, and tax reform became an important part of economic reform. The early tax reform aimed at increasing the economic incentives for the state-owned enterprises, reducing their reliance on public finance, and promoting fair competition. First, the state-owned enterprises were allowed to keep their profit, that is, to gain power and profit. Second, taxes were increased and profits were taxed. Taxes rather than shares of profits became the major source of public finance. Finally, a financial responsibility system was established. From December 1986, enterprises paid income taxes and a profit adjustment tax, and the rest of the profit was retained.

To increase government revenue, China adopted a new tax system in 1989. As a first step, the state-owned enterprises were required to pay income tax and then submit a certain portion of the profit to the state. The basic idea was that the state as the owner of the enterprises had the right to the profit. However, this measure did not reverse the trend of decreasing government revenue. The state's share of revenue over GDP dropped from 31.1 percent in 1978 to 15.8 percent in 1989 and 12.6 percent in 1993. The central government's share of revenue over the total revenue dropped from 40.5 percent in 1985 to 22 percent in 1993. The central government decided to change this trend. China created a tax-sharing system. Tax items were reduced from thirty-seven to twenty-three with three major categories, state tax, local tax, and state-local shared tax. The state tax bureau and local tax bureau were established and a tax redistribution system created.

The central government's revenue situation has greatly improved since then. After the Asian Financial Crisis, the Chinese government adopted an active financial policy, and issued huge debt. Government revenue has increased rapidly in recent years. China has established a large public financial system. China is facing the increasing tension between the demand for public products and transfer payments on the one hand and, on the other hand, the demand for reducing taxes on businesses and individuals. To maintain social order and economic sustainability, China needs to improve its expenditure structure and increase the share of public goods in the total government expenditure so that ordinary citizens can enjoy the benefits of public goods and services provided by the government. It will also have to increase the willingness of citizens to pay taxes. The tax system needs to be improved, and the efficiency of tax collection also needs to be improved. The size of the government and civil servants needs to be reduced. Government also needs to increase payments for poverty relief, establish tax-exemption for private donations, and encourage poverty relief by private forces. The local governments also should play an important role in providing public goods and services as well as raising money.

Reform on Civil Service System

China reformed its civil service system in keeping with the general policy of reform and modernization. The major reforms included establishing an open, equal, competitive, and legal system of personnel management based on the differentiation of government from enterprises and other institutions. A civil service system has been established in government, and a modern personnel system was created for other enterprises and organizations. Market mechanisms have been brought into personnel reform to play the fundamental role of human-resources distribution. Personnel management power is given back to each working unit. Both individuals and working units have freedom in human resources. A salary distribution system was established to match the rules of a market economy, the nature of work, labor's contribution, and production elements. A social security system is being gradually established to suit different types of employees for their retirement, unemployment, and medical needs. The government changed its old human resource concepts and bases all its policies on human resource development. It also formulated a future-oriented strategy for human resources that is aimed at its future position in the world. The government hopes to better predict the growth of talented people in order to better discover and use that talent.

MAIN ACHIEVEMENTS OF CHINA'S PUBLIC ADMINISTRATION REFORM

The achievements over the past three decades are reflected in the changes in government values, major functions, and administrative methods.

Changes in Government Values

The ideas of a service-oriented government, rule of law, accountable government, clean government, and frugal government have been established through administrative reform. Alongside the transformation from a planning economy to a market economy, the government shifted its previous policy to support only the state-owned enterprises to a new policy that supports all positive economic elements including the private economy. It also changed the narrow definition of development as economic development, and shifted the focus from the growth of GDP to coordinated development promoting economic quality, efficiency, and social and economic growth. These changing values helped promote a series of adjustments and reforms in administration.

The Rationalization of Government Functions

The government used to control everything, macro or micro, big or small. However, it started to focus only on economy adjustment, market oversight, social management, and public service through the separation of enterprises from the state, investment from the state, and the reform in state-owned assets. The state is changing from direct production and intervention to effective macro-intervention in order to create an environment for the market mechanism. The old idea of seeking rapid economic growth only has also been replaced by the new idea of balancing economic growth and efficiency, coordinating social and economic growth, and promoting the coexistence of human beings and nature. The state started to emphasize the importance of public service, and worked to establish a public service system.

Change in Administrative Methods

The number of items needing government licensing was reduced by half in both central and provincial governments. New methods of approval have been adopted, and procedures are standardized and simplified, including online approval. The content, meaning, and methods of a system of responsibility have been explored systematically. A performance measurement system combining Chinese characteristics and foreign practices has been carried out in some governments. E-government has been promoted and its general structure is established.

Standardization of Government Behavior

The past six rounds of administrative reform have enhanced the structure of economic adjustment, social and economic management, and public service, reduced administrative overlap, decreased the number of civil servants, and improved the efficiency of government. A legal system for administration has gradually been established. Civil servants, particularly senior ones, have become more aware of the need to administer by law. The decision-making process has been improved to reduce error, which promotes social and economic coordination. The principle of government publicity has brought forth greater policy openness, information openness, procedure openness, and enhanced administration implementation.

The Initial Establishment of a Civil Service System

"The Temporary Regulation of National Civil Servants," which was implemented on October 1, 1993, marks the beginning of the civil service system. It established a restrictive procedure for hiring. All civil servant employment had to undergo a thorough examination. The Civil Servant Law of January 1, 2006, is a milestone in the rule of law in construction and management of a civil service. The hiring, assignment, evaluation, reward and punishment, and training in civil servant management have been gradually improved. The newly established civil servant bureau under the Ministry of Human Resources and Social Security is the specific management agency for civil servants.

MAJOR CHALLENGES FACING THE PUBLIC ADMINISTRATIVE SYSTEM IN CHINA

Although some progress has been made over the past three decades, some areas in the public administration system need to be considered carefully, particularly some deep-rooted challenges with the administrative reform.

Some Defects in the Political System Limit the Deepening of the Administrative Reform

The Chinese political system is huge and complex, including an executive branch, legislative branch, and judicial branch, as well as the party system, media system, nongovernmental system, civic organization system, and their interrelationships. China's administrative reform needs to be examined from a systematic approach, and borrows experiences and lessons from other countries. The public administration system is essentially part of the political system. It is also a special part because it exists between the political sphere and the economic establishment. Administrative reform is limited by political reform, and yet it also promotes political reform.

The reform practices in modern public administration show that it deeply relates to government, society, market, and business, and touches upon the interaction among the political system, economic system, social system, and cultural system. In China, the goal is to coordinate the reforms in the above systems. If the ultimate values for administrative reform are efficiency and justice, the goals of political reform are democracy and rule of law. Because democratic administration and administration by law will inevitably require political reform, democracy and rule of law need to be enhanced. The current corruption among some officials is related to the absence of political mechanism, that is, the absence of a power balance in political system. This shows that the further administrative reform depends on the deepening of the political reform.

Some Government Functions Are Still Lagging Behind

The governmental functions still need further clarification. The problems need to be tackled from the roots, such as the mixtures of government and business, administration and other businesses, and state and other intermediate organizations. Some local governments in particular still intervene in micro-economic affairs, and pay insufficient attention to public service. Investment needs to be increased in the following areas, including social security, employment, basic education, medical service, culture, population and planning, and other public services. Although the government licensing has made great progress, the follow-up oversight and dynamic oversight are still inadequate. The cooperation between the state and social self-governing organization is still at the beginning stage. Nongovernmental organizations (NGO) play little roles due to the absence of law and policy. Civic participation in public affairs and governance is still low, and democratic administration progresses little.

Some Governments Still Lack Clear Definitions of Rights and Responsibilities

Administrative overlapping still exists. Some organizations see the inconsistency of power and responsibility, the overlapping of functions, and fuzziness in functional areas. As a result, some organizations are fighting for power, avoid responsibility, and increase the administrative cost in general. In addition, the administrative structure is inadequate. The definition of government size and expenditure is not scientific. A typical example is the small size of central government personnel versus the large size of local governments. This is different than some other big countries. Another related problem is the small size of civil servants directly providing public service versus the total civil servants that are directly or indirectly supported by the public finance.

Administrative Coordination Is Still Not Smooth in Some Areas

There are three major problems here. First is the lack of an effective mechanism of coordination. The lack of an effective mechanism of coordination sometimes causes obstruction in administrative operation. Different organizations compete for power and responsibility. The national interest is sacrificed as a result of special interests.

Second is the need for the further enhancement of scientific and democratic decision-making processes. Citizen participation in administrative decisions is still low. Interest-representation mechanisms have not been established. The real interest and opinion from the public cannot be reflected through proper channels. The social dispute resolution has not established proper mechanisms.

Third is the need to further strengthen administrative oversight. The major problems in this area include: superficial and procedural oversight is more common than substantive and effective oversight; general oversight is more common than oversight on major affairs; one-time oversight is more common than frequent oversight; too much praise in oversight and too few questions; soft means such as discussion and inspection in oversight are more common than hard means such as testifying and impeachment.

Administration by Law Needs to Be Further Reinforced

The state has issued many laws to implement administrative reform. However, the legal means provided are still inadequate in general. The previous administrative reform, such as the decisions on reform measures, procedure, interest adjustment, and responsibility, was mostly implemented through an ad hoc policy and through top-down authority. Although it is flexible, this method lacks legal authority, and lowers the predictability of the reform. This reduces the trust in reform.

CHINA'S PUBLIC ADMINISTRATION REFORM ALSO BORROWS FROM SUCCESSFUL EXPERIENCES IN THE UNITED STATES AND OTHER COUNTRIES

The world is diverse, as are the world's civilizations. A political system is also an organic unity involving uniqueness and commonality. On the one hand, different political systems have their own character; on the other hand, they share some commonalities. The global village is becoming reality as a result of modern technology and the Internet. Different civilizations need to learn from each other in the face of global challenges. All governments need to borrow from the useful experience of others to enrich and develop their own social governing models. In the administrative reform, China has its own situation, and will not simply copy others' models. However, China also tries to borrow from some foreign experiences, particularly those of Western countries.

The State Council Development Research Center, Tsinghua University, and the Kennedy School of Government at Harvard University have implemented a joint training program for Chinese senior administrators. This program has been running for several years. The China National School of Administration cooperates with Yale University to train several groups of provincial leaders from China. Beijing Administrative College and the University of Georgia have established an academic exchange relationship. The two schools have jointly trained nine groups of middle to senior administrators from Beijing.

In the training courses offered in the China National School of Administration, there are courses on foreign administrative reforms. The author himself has lectured many times on this topic. Students show great interest in "new public management" and "governance" theories and practices. China also holds international conferences with foreign countries. For example, the China National School of Administration has jointly hosted four rounds of a "Sino-Europe Summit" with the European Union to discuss governmental reform and innovation. Through these types of exchanges and cooperation, administrative reform in China is gradually transferring from the goal of government control to the goal of having government serve, and from totalitarian government to limited government, and from government by person to government by law. The administrative reform experience in China also attracted international attention. China has carried out large-scale exchanges with western countries, newly industrialized countries, transitional countries, and developing countries. For example, there are dozens of countries that have sent their civil servants to study at the China National School of Administration in recent years.

CHINA'S FOREIGN POLICY HAS CHANGED ALONG WITH ITS PUBLIC ADMINISTRATION REFORM

Since the People's Republic of China was founded in 1949, its diplomatic policy has undergone a great many adjustments. In the 1950s, China's diplomatic policy was to fight alongside the Soviet Union against the United States; in the 1960s, it was to fight against the United States as well as the Soviet Union; in the 1970s, it was to fight against the Soviet Union with the United States. Since the 1980s, China has established the opening policy, trying to peacefully coexist and develop with the United States and other countries.

The changes in China's diplomatic policy are, on one hand, related to the international environment; on the other hand, they are related to China's domestic situation. They are also related to changes in China's diplomatic philosophy. According to Mao Zedong's diplomatic philosophy, the themes of "war and revolution" and "contradiction dialectic" should be applied to international relations. Mao's diplomatic philosophy shows a special idealism. In Deng Xiaoping's thought, peace and development have substituted for war and revolution. His diplomatic philosophy shows a great deal of realism. Jiang Zemin, recognizing the new situation involving economic globalization, put forward the theory of diversity of world civilizations: each civilization, especially Western and Eastern civilization, should foster mutual trust, mutual benefit, equality, and coordination. Hu Jintao now espouses a diplomatic philosophy of a harmonious world. In his view, China should build up a harmonious society internally and a harmonious world externally.

At the conference of the sixtieth anniversary of the United Nations, Hu Jintao put forward a new view regarding world development, appealing to every country to work toward eliminating poverty and fighting against international terrorism to build up a peaceful and flourishing world. We can see that Chinese leaders' diplomatic philosophy has gradually turned from a philosophy of warfare to a philosophy of harmony. The United States and China are both permanent members of the Security Council of the UN and the Sino-American relationship influences the world's peace and development. Chinese and American leaders should build up a win-win thinking mode to manage their bilateral relationship in the twenty-first century.

Although China and the Unites States disagree on the Taiwan issue, political ideology, and on other issues, the two countries have a common interest regarding many other crucial issues, such as fighting against terrorism, maintaining the stability of northeast Asia, and environmental protection. Even in some disputes, the two share common interests; for example, regarding trade disputes and globalization the two countries' economic interests are more and more related.

NOTES

1. People's Republic of China.
2. The reform in public administration in this article does not include legal, judicial, and political reforms.

3

Grassroots Democracy in China

A Comparative Study of Villagers' and Residents' Committees

Jianfeng Wang

Grassroots democracy is often viewed as a just and effective means to achieve local governance, despite the fact that the concept itself takes different forms in different political and social settings. Ever since the early twentieth century, China has committed to reforming its feudal-based and stagnant local governing structure to match a fundamentally modernizing society. Different experiments were carried out, including the *Bao Jia* system in the 1930s and 1940s, the commune system in rural China from the 1950s to the 1970s, and the *Danwei* system in urban China since 1950s. None of the above qualified as grassroots democracy. Contemporary Chinese society has experienced deep changes as the market economy has gradually established itself in the past three decades. Along the way, grassroots democracy has been gradually accepted as a key means to achieve local governance. Its increasing application now includes villagers' committees, residents' committees, labor unions, local People's Congress elections, township elections, and township public finance reforms. The first two organizations are the nuclei of rural and urban neighborhood management, respectively, through which residents manage neighborhood affairs and state-citizen interactions are carried out. Observers and researchers often credit them as examples of an increasing trend toward grassroots democracy in China. This chapter will compare the two organizations in terms of their history, structural differences, and implications for the further development of grassroots democracy in China.

INTRODUCTION

China's Constitution (1982) promulgated the principle of grassroots self-governance (art. 111). It defined villagers' committees and residents' committees as "autonomous mass organizations" in rural and urban neighborhoods, respectively, through which citizens manage neighborhood affairs by themselves. Based on the Constitution, the National People's Congress (NPC) passed the Organic Law of Villagers' Committees (1987, revised in 1998) and the Organic Law of Urban Residents' Committees (1989). Both laws state clearly that villagers' committees and residents' committees are not part of the state apparatus but grassroots elected self-governing organizations. Local residents should practice the principle of self-governance to manage, educate, and serve themselves (art. 2 in both laws).

Villagers' committees and residents' committees are twins. Figure 3.1 shows that both organizations hold unique positions in China: they are intermediaries between the state and citizens at the neighborhood level. In practice, both organizations serve as the nuclei of neighborhood governance. Despite many inadequacies, both villagers' committees and residents' committees have experienced enormous growth during the reform era. So far, China has established about 1 million villagers' committees with 4.5 million committee members in rural areas and 115,000 residents' committees with half a million members in cities by 2001 (Ministry of Civil Affairs 2002). Despite many inadequacies in practice, both organizations have characteristics of genuine grassroots self-governing organizations. This has significant implications for state-citizen interactions and grassroots democracy in China.

Indeed, many observers have tried to gauge and project the prospects for grassroots democracy through the ups and downs of villagers' committees in recent years (Kennedy 2002; L. Li 2002; Manion 2000; O'Brien and Li 2000; Oi and Rozelle 2000; Pastor and Tan 2000; Shi 1999; X. Wang 1997). The study of residents' committees also reveals their central role in neighborhood service provision and interest representation (Read 2000; J. Wang 2003). However, the field is still at the early stage in learning about China's grassroots democracy. Both villagers' committees and residents' committees vary from neighborhood to neighborhood and village to village, which makes conclusive generalizations premature. However, a pilot comparison between contemporary villagers' committees and residents' committees can provide a unique window for exploring several serious analytical questions. How could villagers' committees and residents' committees originate and then develop? Given the rural-urban dichotomy, what are the differences between these two neighborhood organizations? Do they suggest different directions for China's grassroots democracy? What are the prospects that grassroots democracy will develop through urban residents' committees and

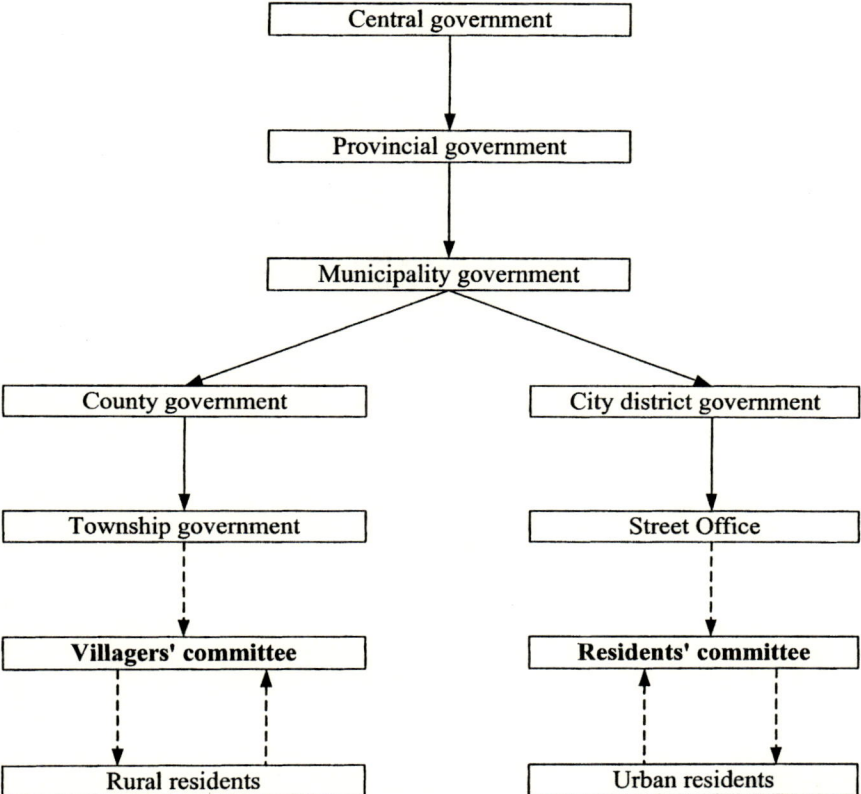

Figure 3.1. The Formal Governing Structure in China

rural villagers' committees? The purpose of this chapter is to lay out these theoretical questions and offer some tentative and partial answers to them.

THE RISE OF VILLAGERS' AND RESIDENTS' COMMITTEES

Before the reform and opening period, the Chinese state controlled urban and rural society through different means. The state penetrated and dominated rural China mainly through the commune system.[1] The commune system was implemented in the mid-1950s. A typical commune had three administrative levels: commune, brigade (*dadui*), and production team (*shengchan dui*).[2] Each commune was a political-social-economic compound. Based upon collective ownership of land, food production, and distribution, a commune effectively controlled individual peasants. Similar to urban society, rural society was also divided into numerous isolated "cells" (communes). Each commune was in the state's shadow and each peasant was the commune's dependent.

In cities, the state penetrated society through the *danwei* (working units) system (Lei 2001; Lu and Perry 1997). Originated from military supply systems, each *danwei* was endowed with not only economic functions, but also political, social, administrative, logistical, and educational functions. *Danwei* controlled and served its employees and their dependents "from cradle to grave." Each *danwei* belonged to a specific level of government and each individual was slotted in a specific *danwei*. Thus, the urban society became a huge "honeycomb," in which numerous cells (*danwei*) encircled the nucleus (state) (Shue 1988). The state controlled *danwei*, and through them, controlled urban residents.

In general, Chinese society was deeply embedded in the state's power structure in the pre-reform era. The state created a minimal, divided, isolated, and dependent society. How could both villagers' and residents' committees have emerged and developed within such a tightly controlled system?

THE RISE OF RESIDENTS' COMMITTEES

The first residents' committees developed as early as 1949. According to the latest archives, Hangzhou City in Zhejiang Province promulgated an administrative order, "*guanyu quxiao baojia zhidu jiangli jumin weiyuanhui de zhishi*" (an order to abolish *Baojia Zhi* and establish residents' committees) (Zhao 1998, 531). The order stated that urban neighborhood management should follow the principle of self-governance. Residents' committees were not part of the state apparatus but self-ruling organizations elected by local residents. Each was responsible for: (1) representing urban residents, publicizing governmental laws and orders, and strengthening connections between governments and residents; (2) assisting governments in urban management and construction; and (3) managing neighborhood affairs. This was the first comprehensive local government order regarding grassroots self-governance. By March 1950, Hangzhou had established 571 residents' committees and 3,802 residential teams (*jumin xiaozu*).[3]

In 1954, the Standing Committee of the NPC adopted the Organic Bylaw of Urban Residents' Committees, which finalized residents' committees' legal status as urban neighborhood self-governing organizations. This law laid the foundation for later legislation governing both residents' and villagers' committees.

However, despite their legally stipulated status, the primary goal of residents' committees was to enhance the state's control over cities. Peng Zhen, one of the Chinese Communist Party (CCP) senior leadership's most vocal and enthusiastic promoters of grassroots self-governance and the rule of law, stated the purpose of residents' committees clearly:

> Since our industrialization is at the beginning period and we are still in transition period to socialism, there are many street residents who are not belong to factory, firm, school, and administration in even relatively industrialized cities. These people even take sixty of total population in some cities. In order to organize and gradually transform them into *danwei*, and to reduce the burdens of district governments and public security dispatching units, we suggest to establish residents' committee, besides street offices. (Peng 1991, 241)

Residents' committees targeted those socially unconnected who could not be absorbed into the *danwei* system, such as private businesses owners and employees, the jobless, housewives, the handicapped, and others socially disadvantaged. Compared with the *danwei* system, residents' committees took only a marginal role in urban neighborhood management. When the socialist reconstruction (1949–1957) was finished, the importance of residents' committees was quickly diminished as the number of socially unconnected decreased. The further politicization during the Great Leap Forward (1958–1960) and the Cultural Revolution (1966–1976) almost changed residents' committees into quasi-government institutions, spending most of their energy in political activities. It is fair to say that the residents' committees' self-governing status had largely remained on paper for its first several decades.

The real growth of residents' committees started in the early 1980s. Several changes pushed the state to re-institutionalize and empower residents' committees in urban neighborhood governance.

As the market started gaining dominance in the economy, the *danwei* system gradually dissolved (Lu and Perry 1997). *Danwei* become *an* actor of the society, primarily taking economic functions, rather than *the* actor that represented the state in controlling urban residents. *Danwei* start peeling off their social responsibilities, such as social welfare, housing, childcare, and so on. Many of these social responsibilities, which are necessary for social integration and deeply connected with residents' interests, fall upon residents' committees.

In addition, the demographic structure of urban society is increasingly complicated during the reform era. Chinese urban society has never been as socially and economically fragmented as it is today, with increases in new vocations and careers, completely new types of working units, labor mobility, the number of rural migrant laborers in cities, new poverty groups and other disadvantaged groups, and an aging population. These are elements that cannot be encompassed by the traditional urban governing structure.

As a result, the state started losing its capacity to effectively manage urban neighborhood affairs (Read 2000). Despite many inadequacies, residents' committees are perhaps the only viable institution that has the legal authority and potential capacity to respond to neighborhood challenges. Filling the power vacuum as the state retreats from the urban neighborhoods, residents' committees have expanded their areas of concern from the socially disconnected to all urban residents. This increase in their constituency naturally strengthens the residents' committees' position as representatives of residents' interests. Meanwhile, residents' feelings of ownership toward local affairs have been increasingly strengthened. More than ever before, local residents are willing to identify themselves with their residential neighborhoods and, therefore, are eager to participate in local decision-making. Local residents' demands for participation also significantly bolster residents' committees' self-governing status. For the state, residents' committees provide a channel to release the political pressure for participation. All of these factors determine the broad context for the rise of residents' committees.

THE RISE OF VILLAGERS' COMMITTEES

If residents' committees emerged as a response to the gradually dissolving *danwei* system and increasing social plurality, villagers' committees arose relatively more quickly when the commune system was abolished in the late 1970s.

The commune system was decollectivized in the late 1970s and replaced by the household contracting system in which peasants gained the usufruct over the land and hence the freedom to dispose of agricultural products after meeting the state's quota. The land reform, marketization, and partial privatization in rural China gradually released peasants from total dependence on the state. In addition, rural economic liberation helped restore a sense of individuality, mostly reflected in individual households.

Facing the "ocean" of a new small-scale farming economy, the state found that the old rural governing structure was inappropriate for handling the new challenges. As the rural economy grew, the state saw growing decay of the state apparatus at the grassroots level and increasing tension in cadre-peasant relations. The elimination of the commune system also quickly induced a decline of social order in the countryside (O'Brien and Li 2000). Both factors contributed to the rising crises of legitimacy and governability of the state in rural China (X. Wang 1997). Therefore, the state needed to fill the grassroots vacuum with some institutions that could reorganize the rural society, and yet not be as costly and destructive as the old state apparatus was.

The earliest villagers' committees spontaneously occurred in Guanxi Province (Yishan and Luocheng) in 1980 and 1981, where the security problems were the worst. The practices in Guangxi were quickly appraised and then introduced to other provinces by Beijing (Kelliher 1997; X. Yu 1983). The villagers' committees' status as self-governing neighborhood organizations was soon ratified by the Constitution (1982). Consequentially, the NPC passed the Organic Law of Villagers' Committees (experimental) in 1987, which provided many detailed articles to boost villagers' committees nationwide. After a decade of active experiments, the Organic Law of Villagers' Committees was finally promulgated in 1998. This law provided a solid base for grassroots democracy in the countryside.

VILLAGERS' AND RESIDENTS' COMMITTEES: WHAT ARE THE DIFFERENCES?

According to the Constitution (1982), both villagers' and residents' committees are nongovernmental organizations, practicing self-governing principles inside neighborhoods. Their legitimacy comes from the recognition of local residents rather than being delegated by the state. Furthermore, both organizations have similar responsibilities: representing and reflecting their constituents' interests to the state, managing organization affairs and welfare, mediating civil disputes, and maintaining public security and order.

In practice, both villagers' and residents' committees represented real progress in the transformation toward grassroots democracy. The structure of neighborhood governance and state-society relations has been reshaped in the retreat of the state. The neighborhood power vacuum was gradually filled by the practice of self-governance, primarily carried through residents' and villagers' committees.

However, despite their similar legal status as well as practical background, there are some distinctions between residents' and villagers' committees.

Involvement versus Indifference

Participation is an important element in grassroots democracy. In general, peasants show much more enthusiasm about participation than do urban residents. Peasants know more about villagers' committee operations and participate more in villagers' committee elections. In contrast, some urban residents cannot even name the members of their residents' committee. The nationwide voter turnout in villagers' committee elections was about 85 percent, while the average voter turnout by urban household representatives in residents' committee elections was lower than 25 percent (Gui and Cui 2001; X. Wang 1997).

History partially accounts for the difference. For example, residents' committees primarily dealt with marginal populations during most of their history; therefore, they were widely viewed by urban residents as dispensable and trivial organizations. In addition, the historically negative image of residents' committees as intrusive instruments of the state in the 1960s and 1970s also prevent some residents from accepting residents' committees today (Read 2000). In contrast, villagers' committees targeted the whole village population since their beginning. Furthermore, villagers' committees have a relatively short history. As the replacement for the commune system, villagers' committees do not have as bad a "reputation" as residents' committees have.

Besides history, an even more important reason is the interest connections between the organizations and residents/villagers. In general, villagers' interests are much more closely tied to the villagers' committee than are urban residents' interests tied to the residents' committee.

When the commune system was abolished in rural villages, collective ownership over village property was retained (Oi 1989). Since villagers' committees inherited the collective property from the former commune system, they maintained a monopoly over the public resources of the village. As a self-governing organization, the villagers' committee manages not only social affairs but also economic affairs in the village. Despite the de facto commercialization of agriculture production in the 1990s, many key properties in a village, including land, schools, roads, the irrigation system, and other infrastructure, are still collectively owned. This collective ownership gives peasants some sense of ownership over village affairs. Since each peasant's welfare depends on the villagers' committee's management over this collective property, he or she often is interested in actively participating in villagers' committee elections and management.

In contrast, urban citizens lack the bond of collective property. In the *danwei* system, one's interest was mostly tied to his/her work unit. Horizontal economic linkages among residents were relatively rare and difficult to establish. Despite the gradual dissolution of the *danwei* system, urban citizens still identify their major economic stakes with their work units. In addition, residents' committees lack the monopolistic status in neighborhoods that villagers' committees have in villages. Residents' interests are diversely tied with many other actors, such as water stations, police, asset managing companies, and the social security administration. Therefore, given the weaker linkage of interests, it is not surprising that urban residents are more apathetic when it comes to neighborhood participation than are peasants.

Direct Elections versus Indirect Elections

Villagers' and residents' committees also differ in their electoral processes. The Organic Law of Villagers' Committees (1998) promulgated a comprehensive electoral procedure for village elections. According to the Organic Law, direct election is the only legitimate method in villagers' committee elections (art. 11). In addition, the Organic Law also accords an independent status to the Villagers' Electoral Committee, which is solely responsible for holding elections. The members of this committee should be elected either directly by the residents or indirectly by their household representatives (art. 13). These are institutional assurances for relatively independent village elections.

In order to promote the transparency and fairness of villagers' committee elections, the Organic Law also enlists several procedures such as open nominations, secret voting, semi-competitive elections (more candidates than the number of positions), and open counts (art. 14). It holds that any threat, bribe, forged ballot, or other improper method that hinders normal elections will be punished (art. 15). So far, most Chinese villagers' committees have been generated through grassroots direct elections, the majority of which held several rounds of election (Z. Wang 2001).[4]

In contrast, members of residents' committees can be elected either directly by local residents or indirectly by household representatives, according to the Organic Law of Urban Residents' Committee (1989) (art. 8). Furthermore, the Organic Law has no provision about the electoral committee or any other specific procedures and requirements concerning residents' committee elections. In practice, most residents' committees have adopted the indirect election procedure. Furthermore, the street office, the lowest level of government in cities, has a huge influence on election results (Xu 2002). It often organizes the election, and sometimes even nominates the candidates for residents' committees. Some of the candidates are not even local residents. Finally, the number of household representatives is small in the indirect election, which makes local government's intervention or manipulation relatively easy.

It is hard to make a normative comparison between direct and indirect elections. Direct elections can increase competition and transparency. They can also increase the accountability of some villagers' committees to their constituents (Oi and Rozelle 2000; Xu 2000). Indirect elections are cheaper and are more likely to produce a consensus.

Villagers often show great enthusiasm about participating in villagers' committees. Therefore, direct elections provide a better means than indirect elections for peasants to express their will and defend their interests. In addition, rural villages are relatively close and most villagers' families have lived in the same villages for many generations. Such familiarity reduces the cost of information for villagers when they cast their ballots. Finally, rural society is relatively homogeneous, and the needs and demands of peasants are relatively similar and simple. Therefore, building consensus in villages is reasonably easier than in cities.

In contrast, urban residents care less about the activities of residents' committees, which increases the difficulty of having a meaningful direct election. Some cities have tried to encourage direct elections. But voter turnout was unsatisfactory (M. Zhang 2001). In addition, urban neighborhoods, especially newly emerged ones, are much more fragmented than rural villages. Many people even do not know their neighbors. Therefore, the cost of information and consensus-building is perceptibly high. Finally, China's neighborhood self-governance, especially in urban areas, is still heavily reliant on the state's support. For example, while villagers' committees' expenses are almost exclusively paid by the peasants, the state is still the largest contributor to residents' committees' funding. The indirect election process is thus a more realistic reflection of the relation among residents, residents' committee, and the state.

The Role of Residents'/Villagers' Assemblies

Villagers' and residents' committees are told to be the executive branches, reporting to Residents'/Villagers' Assemblies consisting of all residents/villagers. Residents'/Villagers' Assemblies are supposed to hold the highest power in urban/rural neighborhoods. However, Villagers' and Residents' Assemblies play quite different roles.

According to the Organic Law of Villagers' Committees, the Villagers' Assembly is the power center in a village. It has legislative power, power of oversight, and even power of decision-making over major substantive issues. It is responsible for creating and modifying the Ordinance of Village Self-Governance (*cunmin zizhi zhangcheng*) and Village Charters and Codes of Conduct (*cungui minyue*) (art. 20). It is also required to check and approve the villagers' committee's annual report and evaluate each committee member's performance (art. 18).

In addition, the Organic Law explicitly requires that each villager's committee submit for a decision eight specific issues that are vital to villagers' interests to the Villagers' Assembly (art. 19).[5] These eight issues cover the most important public affairs in a village. Endowing the decision power over these eight issues to the Assembly elevates the Assembly from a merely legislative and oversight body to the locus of decision-making in the village. In a system like this, the villagers' committee works more like a policy executor, following the substantive orders from the Assembly. Despite some doubts about the actual capacity of the Assembly (Oi and Rozelle 2000), more and more cases show that villagers see the Assembly as the primary place to fight corrupt villagers' committees or township governments (Xin 1999). In a survey conducted in eight provinces in 2000, 77 percent of villagers rank the Villagers' Assembly as the strongest protector for their interests in those villages whose villagers' committee receive residents' evaluations that are "very satisfied" and "satisfied" (Rural Investigation Team

2001). This shows that Villagers' Assemblies take the lead role in those villages that carry out self-governance successfully.

In contrast, the Residents' Assembly is much weaker in the urban neighborhood self-governing system, despite its nominally leading status designated by the Organic Law of Urban Residents' Committee. The law confines the power of the Residents' Assembly to oversight (art. 10). Unlike the Villagers' Assembly, which has decision power over eight substantive issues, the Residents' Assembly does not have clear power over any substantive issues. From a legal perspective, the Residents' Assembly works more like an oversight body, keeping a certain distance from the daily decision-making process.

In addition, the functioning of the Residents' Assembly was made intentionally harder than the Villagers' Assembly. According to the law, the Villagers' Assembly needs only one-tenth of the villagers to be called into session while the Residents' Assembly needs double that number (one-fifth). Given the fact that urban residents have less enthusiasm for neighborhood affairs than rural villagers do, it is clear that the Residents' Assembly is much more difficult to call into session.

In practice, the Residents' Assembly's oversight is rare, passive, and weak (M. Zhang 2001). The Organic Law of Urban residents' Committees (1989) does not mandate meeting times for Resident's Assemblies. Some neighborhoods do not even hold one session a year (M. Zhang 2001). The call for a session can come from either the residents' committee or one-fifth of the residents. Given residents' apathy to residents' committees, most Residents' Assemblies are called by the residents' committees. Therefore, they follow the residents' committee's agenda, which is not necessarily the residents' agenda.

Finally, even the oversight power of the Residents' Assembly was further weakened by the introduction of Residential Consultative Assemblies (*jumin yishihui*) in many cities. The Residential Consultative Assembly consists of residents' representatives, CCP local units, business representatives, representatives from local governments, celebrities, and representatives from other social circles. Many of them are not community residents. The Residential Consultative Assembly is intended to work as a consulting entity for the residents' committee, just like the role of the Chinese People's Consultative Conferences with respect to the central government. However, it is common in rich cities for the Residential Consultative Assembly to seize the oversight position that the Residents' Assembly should perform (X. Zhang 2002). For example, the Residential Consultative Assembly in Dejia Community of Hangzhou City in Zhejiang Province met three times and made fourteen recommendations, while the Residents' Assembly held no meetings in 2001 (X. Zhang 2002). In Shanghai city, the Residential Consultative Assembly is given the power to "advise, bridge communication, and oversight" in urban self-governance (Lin 2002).

Relationship with the State

Villagers' and residents' committees further differ with respect to their relationship with the state.

The villagers' committee has replaced the commune as *the* comprehensive organization for villages. This puts villagers' committees in a very delicate position between the state and the villagers. In one way, despite the state's retreat from the rural grassroots, the state does not leave them unintended. Since the villagers' committee is the only comprehensive organization in the village, the state tries hard to control it primarily through township governments and CCP village committees. On the other hand, the villagers' committee is also supposed to be the defender of villagers' interests. Therefore, the villagers' committee is often caught between the will of the state and the will of the villagers when both are at odds. The relationship between the local governments and these villagers' committees truly fighting for villagers' interests is often strained, sometimes even conflictive, and the committee members bear tremendous pressures from local governments (J. Yu 2000). Those villagers' committees that become the "legs" of the state often encounter resentful and uncooperative villagers.

Residents' committees face a different situation. Historically, residents' committees were marginal actors in urban governance, primarily used for managing social "misfits." The state has maintained a traditionally weak presence in urban neighborhoods up to today. Unlike most rural villages that have CCP grassroots units, many urban neighborhoods simply lack CCP units. That is why CCP units are not even mentioned in the Organic Law of Urban Residents' Committees, while they are supposed to be the "leading core" in rural villages.[6]

Even though residents' committees have become vital institutions for grassroots governance, their status in cities is still less important than the status of villagers' committees in villages. Unlike the villagers' committee, which is the only comprehensive organization in the village, residents' committees are only one among several types of organizations in urban communities. Therefore, the state does not make as great an effort control residents' committees as it does to control villagers' committees.[7]

In addition, residents' committees are taking on more and more responsibilities that the state is either reluctant or unable to handle effectively, such as neighborhood services, cultural entertainment, environment and sanitation, social order, and even re-employment. Residents' committees and the state increasingly have a cooperative relation in which the state would often encourage and support the expansion of residents' committee. Meanwhile, urban residents' low participation also facilitates cooperation between the state and residents' committees. Since the pressure on residents' committees from their constituents is not as strong as that on villagers' committees, residents' committees often have more room to win the state's support while worrying little about alienating their constituents.

Therefore, the state means quite different things to villagers' committees and residents' committees. The relationship between the state and villagers' committees is more strained and even conflictive, while the relationship between the state and residents' committees is more cooperative and mutually enhancing. The further development of villagers' committees faces a less favorable environment with respect to the state than do residents' committees.

Amateurism versus Professionalism

The composition of villagers' residents' committees also diverges.

All villagers' committees and their subcommittee members are village residents. They might not be experts in administration, but they are enthusiastic village "citizens," knowing their constituents and willing to serve voluntarily. According to the Organic Law of Villagers' Committees, membership of villagers' committees and their subcommittees is only a part-time position (art. 9). Villagers' committee members are considered to be passionate amateurs rather than rational professionals. Being a villagers' committee member is an honor and duty rather than a career.[8] When a peasant is elected as a villagers' committee member, he or she still needs to engage in agricultural production. He or she is still a "peasant" or "fellow villager" rather than an "employee" or "bureaucrat." He or she needs to make a living through agricultural production (or other means) rather than through a salary from "office," so this position rests on voluntarism.[9]

In contrast, residents' committee members are not necessarily local residents, the Organic Law of Urban Residents' Committees notwithstanding. In recent years, residents' committees have received increasing complaints about their aging and poorly educated personnel. As a result, residents' committees and their subcommittees in big cities, such as Shanghai, started recruiting personnel through contract rather than election. For example, Shanghai sets limitations on eligibility to serve on residents' committees, including an age limit and minimum education level (Lin 2002). Committee members must show some expertise or experience in local affairs management and they need not be residents of the neighborhood. In addition, positions in residents' committees are treated as full-time jobs so that their members can fully engage in neighborhood affairs. Being a member is a vocation, not a volunteer position.

Amateurism and professionalism reflect the different goals of villagers' and residents' committees. Through amateurism, villagers' committees want to increase accountability while through professionalism residents' committees emphasize efficiency. Peasants have a much higher stake in the villagers' committees; therefore, their demands for accountability are naturally higher. Urban society is more fragmented with constant new challenges; therefore, efficiency is often a bigger concern than accountability in the residents' committee's daily operations, given its apathetic constituents. This is why most residents' committees have started setting prerequisites for membership, such as a minimum level of education and experience, and an age requirement, while villagers' committees are open to all villagers (Lin 2002).

Participatory Democracy versus Representative Democracy

The bottom-up democratization scenario is still an ongoing process in China. In practice, villagers' committees vary from village to village, as residents' committees vary from neighborhood to neighborhood. It is far too early to tell what their explicit impact on grassroots democracy in China will be. However, based upon the rapid progress of villagers' and residents' committees, especially those relatively successful ones, it is possible to point out the probable divergent roads to grassroots democratization in China.

Peasants in a village are relatively homogeneous, despite their increasing differentiation under the economic reform. They have relatively equal status, guaranteed primarily though collective ownership over land, infrastructure, and other property. Most important, villagers' committee operations have a significant impact on each villager's interest. Based upon equality, collectivism, and the bond of property, villagers practice self-governance through active participation. Since peasants live in a relatively close community, familiar with each other, the cost of active participation is low. Through popular discussions in the Villagers' Assembly, average villagers decide important issues. Further, they directly elect and entrust villagers' committees with the power to implement the major decisions they have made. Villagers' committees, compared to residents' committees, have less discretion, as Villagers' Assemblies take more active roles. Villagers' committees are also characterized by amateurism, which is designed to strengthen accountability. However, holding the villagers' committees accountable to villagers' interests often pushes villagers' committees to the forefront of conflict with the will of the authoritarian state. The potential threat from the state, in turn, reinforces the popular nature of self-governance for those villagers' committees that insist on representing villagers' interests. All this suggests a possible transition toward a participatory (popular) democracy at the grassroots.

In contrast, residents' committees reflect a scenario that is more compatible with representative (elite) democracy. Urban residents have fewer connections with residents' committees than do villagers with villagers' committees. In addition, the existence of many other types of institutions in neighborhoods also diverts residents' attention from the residents' committee. In general, residents' participation in residents' committees is inactive.

Given public apathy and the weak role of the state, the residents' committee tries to build its legitimacy based on service provision and problem-solving. The format of the elections is not the major concern. The quality of services matters more. Therefore, efficiency becomes the enemy of urban grassroots democracy. Following the desire for efficiency, the thresholds for residents' committee memberships are raised to recruit people with more expertise. In addition, since the residents' committee is the center of neighborhood life, the Residents' Assembly is marginalized. Urban neighborhoods also create Residential Consultative Assemblies to incorporate nonresidential representatives, hoping to expand the residents' committee's influence and improve the quality of decision-making. Without strong backing from its constituents, the residents' committee chooses cooperation with the state to give itself more room to grow, even though some residents view such coordination as a form of "cozy collusion" (Ling and Jiang 2001). It is a pragmatic choice, but is also a wise policy to enhance the status of urban grassroots self-governance under the authoritarian state.

In general, the practice of some relatively successful villagers' and residents' committees indicates divergent roads to grassroots democratization. However, this argument is only a tentative one, given the fact that the differences between villagers' and residents' committees are far from clear-cut. In addition, between those successful and failed ones, the majority of residents' and villagers' committees have an ambiguous status whose further evolution is still fuzzy. It is uncertain whether (1) current democratic developments at the neighborhood level will eventually flourish, or (2) the future path of grassroots democratization will be exactly as described above. However, the possible divergence between participatory and representative democracy still provides valuable information for forecasts about grassroots democracy in China.

IMPLICATIONS FOR CHINA'S GRASSROOTS DEMOCRACY

While there is serious uncertainty about the ultimate format of grassroots democracy, it is uncontroversial to claim that both villagers' and residents' committees have significantly added to the movement toward democracy. In fact, villagers' and residents' committees are similar in at least three areas, which has important implications for China's grassroots democracy:

First, democracy needs an independent, self-generating, and self-supporting civil society (Havel and Klaus 1996; O'Donnell, Schmitter, and Whitehead 1986). As an intermediary entity between citizens and the state, civil society needs voluntarism as a prerequisite and self-ruling as its basis (Berman 1997; Diamond 1994; Migdal 1988). Neighborhood self-governance strongly facilitates the emergence and growth of civil society in China. Demands on personal freedom arise as a result of free-market-oriented reforms (Tao and Tao 1998).

However, the actual increase of freedom does not come voluntarily. Neighborhood self-governance provides an effective way to promote individual liberty. The state is usually least intrusive at the neighborhood level. By gradually softening and replacing the influence of the state in neighborhoods, both villagers' and residents' committees create a viable free space at the grassroots levels. In this space, individual citizens gain more independence from the state, making free choices and decisions. Both organizations further help to institutionalize civil society by offering a pattern of civil self-management and self-construction, both of which are necessary for the emergence and growth of a vibrant civil society in China.

Second, studies of democracy have repeatedly emphasized the importance of public virtues or social capital in the democratic process (Putnam 1993). Participation is perhaps the only way to develop behaviors and protocols compatible with grassroots democracy (Rousseau 1964; Tocqueville 1899). Both villagers' and residents' committees are dealing with the affairs that are closest to individual citizens. For most citizens in a country as large as China, learning how to manage neighborhood affairs is no doubt the first step in fostering democratic virtues such as tolerance, cooperation, moderation, solidarity, and public awareness.

"All politics are local" (O'Neill and Hymel 1995). Today hundreds of millions of ordinary citizens are learning to practice their rights through residents' and villagers' committees, even though such practices are far from perfect. By civic participation and engagement, villagers' and residents' committees provide millions with training schools for public virtues, which in turn will benefit grassroots democracy in China.

Third, the development of grassroots democracy will keep violence, instability, and disorder to a minimum. Order is especially valuable but fragile when political institutions are insufficiently developed to accommodate the mobilization of social forces into politics (Huntington 1968). Like many modernizing nations, China is facing many unintended and even disruptive consequences in its rapid transformation. The neighborhood is the place where most Chinese can participate in public affairs, express their interests, and defend their rights with the least resistance from the state. It is also the place that eventually will reflect most social and economic pressures. As reforms are deepened, the pressure on current social and political systems will be intensified so quickly that some pessimists even predict that a total crisis is right at the door (Chang 2001). Villagers' and residents' committees constitute a buffer between grassroots pressures and upper political and social structures. Disastrous outbursts might be partially defused, or at least postponed, at the grassroots through self-governance before they escalate. This is a primary reason for the state to promote the principle of grassroots democracy at the neighborhood.

Finally, the rule of law is widely believed to be an integral part of a democracy (Almond and Verba 1963). Efforts to improve the rule of law at national and sub-national levels may contribute to grassroots democracy in China (Tanner 1999). Villagers' and residents' committees offer channels to promote the rule of law at the grassroots.

Neighborhood self-governance is labeled as self-service, self-management, and self-education that are based upon democratic election, decision-making, management and supervision by local residents. Despite the wide variance in practices, both villagers' and residents' committees are increasingly active in constraining the arbitrariness and abuse of local governments with regard to neighborhood affairs. In recent years, many villagers' and residents' committees have defended residents' rights and interests, suggested policy changes, communicated, coordinated, and bargained with local governments, and sometimes even put pressure on certain governmental policies (J. Li 2002; J. Yu 2000). Though these self-governing activities, villagers' and residents' committees have made local officials more effective, responsive, and, in some way, more accountable than that in the past (Oi and Rozelle 2000; X. Wang 1997; Z. Wang 1998).

CONCLUSION

Both rural villagers' and urban residents' committees were created by the state for the purpose of neighborhood control in China. However, as the principle of grassroots democracy started taking root and burgeoning, villagers' and residents' committees started generating centrifugal forces resisting "resolute statecraft" (Gray 1998). The comparison between the two forms of committee indicates distinctive roads to grassroots democratization: a participatory democracy in rural villages and a representative democracy in urban neighborhoods, although such an ideal typology is rough and tentative. However, it offers a new analytic framework to examine democratic development in China. So far, despite many inadequacies, villagers' and residents' committees have played a genuine role in neighborhood governance. As grassroots organizations, villagers' and residents' committees contribute to a rising and vibrant civil society, democratic education, social order, and the rule of law, all of which are vital for grassroots democracy.

NOTES

1. For details about the commune's history in China, see Shue (1988).
2. A commune is equal to a township government, a brigade to an administrative village, and a production team to a natural village.
3. Residential teams (*cunmin xiaozu*) usually consisted of ten to fifteen households working under a residents' committee.
4. Many studies have produced mixed and even contradictory assessments about whether the elections were truly "democratic" (Bai 1997; Carter Center 1997; 1998; International Republican Institute 1994; 1997; O'Brien and Li 2000; Z. Wang 1998).
5. These issues include: (1) The method for gathering fees that are submitted to the township government and retained for village usage (*xiangtongchou yu cuntiliu*); (2) the number of people who can enjoy subsidies for collective services (*wugong butie*) and the level of the subsidy; (3) the use of revenue from the collective economy; (4) the plan for raising funds for public projects, such as schools and roads; (5) the plans for launching and contracting collective economic projects, and construction contracting plans for public projects; (6) the use of collective property; (7) the plans for assigning land for housing (*zhaijidi*); and (8) other issues necessary for the Villagers' Assembly to decide.
6. See the article 3 of the Organic Law of Villagers' Committees.
7. This does not mean that residents' committees are free from the state's intervention. As Wang (2003) discussed, residents' committees, like villagers' committees, still perform many governmental tasks that are essentially irrelevant to grassroots self-governance, such as implementing the so-called one-child policy.
8. There is a debate over whether amateurism increases the accountability of the villagers' committee, since corruption is prevalent in many villagers' committees and rural governments.
9. Villagers' committee members get some subsidies from township governments and from the village's collective funds.

REFERENCES

Almond, Gabriel, and Sidney Verba. 1963. *The Civic Culture, Political Attitudes and Democracy in Five Nations*. Princeton, NJ: Princeton University Press.
Bai, Gang. 1997. *Report on Improving the Legislation of Villagers' Self-Governance*. Working Paper No. 971103. Beijing: Center for Public Policy Research, Chinese Academy of Social Science.
Berman, Sheri. 1997. "Civil Society and the Collapse of the Weimar Republic." *World Politics* 49:401–29.
Carter Center Delegation Report. 1997, 1998. "The Carter Center Delegation to Observe Village Elections in China and Village Elections in China and Agreement on Cooperation with the Ministry of Civil Affairs, People's Republic of China." Washington, DC.
Chang, Gordon G. 2001. *The Coming Collapse of China*. New York: Random House.
Diamond, Larry. 1994. "Rethinking Civil Society, toward Democratic Consolidation." *Journal of Democracy* 5 (3): 5–17.

Gray, John, 1998. *Hayek on Liberty*. New York: Routledge.
Gui, Yong, and Cui Zhiyu. 2001. "Xinzhenghui jinchengzhong de chengshi juweihui tizhi Bianqian" [The Institutional Changes of Urban Residents' Committee in the Bureaucratization]. *Gonggong xingzheng* [Public Administration], no. 1:38–42.
Havel, Václav, and Václav Klaus. 1996. "Civil Society after Communism: Rival Visions. Debate with Commentary by Petr Pithart; Reprint from Gazeta wyborcza." *Journal of Democracy* 7:12–23.
Huntington, Samuel P. 1968. *Political Order in Changing Societies*. New Haven, CT: Yale University Press.
International Republican Institute. 1994, 1997. "People's Republic of China Election Observation Report and Election Observation Report." Fujian, People's Republic of China.
Kelliher, Daniel. 1997. "The Chinese Debate over Village Self-Government." *The China Journal*, no. 37:81–85.
Kennedy, John James. 2002. "The Face of 'Grassroots Democracy' in Rural China: Real Verse Cosmetic Elections." *Asian Survey* 42 (3): 82.
Lei, Jieqiong. 2001. *Zhuanxing zhong de chengshi jiceng zhequ zhuzhi* [The Community Organizations in the Urban Grassroots during the Transition]. Beijing: Peking University Press.
Li, Jingpeng. 2002. "Guanyu shuqu jiangshe de mubiao ji shequ jiangshe zhongde 'xingzheng tuidong' de wenti" [About the Problems in the Objects of Community Development and "Administrative Sponsorship" in Community Development]. *Beijing xingzheng xueyuan xuebao*.
Li, Lianjiang. 2002. "The Politics of Introducing Direct Township Elections in China." *The China Quarterly* 171:704–23.
Lin, Shangli. 1999. "Grassroots Mass Self-Governance: the Practices of Democracy and Political Construction in China." *Zhengzhixue yanjiu* [The Journal of Political Science] 4.
———. 2002. *Shanghai shi jumin weiyuanhui zuzhi jiangshe yu shequ mingzhu fazhan* [Organic Construction of Resident's Committees and Community Democratic Progress in Shanghai City]. Jiangsu: *Nanjing sifaju*.
Ling, Hua, and Jiang Liyong. 2001. "Social and Legal Analysis of Urban Residential Committees." *Dongwu Faxue*.
Lu, Xiaobo, and Elizabeth Perry, eds. 1997. *Danwei: The Changing Chinese Workplace in Historical and Comparative Perspective*. Armonk, NY: M. E. Sharpe.
Manion, Melanie. 2000. "Chinese Democratization in Perspective: Electorates and Selectorates at the Township Level." *The China Quarterly* 163:764–82.
Mao, Yishi, and Zhang Yuren. 2001. "Zhongguo minyin jingji de fazhan he qianjing" [The Development and Prospects of Private Economy in China]. *Guojia xingzhen xueyuan xuebao*, no. 6.
Migdal, Joel. 1988. *Strong Societies and Weak States: State-Society Relations and State Capabilities in the Third World*. Princeton, NJ: Princeton University Press.
Ministry of Civil Affairs. 2002. *China Yearbook of Civil Affairs*. Beijing: Zhongguo Minzheng Chubanshe.
O'Brien, Kevin, and Li Lianjiang. 2000. "Accommodating 'Democracy' in a One-Party State: Introducing Village Elections in China." *The China Quarterly* 162:465–89.

O'Donnell, Guillermo, Philippe Schmitter, and Lawrence Whitehead. 1986. *Transitions from Authoritarian Rule: Tentative Conclusions about Uncertain Democracies.* Baltimore: John Hopkins University Press.

Oi, Jean. 1989. *State and Peasant in Contemporary China: The Political Economy of Village Government.* Berkeley: University of California Press.

Oi, Jean, and Scott Rozelle. 2000. "Election and Power: The Locus of Decision-Making in Chinese Villages." *The China Quarterly* 162:513–39.

O'Neill, Tip, with Gary Hymel. 1994. *All Politics Is Local: And Other Rules of the Game.* New York: Times Books.

Pastor, Robert, and Tan Quingshan. 2000. "The Meaning of China's Village Elections." *The China Quarterly* 162:490–512.

Peng Zhen. 1991. *Pengzhen Wenxuan.* Beijing: Renmin chubanshe.

Putnam, Robert D. 1993. *Making Democracy Work: Civic Traditions in Modern Italy.* Princeton, NJ: Princeton University Press.

Read, Benjamin. 2000. "Revitalizing the State's Urban 'Nerve Tips.'" *The China Quarterly* 163:806–20.

Rousseau, Jean-Jacques. 1964. *Discours sur les sciences et les arts* [The First and Second Discourses]. Trans. Roger D. and Judith R. Masters. New York: St. Martin's Press.

Rural Investigation Team (Agricultural Committee of CCP Central Committee). 2001. "Guanyu Nongcun dangjian wenti de baogao" [A Report about the Problems in Party Construction in the Rural China], internal manuscript.

Shi, Tianjian. 1999. "Village Committee Elections in China: Institutionalist Tactics for Democracy." *World Politics* 51 (3): 385–412.

Shue, Vivienne. 1988. *The Reach of the State: Sketches of the Chinese Body Politic.* Stanford, CA: Stanford University Press.

Solinger, Dorothy J. 2001. "Why We Cannot Count the 'Unemployed.'" *The China Quarterly* 167:671–88

Tanner, Murray Scot. 1999. *The Politics of Lawmaking in Post-Mao China: Institutions, Processes and Democratic Prospects.* Oxford: Clarendon Press; New York: Oxford University Press.

Tao, Dongming, and Tao Mingming. 1998. *Dandai zhongguo de zhengzhi canyu* [Political Participation in Contemporary China]. Zhejiang, China: Zhejiang People's Publishing.

Tocqueville, Alexis de. 1899. *Democracy in America.* New York: D. Appleton and Company.

Wang, Jianfeng. 2003. Unpublished manuscript.

Wang, Xu. 1997. "Mutual Empowerment of State and Peasantry: Grassroots Democracy in Rural China." *World Development* 25 (9): 1431–42.

Wang, Zhenyao. 1998. "Village Committees: the Basis for China's Democratization." In *Cooperative and Collective in China's Rural Development: Between State and Private Interests*, ed. Edward B. Vermeer, Frank N. Pike, and Wei Lien Cheng. Armonk, NY: M. E. Sharpe, 247–52.

———. 2001. "Report on the National Implementation of the Organic Law on the Villager Committees (Provincial) (June 1998–December 1989) (excerpts) (January 1990)." *Chinese Law and Government* 34 (4): 39–48.

Xin, Qiushui. 1999. *Zhongguo cunmin zizhi* [Village Self-Governance in China]. Anhui, China: Huangshan Chubanshe.

Xu, Yong. 2000. "Discussion about Residents' Self-Governance in Urban Community Development." *Hauzhong shifan daxue xuebao (shezhe ban)*, no. 2.

———. 2002. "'Luse jueqi' yu 'dushi tupo': Zhongguo chengshi shequ zizhi yu Nongcun cunmin zizhi bijiao" ["Luse jueqi' yu 'dushi tupo": A Comparison between Urban Community and Rural Village Self-Governance in China]. *Shehui zhuyi yanjiu* [Socialism Study].

Yu, Jianrong. 2000. "Liyi, quanwei he zhixu—dui cunmin jiti duikang jiceng dangzheng Shijian de fenxi" [Interest, Authority and Order—An Analysis on Villagers' Collective Confrontation with Grassroots Party and Administrative Units]. *Zhongguo Nongcun guancha* [Countryside Observation in China] 4.

Yu, Xiangyang. 1983. "Cunmin weiyuanhui banle shier jiang dashi" [Villagers' Committee Do Twelve Jobs]. *Neibu wengao* [Internal Manuscripts], no. 20:17–24.

Zhang, Mingliang. 2001. "Chengshi shequ jiangshe de tanshuo he tuijin" [Exploration and Promotion of Urban Community Construction]. *Beingjing xingzheng xueyuan xuebao*, no. 1:1–3.

Zhang, Xiaolong. 2002. *Shequ jianshe de diaocha yu sikao* [Investigation and Thinking on Community Construction]. Zhejiang: *Hangzhou dianzi gongye xueyuan*.

Zhao, Huicong, ed. 1998. *Current Civil Affairs in Hangzhou*. Zhejiang: Hangzhou Chubanshe.

4

Hayek and the *Daodejing* on Order and Coercion

Daniel Kapust

BACKGROUND

Drawing on Friedrich Hayek's discussion of individualism, endogenous and exogenous orders, coercion, and the rule of law, I will explore the *Daodejing* as a resource for democratic theorizing. I discuss Hayek's account of political liberty, which, while individualistic, does not rest on an atomistic conception of the self, but instead begins with a social self, thus avoiding some of the components of liberalism that critics, be they communitarian or influenced by Chinese philosophy, criticize. In particular, I hope to show that the *Daodejing*'s treatment of naturalness, the concept of *wuwei*, and the proper governance of the sage, when read with Hayek, can provide a non-atomistic—though not anti-liberal—foundation for democratic theorizing. At the same time, a social conception of the self, when combined with an acknowledgement of the limitations of human cognition, creates a justification for liberty. The reading I advance of the *Daodejing* will, however, be more liberal than democratic, viewing democracy with some caution, and as a means for achieving further goods—especially the limitation of coercive power—rather than a good in itself

THE PROBLEM: CHINESE DEMOCRACY AND LIBERAL DEMOCRACY

The importance of looking to Chinese thought as informing or being receptive to democratic theorizing, and of exploring what a democratic theory sensitive to Chinese philosophical traditions might encompass, hardly need be stated; it is, after all, one of the central themes of the present volume. However, some, such as Lucian Pie, view Chinese thought and Chinese political culture as inhospitable to democracy; others hold "that Chinese political culture, particularly Confucianism, was full of humanism and was conducive to democracy" (Zhao 2000, 6). From a broader perspective, it is important to note just how different the dominant philosophical traditions in Chinese and Western thought are, in the opinion of many scholars, as Western understandings of liberal democracy may not be amenable to Chinese conceptions of personhood, society, or the relationship between the individual and the community.

To explore these differences, and their importance, we may turn to *Anticipating China*, written by David Hall and Roger Ames, who argue that Chinese thought differs from Western thought in fundamental ways.[1] First and foremost, Hall and Ames argue that Western thought throughout most of its history has centered on the priority of *cosmos* over *chaos*: "The idea of bringing cosmos out of chaos is at the very root of our conception of beginnings" (Hall and Ames 1995, 4). This idea, in turn, they link to a "rationalism" that characterizes much of the Western philosophical tradition, and which they describe as "second problematic" thinking. They characterize second problematic thinking in the following way:

> the construal of the beginning of things in terms of "chaos" ... the understanding of "cosmos" as a single-ordered word; the assertion of the priority of rest over change and motion [being over becoming] ... the belief that the order of the cosmos is a consequence of some agency of construal such as ... the Unmoved Mover, the Will of God ... the tacit or explicit claim that the states of affairs comprising "the world" are grounded in, and ultimately determined by, these agencies of construal. (Hall and Ames 1995, xvii)

Han Chinese thought, by contrast—including both Daoism and Confucianism—is characterized by what they describe as "first problematic" thinking, which is

> neither strictly cosmogonical nor cosmological in the sense that there is the presumption neither of an initial beginning nor of the existence of a single-ordered world ... [it] accepts the priority of change or process over rest and permanence, presumes no ultimate agency responsible for the general order of things, and seeks to account for states of affairs by appeal to correlative procedures rather than by determining agencies or principles. (Hall and Ames 1995, xviii)

First problematic thinking, characteristic of Confucianism as well as Daoism, while not utterly absent from the Western tradition—indeed, it has witnessed something of a rebirth according to Hall and Ames in twentieth-century thought, especially in the form of pragmatism—is not the dominant mode of thinking in Western thought. Similarly, while first problematic thinking is dominant in classical Chinese thought, second problematic is not entirely absent—one might point, in this regard, to Legalism (Hall and Ames 1995, 203).

Second problematic and first problematic thinking differ with respect to social and political theorizing, just as they differ in ontology and metaphysics. In second order thinking, society and politics are to be given a rational ordering, just as the cosmos is to be rationally ordered, transcending social chaos as physical chaos was replaced with order. That is, faced with the intransigent diversity of society's many different parts, the task of political theorizing is to bring a rationalized order to the potential chaos of a disordered society. First problematic thinking—such as Confucianism or Daoism—sees society as naturally inclined to achieving a spontaneous ordering, and views order as expressing "ritual harmony," rather than "rational certitude" (Hall and Ames 1995, 210).

Keeping in mind this distinction between first and second problematic thinking, and its political implications, it is clear when we turn to dominant accounts of liberal democracy that they fall under the rubric of second problematic thinking. Moreover, this helps us to see the tensions between many conceptions of liberal democracy and Chinese thought. Liberal democracy represents the effort to balance two different values: individual liberty and political equality. The latter value is manifested in the form of some mode of governance that entails political equality—for instance, "one person, one vote"—which is often termed popular sovereignty. The prior value—individual liberty—is manifested in the protections of individuals and groups *from* popular governance (or popular sovereignty), popular governance which in turn is a manifestation of political equality. Democracy seeks to realize the "will of the people"; liberalism seeks to protect individuals *from* their will, often invoking the value of justice to this end. For just as an individual or group may rule tyrannically, so too can the people as a whole. As de Tocqueville put it, writing of nineteenth-century America, "If ever freedom is lost in America, that will be due to the omnipotence of the majority driving the minorities to desperation and forcing them to appeal to physical force" (Tocqueville 1966, 260). De Tocqueville himself cites Madison, who is also worth noting in this regard: "It is of great importance in a republic not only to guard the society against the oppression of its rulers, but to guard one part of the society against the injustice of the other part" (Madison 1987, 323). Popular sovereignty, then, must be balanced against justice, which constrains what majorities may do.

Typically, liberal democratic theories look to individual rights to prevent unjust action on the part of majorities. Ronald Dworkin, a prominent liberal political theorist, provides a representative example. In Dworkin's formulation, rights serve as "trump cards," enabling "individuals to resist particular decisions in spite of the fact that these decisions are or would be reached through the normal workings of general institutions that are not themselves challenged" (Dworkin 1985, 198). Similarly, John Rawls, in *A Theory of Justice*, argues that the first of the two principles of justice that would be chosen in the original position is that "Each person is to have an equal right to the most extensive basic liberty compatible with a similar liberty for others" (Rawls 1971, 60). These rights would include, for example, free speech and free assembly. For Rawls, this principle must precede the second principle that would be chosen—"social and economic inequalities are to be arranged so that they are both (a) reasonably expected to be to everyone's advantage, and (b) attached to positions and offices open to all"—precisely because individual liberty is more important than the social and economic benefits that might be derived from sacrificing individual liberty (Rawls 1971, 60).

Joining the liberal emphasis on individual rights is an emphasis on political and moral neutrality. As Kukathas puts it, "the liberal state must exemplify neutrality inasmuch as its laws must not prefer any particular conception of the good life as superior to others"—this is so because pluralist societies feature a plurality of different ways of life and systems of value, each of which should be treated with "equal respect." Moreover, "the principles governing a liberal polity must be principles chosen under 'neutral' conditions" (Kukathas 2006, 194). That is to say, they should be such that any individual, regardless of his or her conception of the good, could choose them. This emphasis on neutrality, in turn, derives from a view of the individual as autonomous, and of society as an association of autonomous individuals. Such a view, according to critics of liberalism, denies the reality of society: society "is a community that coheres because people share common practices and beliefs" (Kukathas 2006, 195). In addition, the liberal view of pluralism as a problem that must in some way be solved gives rise to the aspiration to neutrality; if we do not view pluralism as a problem, however, neutrality may be less important.[2]

The view of political liberalism, in the language of Hall and Ames, is, as noted, characteristic of second problematic thinking. One is an individual insofar as one is a chooser of one's own ends, or a self-owner. Individuals, as choosers of their own ends, self-owners, or possessors of an inviolable dignity qua individuals, are conceived as surrounded by rights to protect them from illegitimate intrusions upon their core personhood. Given their autonomy or dignity, they ought to be left free to pursue their own ends, and the state should strive to be neutral among the possible ends they may pursue. Whether it is the inhabitant of Hobbes's state of nature, the party to deliberation in Rousseau's *Social Contract*, or the individuals Rawls envisions choosing principles of justice in his original position, the liberal self, according to many scholars, is thus a self prior to her relationships with others. Sandel put it thus in a classic and influential critique of liberal individualism, "The priority of the subject can only mean the priority of the individual, thus biasing the conception in favor of individualistic values familiar to the liberal tradition" (Sandel 1998, 11).

It is precisely on these grounds that liberal political theories, often centering as they do on autonomy and a conception of the self as ontologically prior to society, have come under criticism, whether by communitarian critics or for being hostile to central components of Chinese thought. To be sure, this is in part because "capitalism and consumerism have allowed autonomy to manifest itself as a pursuit of self-interest that threatens social cohesion" (Ackerly 2005, 548). Yet even scholars sympathetic to liberal democracy have noted that the value of autonomy does not feature strongly in Confucian thought (Wang and Titunik 2000, 84). In addition, critics of liberalism have argued that the liberal conception of the self is inimical to other goods, such as the values of community or tradition. Because of this, the *liberal* component of liberal democracy has often been regarded with some suspicion, whereas the *democratic* component seems to move more easily across borders; as Parekh puts it, "It would appear that the democratic part of liberal democracy, consisting in such things as free elections, free speech and the right to equality, has proved far more attractive outside the west and is more universalizable than the liberal component" (Parekh 1993, 172).

The more universalizable concept of democracy, in turn, seems more harmonious with other cultures' understanding of the self insofar as the self is conceived relationally or as ontologically posterior to the community in these cultures. What liberal democrats most feared about democracy—namely, popular sovereignty and its ability to promote particular values or traditions—is, in other conceptions, precisely what is valuable about democracy. We might say that this is especially true of cultures informed by the Chinese philosophical tradition which, in the words of Wong, holds "an inherently social conception of the person" (Wong 2004, 420). Wong means by this term that we "become persons by entering into relationship with others of our kind" (Wong 2004, 420). Such a self is not taken to be autonomous in the way that the liberal self is, and is not conceived of as characterized by reason independent of experience or an existence independent of others.

Faced, on the one hand, with the difficulty of transferring liberal notions of personhood and rights to other cultures and, on the other hand, the desire to enrich both Western political thought and to explore the possibility of democratic theorizing in Chinese thought, some scholars have looked to common ideas in classical Chinese thought, such as *minben*, "the idea that the people are the original source of the political authority of the state" (Wang and Titunik 2000, 74). Other scholars have looked to Confucianism in particular, the most important school of Chinese philosophy. For these scholars, Confucianism serves as a resource for democratic theorizing that is sensitive to the different conceptions of the person that characterize Chinese thought. In some respects, this might appear surprising, given that some Western scholars view Confucianism as largely inhospitable to democracy; Huntington, for instance, argues that Asian—that is, Confucian—"values of consensus and stability" ensure that a Confucian democracy would be a "democracy without turnover" (Tan 2003, 18, 15). Yet Confucianism, according to Tan, is a complex and multifaceted entity and "as a tradition has never been homogenous and monolithic" (Tan 2003, 7). Confucianism, according to many scholars, thus provides resources for democratic theorizing.[3]

Bell, for instance, synthesizes the democratic ideal of popular accountability with the Confucian ideal of the "rule of the wise" (Bell 2006, 165). While emphasizing the importance of "accountability, transparency, and equal political participation," Bell also notes that the problems faced by decision-makers in modern societies might be remedied, in part, by resources from the Confucian tradition of "exemplary persons" (Bell 2006, 160–61). Confucian exemplary persons are not only wise, but also achieve "complete self-realization in their public vocation" (Bell 2006, 153). Thus, Bell argues for a democratically elected representative body combined with a non-elected decision-making body composed of individuals "selected on the basis of competitive examinations."

Brooke Ackerly, in a recent article, has also turned to Confucianism to articulate a conception of democracy "that does not rely on an autonomous liberal rights-bearing individual" (Ackerly 2005, 548). Rather, drawing on Confucianism, Ackerly develops a non-liberal, but not necessarily anti-liberal, conception of democratic theory. This conception is rooted in the concept of *ren* (which Ackerly reads "as concerning the disposition of 'the heart/mind of human beings' [*Mencius* 6A11] toward other human beings"), the Confucian conception of human nature and its cultivation, and what Ackerly views as a Confucian commitment to "a practice of social and political criticism that . . . is democratic" (Ackerly 2005, 558–62). This conception, rooted in Ackerly's reading of Confucianism, is not anti-liberal because it "offers a way of respecting, and a justification for politically protecting, the humanity of people"; it is non-liberal, however, because it does so "without disconnecting them from the familial and other social bonds that sustain their humanity" (Ackerly 2005, 549).

HAYEK ON LIBERTY, ORDER, AND DEMOCRACY

I will turn, as was noted, to Daoism to address the possibility of a non-atomistic self upon which democracy might be built, but I will take what might seem an unlikely route by turning to a thinker—Friedrich Hayek—renowned not only for his anti-centralism, but also for his anti-collectivism. Such a theorist might not seem a likely bridge to a liberal democratic reading of the *Daodejing*, given the apparent priority of the individual over the group in the liberal tradition, and the *Daodejing*'s status as a first problematic text. Yet Hayek, according to Kukathas, while a liberal, is a liberal of a different kind than the more dominant figure of John Rawls. Like Rawls, Hayek argues "that it is vital that society not be brought under the governance of a single conception for the ends of life"; unlike Rawls, however, this is because a single conception of the ends of life would impede the development of knowledge (Kukathas 2006, 184). Moreover, rather than view the problem that political liberalism needs to confront as pluralism, Hayek views it as totalitarianism. This, in turn, means that pluralism is not a problem to solve by rights or justice, but "was potentially a solution—provided the right institutions were in place" (Kukathas 2006, 196). Chief among these institutions, as we will see, was a sphere of protection that prevented others from interfering with individuals, which in turn would allow the individual to "engage in his pursuits in accordance with his own purposes" within the confines of a democratic polity structured by the rule of law (Kukathas 2006, 184).

Why does Hayek make these arguments? Answering this question requires that we begin with Hayek's understanding of the limitations of human knowledge and what this means for how we theorize about society and order. To do so, we may turn to one of Hayek's earlier works, a published lecture entitled "Individualism: True and False." In this lecture, we encounter a number of arguments that will be developed more fully in two of Hayek's later works, which we shall subsequently consider—*The Constitution of Liberty* and *Law, Legislation, and Liberty*. In "Individualism: True and False," Hayek distinguishes between what he terms "true individualism" and "rationalistic individualism" (Hayek 1948, 4). Though the former is a theory of individualism, it does not entail "the existence of isolated or self-contained individuals," but instead starts "from men whose whole nature is determined by their existence in society" (Hayek 1948, 6). Thus, unlike the liberal assumptions about the self which critics influenced by Chinese philosophy or communitarians view with some caution, Hayek premises his account of society upon social individuals. Yet in spite of his conception of the self as having a social nature, Hayek argues that we can only understand society by "our understanding of individual actions directed toward other people and guided by their expected behavior" (Hayek 1948, 6).

Such a foundation indicates that the order we perceive in society is not to be traced "to deliberate design," as rationalists postulate, but rather is "the unforeseen result of individual actions" (Hayek 1948, 8). This understanding of order is, in turn, based upon an awareness of the limits of human cognition; the rationalist claim "is the product of an exaggerated belief in the powers of individual reason" (Hayek 1948, 8). Precisely because of its limited view of the capacity of human reason, true individualism holds that "if left free, men will often achieve more than individual human reason could design or foresee" (Hayek 1948, 11). It is beyond the capacity of any individual mind, or set of minds, to comprehend the complex, multiple, purposive, and spontaneous forces giving rise to social order. Moreover, because no single mind or set of minds could comprehend the totality of human endeavor, we are better off allowing individuals who understand their own circumstances to act on their particular knowledge. Thus we see the link between Hayek's account of individualism and political freedom: "From the awareness of the limitations of individual knowledge and from the fact that no person or small group of persons can know all that is known to somebody, individualism also derives its main practical conclusion: its demand for a strict limitation of all coercive or exclusive power" (Hayek 1948, 16).

Hayek is not an anarchist, and is acutely aware of the need for order and predictability in our pursuit of our own purposes, guided by our own knowledge. This requires a system of rules "which, above all, enable man to distinguish between mine and thine, and from which he and his fellows can ascertain what is his and what is somebody else's sphere of responsibility" (Hayek 1948, 18). Rules are different from orders, or commands, which provide specific information as to what is or is not to be done. Rules, by contrast, supply a general framework within which individuals pursue their own purposes. In addition, Hayek is careful to argue that true individualism positively values community belonging and family, as opposed to the rationalist individualism that he suggests "wants to dissolve all these smaller groups into atoms which have no cohesion other than the coercive rules imposed by the state" (Hayek 1948, 23). And while such a theory of individualism is amenable to democracy, it does not ascribe to majorities any great wisdom, but rather holds that "the whole justification of democracy rests on the fact that in course of time what is today the view of a small minority may become the majority view" (Hayek 1948, 29).

Hayek's account of the individual, liberty, order, and the value of democracy does not, then, rest on a conception of the self as prior to or easily discernable from the society in which it resides, but rather rests on an awareness of the finitude and imperfection of human knowledge. Such an understanding of individualism and liberty is evident in Hayek's later writings, *The Constitution of Liberty* and *Law, Legislation, and Liberty*, to which we turn to explore his views further. In these works, as with "Individualism: True and False," Hayek distinguishes between two broad modes of political and social theorizing: on the one hand, we have a rationalist constructivist approach, including figures such as Descartes, Hobbes, and Rousseau; on the other hand we have an empirical evolutionary approach. In the latter tradition, Hayek includes thinkers such as Cicero, Locke, Hume, Smith, Ferguson, Burke, and Paley (Hayek 1973, 52; Hayek 1960, 56). The rationalist holds that "human institutions will serve human purposes only if they have been deliberately designed for these purposes"; he believes that "the fact that an institution exists is evidence of its having been created for a purpose," and "that we should so re-design society and its institutions that all our actions will be wholly guided by known purposes" (Hayek 1973, 8-9). For Hayek, the rationalist view of society is factually erroneous: while humans have *made* civilization, this does not mean "that civilization is the product of human design"; to view civilization as the product of abstract reason is, for Hayek, an "erroneous intellectualism," an intellectualism evident in the rationalist view of reason as having a "capacity independent of experience" (Hayek 1960, 23, 24).

For Hayek, the human mind has no capacity to reason independent of experience, and—more importantly—is simply incapable of knowing all of the particular facts that structure civilization; the limitations upon the human mind increase with the complexity of society and the amount of knowledge collectively held: "The more civilized we become, the more relatively ignorant must each individual be of the facts on which the working of his civilization depends." Because all humans are ignorant of many of the factors "on which the achievement of our ends and welfare depends," Hayek argues that individual liberty is desirable because it leaves room for the "unforeseeable and unpredictable." And freedom involves "the renunciation of direct control of individual efforts"; this renunciation allows for the advance of civilization precisely because it allows society as a whole to utilize more knowledge than "the mind of the wisest ruler could comprehend" (Hayek 1960, 26, 29, 31).

Hayek's description of the benefits of freedom is somewhat paradoxical; on the individual level, "The benefits I derive from freedom are thus largely the result of the uses of freedom by others, and mostly of those uses of freedom that I could never avail myself of" (Hayek 1960, 32). At the societal level, however, Hayek conceives of the interactions of free individuals as facilitating a process of adaptation and selection; for this process to bring about the advance of civilization, individuals ought to be able to act and think freely. Civilization advances by the selection of behaviors and ideas through a process of individual and group competition. Its outcome cannot be known in advance, yet this process is not opposed to cooperation precisely because of the mutual benefits that it entails, the trust it requires, and the voluntary (general) compliance with social norms that facilitates it.[4] The danger is less unbridled competition than the effort to exclude others from the possibility of experimentation and independent action; as Hayek puts it, we must be on guard "against all exclusive, privileged, monopolistic organization, against the use of coercion to prevent others from trying to do better." For reason, influenced by our interactions with others, to advance, "freedom and the unpredictability of human action" are thus necessary (Hayek 1960, 37–38).

Freedom is thus necessary given the limitations of individual and collective human minds, and freedom, for Hayek, is "independence from the arbitrary will of another." Freedom thus refers explicitly to "a relation of men to other men"; one can only be deprived of freedom if interfered with arbitrarily by others. One is free, then, according "to what extent the pattern of his conduct is of his own design" (Hayek 1960, 12, 13). Such a conception of freedom, for Hayek, necessarily entails the existence of a protected private sphere. The harm of coercion—which compels an agent "to not act according to a coherent plan of his own but to serve the ends of another"—is that it eliminates central aspects of the individual "as a thinking and valuing person and makes him a bare tool in the achievement of the ends of another" (Hayek 1960, 21). The coerced individual is unable to pursue his or her own aims, and in doing so, coercion prevents the individual from utilizing his mental powers to the fullest extent and hence "making the greatest contribution" to civilization as one could (Hayek 1960, 134). Coercion and dependence are distinct phenomena: for instance, we may well depend on others for particular services in the context of the market, but the "mere power of withholding a benefit will not produce coercion." Rather, "coercion is the control of the essential data of an individual's action by another"; preventing this requires that we each be surrounded by a protected private sphere which allows us to formulate and pursue our own ends (Hayek 1960, 137, 139).

A system in which individuals, possessing limited and local knowledge, pursuing their own ends and purposes, freely interact generates its own, spontaneous order. We may turn to Hayek's later *Law, Legislation, and Liberty* for illumination. In this work, Hayek distinguishes between two kinds of order—made, or exogenous, order, and grown, endogenous, or spontaneous order. For Hayek, an order is *"a state of affairs in which a multiplicity of elements of various kinds are so related to each other that we may learn from our acquaintance with some spatial or temporal part of the whole to form correct expectations concerning the rest, or at least expectations which have a good chance of being correct"* (Hayek 1973, 36; italics in original). All societies, for Hayek, possess some order, and often—though not always—this order will not have been created by *deliberate* human agency. From what Hayek terms an "authoritarian" perspective, order that has not been deliberately planned seems paradoxical; for the authoritarian, "order in society must rest on a relation of command and obedience, or a hierarchical structure of the whole of society in which the will of superiors, and ultimately of some single supreme authority, determines what each individual must do." (We might note the parallel here to Hayek's description of rationalism, for which order is external, not internal.) It is this kind of order that Hayek terms "exogenous," as it is imposed from without; the non-deliberately planned order is, by contrast, "endogenous," or "spontaneous" (Hayek 1973, 36).

What might be an example of a spontaneous order? Hayek points to language which, apart from Esperanto, is not the subject of the deliberate planning or agency of any one or even many individuals, but rather the product of the action of many individuals acting purposively but without a single over-arching purpose and without being subject to any particular designs We might also point, more obviously, to the market. Both cases, however, suggest that "the patterns of interaction of many men can show an order that is of nobody's deliberate making" (Hayek 1973, 37). To many, the idea will seem strange—we tend to think of orders as being the product of deliberate arrangement and, like the ordered parts of a geared watch, "simple," "concrete," and serving "a purpose of the maker"—or in the sense of *taxis*, the Attic Greek term. A spontaneous order, or "*kosmos*," will likely be too complex for any mind or set of minds to master, and "Its existence need not manifest itself to our senses but may be based on purely *abstract* relations which we can only mentally reconstruct." Such an order cannot be described (legitimately) as having any particular purpose, though such orders may enable us to pursue many "different purposes" (Hayek 1973, 40). The spontaneous order is itself "an adaptation to a large number of particular facts which will not be known in their totality to anyone" (Hayek 1973, 40).

Precisely because of the complexity of such an order and the immense number of particular facts that structure its organization, "the degree of power or control over the extended and more complex order will be much smaller than that which we could exercise over a made order or *taxis*" (Hayek 1973, 42). Indeed, the rules that exist in a *kosmos* are somewhat different than those that exist in a made order, as they need not be known to the elements of the order, but rather "it is sufficient that the elements actually behave in a manner which can be described by such rules" (Hayek 1973, 43).

Hayek is perhaps most clear in describing what he means in this passage:

> in a social order the particular circumstance to which each individual will react will be those known to him. But the individual responses to particular circumstances will result in an overall order only if the individuals obey such rules as will produce an order. Such an order will always constitute an adaptation to the multitude of circumstances which are known to all the members of that society taken together but which are not known as a whole to any one person. (Hayek 1973, 44)

Given the nature of society, spontaneous order necessarily plays some role; yet "collaboration will always rest both on spontaneous order as well as on deliberate organization"—for instance, particular laws (Hayek 1973, 46). Indeed, government is precisely useful because it helps "to assure that those rules are obeyed"; in this regard, government is like "a maintenance squad of a factory, its object being not to produce any particular services or products to be consumed by the citizens, but rather to see that the mechanism which regulates the production of those goods and services is kept in working order" (Hayek 1973, 47). Such rules are normally the same for all members, and exist independent of members' particular purposes (Hayek 1973, 50). Their utility is evident in the fact that "we can preserve an order of such complexity [as modern society] not by the method of directing the members, but only indirectly by enforcing and improving the rules conducive to the formation of a spontaneous order" (Hayek 1973, 51). In this respect, law is not inimical to liberty, but rather a certain kind of law—the kind of law that enables individuals to use "their knowledge for their purposes"—is in fact necessarily linked to liberty (Hayek 1973, 51).

Law, then, is abstract; in this regard, it is different from commands, which are necessarily particular, and which, unlike law, require an agent to issue them. A command, unlike a law, determines our actions and leaves little leeway to the subject of the command; laws are rather general rules that create a framework within which we are able to pursue our own ends. As Hayek puts it in *The Constitution of Liberty*, "The rules merely provide the framework within which the individual must move but within which the decisions are his" (Hayek 1960, 152). Indeed, while obeying rules, we are in fact pursuing our own ends; hence, "we are not subject to another man's will and are therefore free" precisely because we are not subject to the arbitrary interference of another (Hayek 1960, 153).

What place, then, does democracy occupy in Hayek's conception of liberalism? Democracy is, for Hayek, a method of making decisions, and democracy itself "indicates nothing about the aims of government" (Hayek 1960, 104). The aims—or rather limits—of government are, instead, provided by liberalism; indeed, the liberal "is concerned with preserving the conditions that make democracy workable" (Hayek 1960, 117). This is so because a belief that *whatever* decision a majority makes is right has the potential to undermine both liberty and democracy, as democracy can only serve "as a safeguard of personal freedom because it accepts the limitations of a higher nomos" (Hayek 1979, 2). That is to say, democracy requires a limit if it is to assist us in preventing "the absence of arbitrary power," and this limit is provided by the rule of law; law, in this sense, is defined by its attributes, rather than its source (Hayek 1979, 5). Such laws are negative in character, making it possible to form "a self-generating order, utilizing the knowledge, and serving the desires" of the many individuals that compose it (Hayek 1979, 129). Negative rules, unlike the commands we have earlier encountered, do not prescribe particular ends, but rather allow for the free pursuit of multiple ends precisely because they create "a domain protected against unpredictable disturbance caused by other men" (Hayek 1979, 31). In this regard, then, democracy itself is largely negative in its value; democracy provides no guidance as to what the majority *ought* to want, but it is instead "the only convention we have yet discovered to make peaceful change possible" (Hayek 1979, 137).

THE *DAODEJING* AND HAYEK'S LIBERAL DEMOCRACY

Having explored Hayek's account of individualism, freedom, order, law, and democracy, we may now turn to the *Daodejing* and Daoism. Why turn to Daoism as a resource for democratic theorizing in the first place? First, and perhaps most obviously, Daoism is one of the three most important strands in Chinese thought, along with Confucianism and Buddhism. In addition, much recent theorizing on the potential for Chinese democracy and what a Chinese democratic theory might entail has centered on Confucianism. Finally, as numerous scholars have noted, Daoism has what we might term a "libertarian" bent, a term which Hayek uses—with some reluctance—to describe himself in *The Constitution of Liberty*.[5] Indeed, many commentators read the *Daodejing* as advocating a kind of "negative liberty," which Isaiah Berlin described as the condition by which "no man or body of men interferes with my activity"; this interference, moreover, was characterized by the "deliberate interference of other human beings within the area in which I could otherwise act" (Berlin 1997, 194). In this vein, readings of the *Daodejing* emphasizing negative liberty are not uncommon—for instance, Ivanhoe writes that the *Daodejing* aims to allow "one's spontaneous, prereflective nature to operate unencumbered and guide one's life" (Ivanhoe 1999, 246). A reading of the *Daodejing* which views it as embodying "negative liberty" is certainly amenable to democratic theorizing, as Berlin's discussion of the concept demonstrates, though it is not *necessarily* committed to democracy—as Berlin himself noted, negative liberty is "not incompatible with some kinds of autocracy, or at any rate with the absence of self-government" (Berlin 1997, 201).

Yet despite its apparent amenability to negative liberty, which we might associate with liberalism, Daoism, like Conufucianism, is not characterized by the separability and autonomy of individuals, as with most liberal theories, but rather by the broader Chinese "cultural tradition in which persons are understood to be irreducibly social, constituted by the pattern of roles and rituals of their lives' narratives" (Ames and Hall 2003, 129).Thus we see in chapter 33 of the *Daodejing*:

> To know others is wisdom;
> To know oneself is acuity (*ming*).
> To conquer others is power,
> To conquer oneself is strength.
> To know contentment is to have wealth.
> To act resolutely is to have purpose.
> To stay one's ground is to be enduring.
> To die and yet not be forgotten is to be long-lived.

What we see in this chapter, suggest Hall and Ames, is that knowledge entails grasping "the reflexivity and mutually shaping relationships between self and other" (Ames and Hall 2003, 128). The individual is situated in constitutive relationships with others, and her identity emerges in relation to these others. Self-knowledge is a function of understanding oneself in relation to others, just as understanding relations to others entails an understanding of oneself. Individuals are interdependent, not independent, and selves emerge through mutual interaction and accommodation.

We do not, then, find atomistic selves in Daoism—the Daoist self does not reason independent of experience or situation; such selves, however, acting in local and unique situations, have a natural way of being. Indeed, Xiaogan argues that the core value of Laozi's philosophy is *"ziran er ran,"* naturalness, by which we may understand "the state of 'acting naturally' or 'letting things develop by themselves'" (Ames and Hall 2003, 212). We find other scholars emphasizing, in addition to naturalness, spontaneity—the spontaneously emerging harmony of individuals acting naturally and the spontaneous actions of natural individuals (Fung 1948, 100; Wong 1984, 174; Xiaogan 1999, 214). Naturalness pairs with *wuwei*, which Hall and Ames define as "noncoercive actions," to form the central values of the *Daodejing* (Ames and Hall 2003, 28). The prior "is a positive term used to describe the progression of a certain state of affairs or things," while *wuwei* is the means of achieving this state of affairs and incorporating limits on human behaviors such that naturalness may be promoted (Ames and Hall 2003, 214).

What is natural is spontaneous, but not all that is spontaneous would be of equal value; while *wuwei* promotes spontaneity, it would impede certain forms of spontaneous action, such as "those motivated by desire for and pursuit of fame or profit," because they would diminish the potential field of others' spontaneity (Xiaogan 1999, 214). What this might mean is, admittedly, not immediately clear, but Xiaogan suggests that living naturally would entail that we "give up interfering with other people and things," just as other people and things should not interfere with us; thus naturalness entails a kind of negative liberty, or the absence of coercive interference (Xiaogan 1999, 227). Naturalness, then, provides an ideal by which we may criticize and evaluate behaviors, practices, and institutions, and it entails minimizing interference to foster spontaneity.

Wuwei, along with what Hall and Ames term the "*wu*-forms" (*wuzhi*, "knowing without resort to rules or principles," and *wuyu*, "desiring which does not seek to possess or control its 'object'"), points toward a mode of activity that enables us "to optimize relationships through collaborative actions that, in the absence of coercion, enable one to make the most of any situation" (Ames and Hall 2003, 38, 48). We may be reminded here of Hayek's own desire to foster action based on local knowledge, given his distrust of claims to centralized knowledge or the desire to impose single ends or sets of ends on diverse individuals by single minds or groups of minds. The Daoist analogue to Hayek's value, in its social and political aspect, is evident in chapter 17 of the *Daodejing*:

> With the most excellent rulers, their subjects only know that they are there,
> The next best are the rulers they love and praise,
> Next are the rulers they hold in awe,
> And the worst are the rulers they disparage.
> Where there is a lack of credibility,
> There is a lack of trust.
> Vigilant, they are careful in what they say.
> With all things accomplished and the work complete
> The common people say, "We are spontaneously like this."

This is a passage to which we shall return, but we may provisionally note several points. First, the best ruler rules least, and is credible for doing so—thus, we are not presented with *an*archy, but a different kind of order, one that facilitates the actions of others rather than prescribe specific actions. Second, sage rulers facilitate spontaneous action not through inaction, but through avoiding coercive action, thus allowing the ruled to pursue their own purposes.

Expectations of the sage ruler thus center around the promotion of spontaneity and naturalness; *wuwei*—noncoercive action—is the means by which the sage ruler achieves these ends. Given the Daoist conception of the interrelationship among opposites, and the fact that distinctions produce opposites—for example, "determinacy and indeterminacy give rise to each other/difficult and easy complement each other/long and short set each other off"—*wuwei* seems paradoxical:

> It is for this reason that sages keep to service that does not entail coercion (*wuwei*)
> And disseminate teachings that go beyond what can be said.
> In all that happens,

The sages develop things but do not initiate them,
They act on behalf of things but do not lay any claim to them,
They see things through to fruition but do not take credit for them.
It is only because they do not take credit for them that things do not take their leave.

Too much action, action that is overly vigorous, or the wrong kind of action, produces undesired—and opposite—effects. Moreover, the knowledge of the sage ruler is not a total or totalizing knowledge, but it facilitates the fruition of the knowledge and action of the ruled. It does not teach them in any formal way, but makes possible mutual learning and discovery among the common people. Actions and processes find their origins in the people, and it is not the part of the sage to seek to supplant their spontaneous activity. This is so because things have their own purposes and places; left to their own devices, they move naturally. As Hall and Ames note in their commentary on this chapter, rather than taking sides, sages "are catalytic in facilitating the flourishing of the process as a whole" (Ames and Hall 2003, 81).

We see a similar set of concepts in chapter 3:

> Not promoting those of superior character
> Will save the common people from becoming contentious.
> Not prizing property that is hard to come by
> Will save them from becoming thieves.
> Not making a show of what might be desired
> Will save them from becoming disgruntled.
> . . . .
> It is simply in doing things noncoercively (*wuwei*)
> That everything is governed properly.

With regard to this chapter, Hall and Ames suggest that the successful ruler is not engaged in "foisting an agenda on the community," but instead looks to basic needs of the community, and then allows "the character of the community to emerge synergistically out of the associated living of the people" (Ames and Hall 2003, 82). The ruler provides the framework within which people can pursue their ends and purposes which the ruler does not prescribe or limit these purposes or ends; the sage ruler allows individuals to flourish naturally and spontaneously. In doing so, the sage promotes the well-being of the common people through effective negative action; that is, by not imposing an overarching end or purpose on society, society achieves the best outcome.

Again, Hall and Ames argue—with respect to chapter 9—that "The greatest obstacle to optimizing relationship is coercion." This is so because coercion has a limiting aspect to it, as it "entails a diminution in the creative possibilities of both" the one coercing and the one being coerced (Ames and Hall 2003, 88). Coercion eliminates possibilities of action; it forces an unnatural and enervating order rather than facilitating its spontaneous emergence through the free play of society's component parts. Right rule, by contrast, does not force order, but opens up possibilities of natural action, which give rise to spontaneous order. This is clearly illustrated in chapter 17, which we have noted, but which is worth noting again briefly:

> With the most excellent rulers, their subjects only know that they are there,
> The next best are the rulers they love and praise,
> Next are the rulers they hold in awe,
> And the worst are the rulers they disparage.
> . . . .
> With all things accomplished and the work complete
> The common people say, "We are spontaneously like this."

It is important to note that we are not presented in this chapter with an image of anarchy, per se; the *Daodejing* certainly features sage rulers—they are simply hard to detect in their activity if they are acting rightly. But we are presented with a polity characterized by "the absence of coercion."

If rulers rule as effectively as possible—that is, they are hardly detected and make possible the activities of the common people—"social order emerges from the bottom up." What the ruler does, in other words, is serve as "the coordinate around which [the people's] contributions are synchronized to maximum benefit" (Ames and Hall 2003, 102, 103). In this respect, the sage functions in a way analogous to Hayek's conception of the rule of law, and the order the sage facilitates is analogous to his conception of spontaneous order as opposed to what Hayek termed made, or exogenous, order.

Chapter 29 of the *Daodejing* provides further illustration:

> If someone wants to rule the world, and goes about trying to do so,
> I foresee that they simply will not succeed.
> The world is a sacred vessel,
> And is not something that can be ruled.
> Those who would rule it ruin it;
> Those who would control it lose it.

We may note again the perverse consequences of overly assertive individual action, as well as overly assertive rule that, in seeking to achieve a single purpose in a world of purpose-seeking individuals, bring about an even worse outcome. Hall and Ames note that "the human world," like the natural world, "will flourish if left to its own internal impulses" (Ames and Hall 2003, 123). That is to say, both persons and nature, acting in their own spheres and for their own purposes, achieve a rich and vital order without the coercive ordering of external agents. Similarly, we see the following in chapter 57:

> ... in ruling the world be non-interfering in going about its business (*wushi*).
> How do I know that this is really so?
> From the following.
> The more prohibitions and taboos there are in the world,
> The poorer the people will be.
> The more sharp instruments in the hands of the common people,
> The darker the days for the state.
> The more wisdom hawked among the people,
> The more that perverse things will proliferate.
> The more prominently the laws and statutes are displayed,
> The more widespread will be the brigands and thieves.

Wuwei does not mean here non-action or inaction, but rather, avoiding a certain kind of action: namely, coercive action, or action that limits the actions of others. Thus, the *Daodejing* emphasizes the dangers of coercion, or what Hsu describes as "the assertive use of the human will" (Hsu 1976, 301). This ideal is most evident, again, in the concept of *wuwei*, "noncoercive actions."

We may turn to chapter 57 for further illustration:

> Hence in the words of the sages:
> We do things noncoercively (*wuwei*)
> And the common people develop along their own lines;
> We cherish equilibrium (*jing*)
> And the common people order themselves;
> We are non-interfering in our governance (*wushi*)
> And the common people prosper themselves;
> We are objectless in our desires (*wuyu*)
> And the common people are of themselves like unworked wood.

Noncoercive action on the part of the sage allows the common people to act with a natural spontaneity. Left to their own devices, the common people will achieve their own order, developing in their own way, a way that cannot be imposed upon them by even a sage ruler. Non-interfering government produces better outcomes than interfering government, fostering prosperity. Because it allows purpose-seeking individuals to act freely for their own purposes, it fosters a spontaneous harmony among them, an order that is not made, but rather that emerges.

CONCLUSION

I have argued that Hayek's liberalism, founded not on claims of individual autonomy or the isolation of selves, but rather on the limitations of knowledge and the need to allow experimentation and spontaneous action to foster the development of knowledge, provides resources for a liberal democratic reading of the *Daodejing*. Faced with a pluralistic social world of purpose-seeking individuals, law and the sage ruler ought to allow society to achieve its own order, rather than imposing order from without. Indeed, we may think of a certain kind of law as a stand-in for the sage, embodying the sage's wisdom and the value of *wuwei*. In doing so, both individuals and society benefit, the prior from the ability to pursue their own purposes based upon their own knowledge and aspirations, the latter from the mutually advantageous spontaneous ordering that emerges from the action of such individuals. For Hayek, the flourishing of human activity, spontaneity, and the growth of knowledge are the values that the rule of law protects and promotes; democracy, then, is not a mechanism for deciding what is and is not to be valued, but rather a method by which decisions may be made and, more importantly, to provide a peaceful transfer of power. So, too, with the *Daodejing*, the sage ruler promotes the flourishing and spontaneity of the common people through noncoercive governance.

Both Hayek and the *Daodejing*, then, reject the mode of reasoning that seeks to impose order from above, and instead seek to foster spontaneity and creativity through a certain mode of rule. To be sure, the role of democracy in Hayek's thought is quite clear, whereas in the conception of the *Daodejing*, democracy is absent. However, given my discussion of Hayek's thought, analogous concepts in the *Daodejing*, and how Hayek's thought leads to his cautionary view of democracy—and its value as a method of the peaceful transfer of power—a Hayekian theory of liberal democracy might find support in the *Daodejing*. Indeed, too strong a faith in democracy, and too high of an expectation of its outcomes, would create a new space for coercion and potentially diminish the benefits of *wuwei*.

NOTES

1. In addition to this work, see Hall and Ames (1987).
2. One might point, in this regard, to Gutmann and Thompson's account of the distinction between toleration and mutual respect. See chapter 2 of Gutmann and Thompson (2004).
3. Hu (2000) is a notable exception.
4. For a discussion of the importance of cooperation in Hayek's social theory, see Boyd (2004, 275–77).
5. See Rick Parrish's unpublished working paper, "Sages and Straw Dogs: Isaiah Berlin and Political Violence in the Laozi." Hayek's self-description as a libertarian, and his reluctance to do so, are most evident in the postscript to *The Constitution of Liberty*, entitled "Why I Am Not a Conservative."

REFERENCES

Ackerly, Brooke A. 2005. "Is Liberalism the Only Way toward Democracy? Confucianism and Democracy." *Political Theory* 33 (4): 547–76.

Ames, Roger T., and David L. Hall. 2003. *Daodejing: "Making This Life Significant": A Philosophical Translation*. New York: Ballantine Books.

Bell, Daniel A. 2006. *Beyond Liberal Democracy: Political Thinking for an East Asian Context*. Princeton, NJ: Princeton University Press.

Berlin, Isaiah. 1997. "Two Concepts of Liberty." In *The Proper Study of Mankind: An Anthology of Essays*, ed. Henry Hardy and Roger Hausheer. New York: Farrar, Straus and Giroux.

Boyd, Richard. 2004. *Uncivil Society: The Perils of Pluralism and the Making of Modern Liberalism*. Lanham, MD: Lexington Books.

Dworkin, Ronald. 1985. *A Matter of Principle*. Cambridge, MA: Harvard University Press.

Fung, Yu-Lan. 1948. *A Short History of Chinese Philosophy*. New York: The Free Press.

Gutmann, Amy, and Dennis Thompson. 2004. *Why Deliberative Democracy?* Princeton: Princeton University Press.

Hall, David L., and Roger T. Ames. 1987. *Thinking through Confucius*. Albany: State University of New York Press.

———. 1995. *Anticipating China: Thinking through the Narratives of Chinese and Western Culture*. Albany: State University of New York Press.

Hayek, Friedrich A. 1948. "Individualism: True and False." In *Individualism and Economic Order*. Chicago: University of Chicago Press.

———. 1960. *The Constitution of Liberty*. Chicago: University of Chicago Press.

———. 1973. *Law, Legislation and Liberty: Rules and Order*. Vol. 1. Chicago: University of Chicago Press.

———. 1979. *Law, Legislation and Liberty: The Political Order of a Free People*. Vol. 3. Chicago: University of Chicago Press.

Hsu, Sung-peng. 1976. "Lao Tzu's Conception of Evil." *Philosophy East and West* 26 (3): 301–16.

Hu, Shaohua. 2000. "Confucianism and Western Democracy." In *China and Democracy: The Prospect for a Democratic China*, ed. Suisheng Zhao. New York: Routledge.

Ivanhoe, Philip J. 1999. "The Concept of *De* ('Virtue') in the *Laozi*." In *Religious and Philosophical Aspects of the Laozi*, ed. Mark Csikszentmihalyi and Philip J. Ivanhoe. Albany: State University of New York Press.

Kukathas, Chandran. 2006. "Hayek and Liberalism." In *The Cambridge Companion to Hayek*, ed. Edward Feser. Cambridge: Cambridge University Press.

Madison, James. 1987. "Federalist 51." In *The Federalist Papers*, ed. Isaac Kramnick. New York: Penguin.

Parekh, Bhikhu. 1993. "The Cultural Particularity of Liberal Democracy." In *Prospects for Democracy: North, South, East, West*, ed. David Held. Stanford, CA: Stanford University Press.

Parrish, Richard. "Sages and Straw Dogs: Isaiah Berlin and Political Violence in the *Laozi*." Unpublished working paper.

Rawls, John. 1971. *A Theory of Justice*. Cambridge, MA: Harvard University Press.
Sandel, Michael. 1998. *Liberalism and the Limits of Justice*. Cambridge: Cambridge University Press.
Tan, Sor-hoon. 2003. *Confucian Democracy: A Deweyan Reconstruction*. Albany: State University of New York Press.
Tocqueville, Alexis de. 1966. *Democracy in America*. Ed. J. P. Mayer. New York: Perennial Classics.
Wang, Enbao, and Regina F. Titunik. 2000. "Democracy in China: The Theory and Practice of *Minben*." In *China and Democracy: The Prospect for a Democratic China*, ed. Suisheng Zhao. New York: Routledge.
Wong, David B. 1984. "Taoism and the Problem of Equal Respect." *Journal of Chinese Philosophy* 11 (2): 165–83.
——. 2004. "Relational and Autonomous Selves." *Journal of Chinese Philosophy* 31 (4): 419–32.
Xiaogan, Liu. 1999. "An Inquiry into the Core Value of Laozi's Philosophy." In *Religious and Philosophical Aspects of the Laozi*, ed. Mark Csikszentmihalyi and Philip J. Ivanhoe. Albany: State University of New York Press.
Zhao, Suisheng. 2000. "Introduction: China's Democratization Reconsidered." In *China and Democracy: The Prospect for a Democratic China*, ed. Suisheng Zhao. New York: Routledge.

II

THE RULE OF LAW

5

Legal Reform in China

John Anthony Maltese

By almost any standard, China's legal system has made remarkable progress over the last thirty years. It has moved from virtual nonexistence during the Cultural Revolution—a period when law and lawyers were reviled and persecuted—to an essential component of economic reform initiated by Deng Xiaoping. As recently as 1976, when Mao Zedong died, China had no legal system worth speaking of. The Ministry of Justice had been closed since 1959. There were no functioning law schools, only a miniscule number of lawyers, virtually no legal institutions, and no semblance of the rule of law. Under the Communist dictatorship, no system of civil law existed, nor was there was a comprehensive criminal code.

The years since then have brought enormous change. The 1978 Constitution recognized the need for a legal system and reinstituted the system of advocacy. A series of laws passed in 1979, including the Criminal Law and the Criminal Procedure Law, began to establish some basic rights of criminal defendants. That same year the Ministry of Justice reopened and law schools began to proliferate. China's Constitution officially embraced the rule of law in 1999. Serious efforts began to create a body of criminal, civil, and administrative law. Between 1979 and 1983, over 4,000 laws and regulations were enacted. By 2004, that number exceeded 135,000.[1] Likewise, the number of lawyers jumped from as few as 200 in the wake of the Cultural Revolution to about 11,000 in 1984, and then multiplied by leaps and bounds (Li 2000).[2] Today there are over 600 law schools in China and between 118,000 and 140,000 lawyers work in some 11,000 law firms. There are also roughly 200,000 judges and 160,000 prosecutors (Cohen 2007, 399).[3]

Despite these changes, China's legal system is still in a state of transition. Observers vigorously debate how meaningful the changes have been and how far they will go. Some see a genuine commitment by the Chinese government to the rule of law—even if its version of the rule of law does not contain all of the attributes that the Western liberal tradition has come to expect.[4] They point to apparent success stories. For example, laborers and migrant workers have been granted significant rights by the government (including the recent Labor Contract Law that went into effect on January 1, 2008) and they appear to be successfully exercising those rights through the legal system.[5] The July 2001 choice of China to host the 2008 Summer Olympics followed by China's entry into the World Trade Organization as a full member in November 2001 are also touted as symbols of China's legitimacy on the world stage and a belief by the international community that progress is genuine (Chow 2003, 3). This has led to claims that the transition from "rule of man" to "rule of law" is irreversible, even if the current system is best characterized as "rule of the Party by law" (Zou 2007, 56).

Other observers, however, allege ongoing human rights abuses by the Chinese government, including harsh treatment of labor activists, and they question whether the rule of law can really take root under the current regime in China.[6] They see China's legal reforms as a calculated effort to bolster the legitimacy of the Chinese Communist Party, rein in local governments, and promote economic development (Hand 2007, 116). Such critics contend that legal reform in China—especially the commitment to the rule of law—is more illusory than real.

Even if the changes are calculated and far from perfect, it is hard to deny that some genuine reform has taken place. Even so, ongoing structural and cultural impediments continue to limit the effectiveness of that reform. These impediments include such things as corruption, local protectionism, the lack of independence of judges and lawyers, concerns about the training and qualifications of legal professionals, laws that are poorly drafted and inconsistent, and the absence of a deep-seated "culture of legality" (e.g., Peerenboom 2002, 12–19).

Before discussing the reforms more directly, it is important to put the current Chinese legal system into some context. It is, after all, a system that is influenced by over two thousand years of Chinese history and experience. As defined by Martin Shapiro, the Western ideal or prototype of courts involves "(1) an independent judge applying (2) preexisting legal norms after (3) adversary proceedings in order to achieve (4) a dichotomous decision in which one of the parties was assigned the legal right and the other found wrong" (Shapiro 1981, 1). The traditional understanding of China is that for most of its history, mediation served as a substitute for the type of judging assumed by this prototype of courts. Even today, one of the lingering questions is how well Chinese courts conform to that prototype.

The tradition of mediation in China reflects the impact of Confucius (551–479 BC). Confucianism emphasized harmony and ethical behavior through the concept of *li*, which stressed morality, conscience, and virtue as a means to achieve social order. This stood in contrast to a system of codified law and punishment, known as *fa*, which was thought to bring disharmony and undermine social relationships through coercion. When faced with conflict, the goal of Confucianism was to restore harmony through compromise rather than to decide who was right or wrong (Shapiro 1981, 158). The result was a strong emphasis on mediation, with great deference being paid to wise and virtuous family or community elders who sought a harmonious resolution to disputes rather than imposing a solution based on an impersonal law or regulation (Perkovich 1996, 315). This emphasis on *li* over *fa* is reflected in 2:3 of the *Analects* of Confucius:

> If the people be led by laws, and uniformity sought to be given them by punishments [*fa*], they will try to avoid the punishment, but have no sense of shame. If they be led by virtue, and uniformity sought to be given them by the rules of propriety [*li*], they will have the sense of shame, and moreover will become good.[7]

This does not mean that Imperial China was devoid of legal codes. Such codes date back at least as far as the Tang Dynasty (618–907 AD) and continued in subsequent dynasties. Indeed, observers note that Imperial China combined the traditions of Confucianism (which emphasized *li*) and Legalism (which emphasized *fa*). Even Confucius recognized that it may be impossible to abandon law completely. Still, he criticized the codification of laws and their public dissemination; if used at all, law should be a last resort, with cooperative solutions that promote a humane society always being preferred (Peerenboom 2002, 29).

In Imperial China, legal codes were mostly criminal codes. Although Shapiro argues that the Chinese code also contained "preexisting legal rules for a wide range of civil relationships and wrongs," he also admits that "the Chinese preferred the restoration of harmony between the parties to the assignment of legal right and wrong under them" (Shapiro 1981, 169). Indeed, many believed that it was a disgrace to be involved in any kind of lawsuit, even as a plaintiff in a civil case (Peerenboom 2002, 39). And as for criminal cases, punishments were cruel, torture was common to extract confessions, and corruption was widespread. That simply reinforced the idea that law was something to be feared, and that avoiding the legal system was something that one should do at all cost (Chow 2003, 50–51). Despite the criminal code and a bureaucracy that emerged to enforce it (Shapiro 1981, 171ff), there was no recognition of law as a profession. No law schools existed and though some litigation experts emerged, they were not officially recognized and had no right to represent clients in legal proceedings (Chow 2003, 53).

Confucianism assumed a paternalistic, hierarchical system. Deference to one's superiors was expected. China's legal system reflected this. Neither Confucianism nor Legalism in China assumed equality before the law. This is another sharp contrast with law in the United States (and one, as we shall see, that persists to some extent even today). In Imperial China, penalties for the same crime varied according to the social status or familial relationship of the person committing the offense. Crimes against a superior led to especially harsh penalties. As Daniel C. K. Chow has written:

> The most heinous crimes were those that subverted the social hierarchy as in the case where an inferior in a relationship committed an offense against a superior. For example, a son who struck his parent could face death by decapitation whereas a parent who killed a child for disobedience might receive a light physical punishment only. (Chow 2003, 47–48)

Moreover, neither *li* nor *fa* assumed rights, which are an essential element of the Western conception of the rule of law. Instead, Confucianism emphasized duty to the community over rights of individuals. Likewise, law in Imperial China stressed substantive justice at the expense of procedural due process, and was motivated by top-down efforts by the government to maintain social order rather than bottom-up efforts of the people to maintain individual rights (Huang 2006, 277–78). The emperor ruled with divine authority and stood at the apex of the social hierarchy. A natural law tradition did not emerge, and the idea of government limited by law (another essential element of the Western conception of the rule of law) did not exist. There was, of course, neither separation of powers nor a system of checks and balances and, with neither capitalism nor a merchant class, no system of commercial law took root in Imperial China (Chow 2003, 45–52).

Only in the late nineteenth century, during the waning years of the Qing Dynasty, did China begin to take some interest in Western—mostly Continental European—law. The impetus was largely to deal with the problem of foreign extraterritorial jurisdiction. It was also part of an attempt to strengthen China's position in the world (much as Japan had seemingly done through a similar infusion of Western law). Nonetheless, the first legislation recognizing lawyers was not passed until 1912, the first year of the Chinese Republic. Thereafter, lawyers were allowed to represent the accused at trial. The influence of Western law accelerated when Chiang Kai-shek seized power in 1927–1928, but his reforms—including steps toward a more comprehensive legal code—were never fully implemented (Cohen 2007, 395). The populace continued to hold lawyers in low esteem during this period, and studies of both fiction and cinema in Republican-era China note that lawyers were often portrayed negatively: for example, as agents of a repressive system, representatives of the rich and powerful, and sophists (Kinkley 2000; Conner 2007, 209).[8]

The years from 1937 to 1949 were difficult ones for China. Japan launched a full-scale invasion of China in 1937, which resulted in the bloody War of Resistance—a massive conflict that lasted until September 1945 when Japan finally surrendered. Japan's ruthless tactics during the war led to the deaths of as many as 20 to 35 million Chinese people. The invasion led to a temporary united front between the Chinese Nationalist Party, or Kuomintang (KMT), of Chiang Kai-shek, and the rival Chinese Communist Party (CCP) of Mao Zedong. Over time, however, the CCP took more and more credit for the resistance against the Japanese. A civil war between the KMT and CCP ensued when Japan surrendered, and the CCP won. Mao formally proclaimed the founding of the People's Republic of China on October 1, 1949.

Law suffered under the new People's Republic of China. Mao immediately abolished the laws implemented under Chiang Kai-shek. He initially set out to create a new socialist legal system—one designed, at least in theory, to aid the proletariat in its class struggle. But revolutionary justice came to mean mass trials, which, by Mao's own estimate, led to some 800,000 people being sentenced to death (others say the numbers may be in the millions). Far more were sentenced to hard labor than were sentenced to death. And even though a procuracy and court system were established and laws were enacted, arbitrary arrests and detentions were common, with the police dispensing justice without resort to those institutions (Dreyer 2006, 168–69).

Things improved for a few years following the enactment of the 1954 Constitution, which included a bill of rights and a specific guarantee against arbitrary arrest. Substantive and procedural laws modeled after the codes of the Soviet Union were enacted, a Ministry of Justice was created, and the court system was more fully delineated. Law schools also began to open (Dreyer 2006, 169–70). Encouraged by Mao's promise to "let a hundred flowers bloom," lawyers—who numbered about 3,000 by 1957 (Peerenboom 2002, 347)—began to call for steps to increase the legitimacy and independence of the legal system. That led Mao to turn on them. In July 1957 he began efforts to purge "rightists" from the CCP. This so-called Anti-Rightist Movement may be seen as a reaction against the Hundred Flowers Campaign. One of the movement's primary targets was the legal system, which Mao believed was becoming too independent and too much of a threat to the CCP. Judges, lawyers, and academics now found themselves persecuted, and Mao disbanded the Ministry of Justice in 1959 (Peerenboom 2002, 44–45). Moreover, he jettisoned the right of criminal defendants to be represented by a lawyer (a right that was assumed between 1954 and 1957).

It was, however, the Cultural Revolution (1966–1976) that really sounded the death knell for the legal system. One of the goals of the

Cultural Revolution was the destruction of all formal law. At the outset of the Cultural Revolution, Mao ordered that all law schools be closed and instructed Red Guards to "smash" the judicial system. They took him at his word, destroying offices of the courts, procuracy, and public security and attacking their personnel (Dreyer 2006, 170). Lawyers, judges, and law professors were rounded up from their homes and forced to work in the countryside under harsh conditions. This so-called reeducation program led to many deaths, and it decimated the already small legal profession. Throughout the Cultural Revolution, Red Guards searched any home, arrested whomever they pleased, and executed individuals at will—all without the constraints of legal procedure (Folsom and Minan 1989, 12).

The legal system was not the only casualty of Mao's reign. Despite his goal of transforming China into a major economic power, Mao left China impoverished and isolated from the world community when he died in 1976. His Great Leap Forward, launched in 1958, was designed to transform China's agrarian economy into an advanced industrialized society practically overnight. Mao set in motion efforts to increase dramatically both grain and steel production (which he called the "two generals" of modernization) (Becker 1996, 63), but the initiative ended in disaster. A combination of poor planning (such as diverting too much labor from agriculture to industrial production), bad weather, and the withdrawal of Soviet advisers led to a famine of monumental proportions that killed somewhere between 14 to 30 million people.[9]

Under Mao, China became a command economy. Farms were collectivized into communes and industry was nationalized. These state-owned enterprises took on social welfare functions. They provided not only employment, but also services such as housing, schooling, and medical care that ultimately proved to be more important than profits, efficiency, and productivity. Poor management of state-owned enterprises compounded the problem, thereby adding to China's economic woes (Chow 2003, 25–26).

In 1978, Deng won the power struggle that ensued after Mao's death and set out to implement major economic reform. At the heart of the reform was a shift of focus from class struggle to economic development. Deng introduced elements of a free market and reform of state-owned enterprises, which were given more autonomy and profit incentives. Now those enterprises were allowed to sell products in the market after quotas were met, and to retain profits from those sales. Such changes had spread to about 60 percent of state-owned enterprises by 1980. Non-state-owned enterprises also began to emerge at a rapid rate (Qian 2006, 234, 236). In the agricultural sector, the communes established under Mao were dismantled and control over agricultural production was returned to farm families. As Roderick MacFarquhar has noted, this not only had a "massive impact on production and rural incomes," but served to give 800 million peasants a major stake in the reform (MacFarquhar 1997, 335–36). Deng did not focus only on domestic reform. In 1978, China's isolation from the rest of the world made it one of the most closed economies in the world. Deng's goal was to open China's economy by encouraging foreign trade and investment (Qian 2006, 232). This, of course, necessitated a system of commercial law. In short, economic reform set China on the path toward the rule of law. Yet all of this was designed to take place within what would remain a Communist, authoritarian state.

The Third Plenum of the Eleventh Chinese Communist Party Congress in December 1978 is usually cited as the beginning of this reform movement. To many, it ranks with the revolutions of 1911 and 1949 as one of the great turning points in twentieth-century China (Goodman 1994, 90). The timing could not have been better. Reaction against the Cultural Revolution and the arbitrary and abusive state action carried out during those years made a commitment to the rule of law attractive to the citizenry and palatable to party leaders since it would help to restore the legitimacy of the government. Likewise, the economic failure experienced by China during the period from the Great Leap Forward through the Cultural Revolution—especially when juxtaposed with the extraordinary economic success of its Asian neighbors—convinced both China's leaders and its people that economic reform was needed (Qian 2006, 231).

Prior to the Third Plenum, the National People's Congress adopted a new constitution. This 1978 constitution was the third in the history of the People's Republic of China. The first was adopted in 1954. The second, adopted in 1975 during the Cultural Revolution, was an extreme and anarchic document reflecting the lawlessness of those years. In contrast, the 1978 constitution is significant because it restored a role for law. It reaffirmed the concept of equality before the law (which the 1975 constitution had specifically rejected) and, as mentioned above, it reinstated a system of advocacy. However, it still assumed the primacy of class struggle. That did not change until the 1982 constitution, which downplayed the importance of class struggle and clearly emphasized economic development and modernization as China's top priorities.

China's constitution continues to be subordinate to the Communist Party. As a result, it serves a different purpose than the constitution of the United States. In the United States, the constitution is considered to be one component of the rule of law. Thus, the constitution is thought to be superior to government, with the constitution limiting government by spelling out its powers and enumerating individual rights which government cannot intrude upon.

Thomas Paine famously articulated the American view of constitutionalism in *Rights of Man* (1792): "A constitution is a thing *antecedent* to a government, and a government is only the creature of a constitution. The constitution of a country is not the act of its government, but of the people constituting its government" (Paine 1994, 41). China's constitution, on the other hand, remains an act of the Communist Party. Although it contains lofty platitudes (including an enumeration of rights), it is a document that is part of a system that still falls largely in the rule *by* law tradition. Thus, the Chinese constitution should not be read too literally. Nonetheless, the evolving language in China's constitutions is significant because it reflects some important changes in the official ideology of the Party (Chow 2003, 70–75).

The 1982 constitution remains in effect, but it was amended in 1988, 1993, 1999, and 2004. The 1988 and 1993 amendments focused on steps toward economic reform: affirming the legal status of the private sector in 1988, and specifically embracing a socialist market economy rather than a planned economy in 1993. For our purposes, the 1999 amendments were particularly significant because they contained the first specific mention of the rule of law in China's constitution. Specifically, the following sentence was added to article 5: "The People's Republic of China shall be governed according to the law and shall be built into a socialist country based upon the rule of law" (quoted in Chow 2003, 78).[10]

The emphasis in this language on *building* the country into one based upon the rule of law is significant. It suggests that the amendment may be more prescriptive than descriptive. Indeed, critics are quick to point out that the CCP has not always lived up to the lofty goal embodied by that amendment. Nonetheless, the new language in article 5 marked an important step. First, it was a concrete reflection of the belief among party leaders that at least some legal restraints were needed in order to assure economic development. Second, the language of article 5 gave at least some potential leverage to individuals seeking protection from arbitrary state action (Peerenboom 2002, 61–62).

The 2004 amendments to the constitution mark another important step. For one thing, it incorporated Jiang Zemin's concept of the Three Represents into the preamble of the constitution. First articulated by Jiang Zemin in 2000, the Three Represents can be viewed as a continuation of Deng Xiaoping's reform. They call upon the party to represent the development of (1) advanced productive forces, (2) advanced culture, and (3) the fundamental interests of the majority of the people. The precise meaning of the Three Represents is open to interpretation, but they seemed to signal a further embrace of capitalism, openness to Western culture, and democratic principles (Dreyer 2006, 128).[11] The 2004 amendments are also important because they added language strengthening property rights (article 13) and human rights (article 33).

As with earlier amendments, no clear enforcement mechanism is specifically enumerated. For example, there is no provision for judicial review.

This has led to the criticism that China's constitution only provides conceptual rights that are incapable of being safeguarded—ones that are semantic rather than normative (Killion 2005, 46–47). In the United States, judicial review is closely associated with the rule of law and with the protection of individual rights. Even acts of Congress and actions of the president can be invalidated if a majority of the Supreme Court finds them to violate the Constitution. It is, of course, worth remembering that other Western liberal democracies, such as Great Britain, have survived quite well without judicial review. Even within the United States, pundits and politicians sometimes take aim at "activist judges"—the implication being that judicial review allows them to "legislate from the bench."

It is hard to imagine the National People's Congress allowing a court to invalidate its actions, but some have argued that courts in China should be able to use a form of judicial review to make sure that provincial laws comply with superior legislation (see, e.g., Peerenboom 2002, 264ff). The United States, for example, could probably have survived, and perhaps survived quite well, had the Supreme Court not established the basis for judicial review of acts of co-equal branches (such as Congress) in *Marbury v. Madison* (see *Marbury v. Madison*). But had the Supreme Court not reaffirmed the power of the Supreme Court to invalidate state laws that conflicted with superior legislation in cases such as *Martin v. Hunter's Lessee* and *Cohens v. Virginia*, the future of the United States would probably have been less secure (see *Martin v. Hunter's Lessee*).

Conflicting legislation is a problem in China. Too many entities have been given "expansive and vaguely defined rule-making authority" (Peerenboom 2002, 262). Local protectionism adds to this problem and has helped to foster inconsistency in the law. The Law on Legislation has attempted to limit delegation of rule-making authority in an effort to minimize such inconsistency, and it allowed various entities to petition the Standing Committee of the National People's Congress for review of lower-level legislation thought to be at odds with superior law. But it gave courts no power of judicial review to invalidate lower-level laws that violate superior law, and even the Standing Committee was not required to accept petitions for review (Peerenboom 2002, 264–66). Giving courts that power could help further the rule of law by imposing consistency in the law and counteracting extra-legal factors (such as local protectionism) that might influence lower court decisions. It is important to remember, though, that increased centralization of power can also pose potential threats. For example, it may reinforce the dominance of the Communist Party over lower-level decisions. It could also lead to a situation where higher-level courts are used to promote stability and social control at the expense of protecting freedom and individual rights (Peerenboom 2002, 80–82).

In China there are four levels of courts: the Supreme People's Court at the top of hierarchy followed in descending order by the High People's Courts (the appellate courts for each province), Intermediate People's Courts (the appellate courts for each prefecture), and Basic People's Courts. China continues to lack separation of powers. At every level of government, courts are subordinate to the people's congresses. This subordination of law to politics has deep roots in China, and it raises a concern more serious than the absence of judicial review: lack of judicial *independence*.

Lack of judicial independence is antithetical to the rule of law. Even with real progress toward the rule of law, the subordination of courts to people's congresses may foster popular distrust of the judiciary by perpetuating the belief that judges are mere agents of political leaders. A judge on the Supreme People's Court identified this concern in a September 2006 speech to the University of Maine School of Law. Judge Jianli Song cited "insufficient institutional independence in China for the judiciary," and said that as a result "the robust institutional guarantees needed for the impartiality of procedures and adjudications cannot be implemented" (Song 2007, 141).

Language in article 126 of the Chinese constitution seems to call for judicial independence. It states that courts shall "exercise judicial power independently and are not subject to interference by administrative organs, public organizations or individuals." However, the prevailing interpretation of article 126 is that it does not apply to the CCP since involvement by the party leadership in court decisions is deemed "leadership" rather than "interference." In fact, individual judges are expected to change their decisions if court leaders so instruct. As Andrew Nathan has put it, in China it is an individual judge "sticking to his own decision, rather than court authorities changing it, that constitutes interference" (Nathan 2006, 184). Indeed, the preamble of the Constitution seems to conflict with article 126. It requires that legal decisions be based on four principles: (1) "the leadership of the Communist Party," (2) "the guidance of Marxism-Leninism and Mao Zedong Thought," (3) "the people's democratic dictatorship," and (4) "the socialist road" (Monnin 2007, 761).

In the United States, judicial independence has long been considered a paramount value. One aspect of judicial independence in the American system is separation of powers. It is believed that the institutional independence of the judiciary from the executive and legislative branches is essential to the exercise of judicial power. Thus, in *Federalist* 78, Alexander Hamilton (quoting Montesquieu) wrote that "'there is no liberty, if the power of judging be not separated from the legislative and executive powers.'" Hamilton then added: "The complete independence of the courts of justice is peculiarly essential in a limited Constitution"—that is, "one which contains certain exceptions to the legislative authority" (Hamilton 2000, 497).

Article 3, section 1 of the U.S. Constitution includes specific guarantees that are designed to promote judicial independence. First, federal judges "hold their offices during good behaviour" (which, short of impeachment, gives them life tenure). Second, federal judges are guaranteed compensation "which shall not be diminished during their continuance in office"—thereby preventing Congress from using a pay cut to punish judges for decisions they have handed down. These guarantees not only reinforce the institutional independence of federal courts from the other branches, but also reinforce the concept that judicial independence means that judges must be free from coercion or threats of retaliation.

Chinese judges do not enjoy the same degree of protection. Local governments in China control the budget of courts under their jurisdiction and can use that control to retaliate against judges who rule in ways that they disapprove of. Moreover, people's congresses at every level of government in China appoint and remove judges of the corresponding people's courts for that level. In contrast to the life tenure enjoyed by federal judges in the United States, Chinese judges can be removed by the people's congress overseeing that court. One might retort that the U.S. Congress also has the power to remove federal judges through impeachment. But impeachment is a difficult, time-consuming process that is seldom used against judges. Of the twelve federal judges impeached by the House of Representatives in the entire history of the United States, only seven have been removed after a Senate trial. Two others resigned, and three were acquitted and remained on the bench. The only Supreme Court justice ever impeached by the House was acquitted by the Senate and also remained on the bench. In contrast, it is much easier for people's congresses to remove Chinese judges. Although the Judges' Law does provide some standards governing the appointment and removal of judges in China, those criteria are vague enough that people's congresses have wide leeway (Hung 2008, 234). As a result, judges could be removed for ruling in ways that anger local party leaders.

Of course, the power to impeach could be abused in the United States. Attempts to use impeachment for political reasons are not unheard of. For example, Jeffersonian Republicans in Congress unsuccessfully mounted politically motivated impeachment proceedings against Justice Samuel Chase in 1804 (the House voted to impeach, but the Senate voted to acquit Chase on all eight charges). Nor is the United States immune from such threats today. In 1997, Rep. Tom DeLay (R-Tex.), the Majority Whip in the U.S. House of Representatives, suggested that congressional Republicans should begin efforts to impeach liberal federal judges (nothing came of his suggestion) (Kelly 1997, 3). Despite such threats, removing federal judges in the United States via impeachment continues to be a rare event, and will probably remain so.

Judicial independence is occasionally threatened in the United States in other ways. For example, article 3, section 2 of the Constitution gives Congress the power to make "exceptions" and "regulations" concerning the Supreme Court's appellate jurisdiction. This has led members of Congress to introduce jurisdiction-stripping legislation designed to keep the Court from ruling on certain controversial issues. In the 1970s and 1980s, for example, conservatives such as Senator Jesse Helms (R-NC) introduced dozens of bills designed to strip the Supreme Court of its power to review cases involving issues such as school prayer, busing to achieve racial integration in the public schools, and abortion (Ducat 2009, 25). More recently, the Republican Platform in both 2004 and 2008 included specific calls for Congress to strip the Supreme Court of jurisdiction to hear cases involving the Defense of Marriage Act (*2008 Republican Platform*, 53; *2004 Republican Platform*, 84). Congress, however, has almost never followed through with threats to strip the Court of appellate jurisdiction.

Of course, attacks on judicial independence have come, at various points in U.S. history, from both ends of the political spectrum. For example, President Franklin Delano Roosevelt famously called upon Congress to expand the size of the Supreme Court in the 1930s so that he could pack it with fellow Democrats. But recently, several U.S. Supreme Court justices have publicly criticized what they perceive to be a rise in the number of threats to judicial independence. In 2006, Chief Justice John Roberts (who had just been appointed by President George W. Bush) went so far as to urge fellow conservatives to stop their attacks on the Court. Roberts quoted former president Ronald Reagan: "'The judge's commitment to the preservation of our rights often requires the lonely courage of a patriot.'" Roberts then added: "To the extent that attacks on judicial independence come from conservative quarters, I would commend to those quarters the words of the leading conservative voice of our time" (quoted in Mauro 2006). Similarly, former Justice Sandra Day O'Connor has frequently criticized attacks on judicial independence, sometimes in forums with Justice Stephen Breyer (e.g., Mauro 2005).[12] Concerned about threats to judicial independence, the American Judicature Society recently created a Task Force to monitor and respond to attacks on the judiciary.[13] Likewise, the American Bar Association has had a Standing Committee on Judicial Independence since 1997.

Despite such concerns, judicial independence is much more deeply entrenched in the United States than it is in China. There does, however, appear to be increasing awareness in China of the need for judicial independence and the impartial application of the law. For example, the president of the National Judges College in Beijing (one of the primary centers for the continuing education of judges in China) said in 2005 that the college trains judges "with a modern theory of law: that the courts are impartial. . . . We stress that during a trial, you cannot favor the government or the National People's Congress. In the past, they told them to emphasize the political qualities" (quoted in Yardley 2005, 1).

In spite of such education, judicial independence in China continues to be threatened by factors such as local protectionism (Chow 2003, 221). Indeed, local officials now appear more likely to put pressure on judges than central Party leaders (Peerenboom 2002, 311). Institutional norms in China increase the likelihood of such pressure. For example, it is common for Chinese judges to have their rulings reviewed by supervisors or private trial committees of court officials, and judges are subject to discipline for issuing "erroneous" judgments (which could include rulings that anger political leaders, including local officials). Moreover, it is common for judges to engage in *ex parte* communications with government officials (and with litigants and lawyers in cases before them). Such "consultations" can influence the outcome of pending cases (Hung 2008, 236).

Even if local officials do not apply pressure (or if judges fail to bow to it), those officials may simply refuse to enforce court judgments. Like courts in the United States, courts in China have little power to enforce their rulings. Since Chinese courts are new players in the system—ones that have not built up a long history of institutional legitimacy—agencies and other political entities often disregard their directives (Lubman 2006, 29). Failure to enforce court rulings is an especially common problem in civil cases involving economic issues (Chow 2003, 223). Randall Peerenboom suggests that the devolution associated with economic reform has contributed to this problem. For example:

> Local governments worry that enforcement of an adverse judgment or award could result in the loss of key equipment or the closing of a factory. Increased unemployment not only causes budgetary problems but may lead to social unrest. To further complicate matters, in some cases, local governments may be a shareholder of the defendant and thus have a direct economic interest in the outcome. (Peerenboom 2002, 311)

Stanley Lubman agrees and adds that decentralization and the close ties between local government and local business have led to increased parochialism, made China more fragmented, and contributed to legal uncertainty. All of this, he concludes, obstructs "the maturing of a legal and business culture that supports legality" (Lubman 2006, 6).

Other factors beside local protectionism can also undermine judicial independence in China. One is the poor training of judges. Especially in the early days of reform, when the legal system was being put together essentially from scratch, there was no pool of qualified professions to fill judicial posts. Until the 1995 Judges Law, there were virtually no qualifications necessary to become a judge. Many of those initially appointed to judgeships were former military officers with little or no legal training (Peerenboom 2002, 14, 290). Interestingly, the United States has almost no formal legal qualifications for people to become a judge. For example, the U.S. Constitution provides no specific qualifications for being a justice of the United States Supreme Court—not even age or residency requirements. (This stands in stark contrast to the very specific constitutional qualifications for the president, senators, and members of the House of Representatives.) Federal law has not mandated specific qualifications either, but informal norms (including ratings by the American Bar Association) have emerged to help guarantee that judges are sufficiently qualified. Only at the lowest level of state courts in the United States do some judges serve without a law degree (Provine 1986).

In China, the problem went beyond lack of formal legal qualifications (an issue largely solved in the United States by the emergence in informal norms and procedures) to the widespread appointment of judges who were simply ill equipped to perform their duties. Lack of legal training of judges in China not only undermined the competence—and thus the legitimacy—of the courts, it also made judges more susceptible to outside influences when deciding cases (thereby eroding judicial independence).

For example, Chinese judges developed a practice known as *qingshi*, whereby lower-level judges seek advice from higher-level judges about how to decide a case. Poor training is arguably one reason this practice emerged. Of course, even well-trained judges might confront ambiguous legislation and use *qingshi* as a way to decide how to apply it in a particular case. But for whatever reason it is used, *qingshi* poses a problem: the judges consulted for advice are often those who have appellate review over the judges seeking the advice. Thus, even if used with the best of intentions (to assure a correct legal outcome), *qingshi* prevents the lower court from applying a truly independent judgment (Hung 2008, 231). An even greater threat to judicial independence is when *qingshi* is used not to promote the law, but to guarantee a palatable political outcome in a case. Quite simply, some judges have used *qingshi* to avoid political as well as legal errors that might cause them to face judicial discipline. In such instances *qingshi* provides an opportunity for party organs in the higher-level courts to influence lower-level judicial decisions for political purposes (Nathan 2006, 184).

The Judges Law and subsequent amendments to it have sought to improve the quality of judges by creating minimum qualifications for becoming a judge, mandating that new judges pass a national examination, moving toward merit-based promotion, and requiring continuing legal education. Judges who were appointed prior to the Judges Law were also expected to meet the new standards or be removed (Peerenboom 2002,

290–92). This led to dramatic improvements. In 1987, for example, only 17 percent of judges in China had received post-high school education, but by 2000 100 percent had (Dickinson 2007). Later, the Judges Law was amended to require legal training at the bachelor's level along with prior legal experience before becoming a judge (Peerenboom 2002, 291). This has led at least some to argue that the problem of poorly trained judges is a thing of the past in China (Dickinson 2007). Lingering problems would not be unexpected, however, in a legal system that is only about thirty years old. Moreover, the requirement of legal training does not necessarily guarantee good legal training.

The problem of poorly trained judges is compounded because of the extraordinary amount of legislation enacted in China since the beginning of reform in 1978. Entire areas of the law have emerged almost overnight involving subject matter and transactions that would have been unthinkable a few years earlier (Lubman 2006, 7). Mastering this new terrain is a hurdle for new judges who do not have a long tradition to fall back on (a factor that no doubt contributed to the practice of *qingshi*). Further compounding the problem is the fact that the laws themselves have often been ambiguous, poorly drafted, and subject to frequent change (Peerenboom 2002, 13). This, itself, serves as a threat to the rule of law, which assumes that laws should be clear, consistent, and stable (Peerenboom 2002, 65).

Corruption is yet another impediment to judicial independence. Corruption within government has been an ongoing problem in China (Lubman 2006, 75–76). Courts do have some power to sanction officials for corruption, but judges themselves are not immune from the problem. Connections have sometimes seemed more important than the law in determining the outcomes of cases, and *ex parte* communication between judges and litigants increases the likelihood of bribes in return for favorable rulings. Complaints about judicial misconduct are decreasing, but courts in 2005 found that 378 judges had abused their power in return for personal gain (Hung 2008, 237). When one recalls, however, that China has some 200,000 judges, that number is quite miniscule. Probably more rampant than bribery is favoritism based on personal relationships between judges and lawyers. This reflects the emphasis on *guanxi* in Chinese culture, in which personal connections lead to favors. As Melissa Hung puts it, a reliance on *guanxi* means that one's "familiarity with influential persons who can bend the rules, rather than the rules themselves, determines the outcome" (Hung 2008, 237–38).

In short, institutional and systemic factors have served as obstacles to China achieving even the basic procedural requirements of the rule of law. The problem from the perspective of the Western liberal tradition is that the rule of law embodies more than just these basic procedural requirements. The supremacy of clear, consistent, and stable laws fairly applied by independent judges—even ones that impose meaningful limits of state actors—is not enough. The Western liberal tradition assumes that the rule of law requires, beyond all that, a civil society that consists of such things as democracy and the legal development of civil liberties. In other words, it moves beyond a positivist conception of law to one that stresses a normative conception of law that includes the idea of *justice*. Peerenboom has written extensively about this distinction between "thin" procedurally based theories of the rule of law and "thick" theories that add substantive elements of political morality to the mix (Peerenboom 2002, especially chapters 3–4). Although Peerenboom suggests that it may be unfair to judge China by the "thick" conception of the rule of law embodied by the Western liberal tradition, critics of China frequently resort to such judgments.

Critics, for example, point to China's record on freedom of speech. Article 35 of the Chinese Constitution clearly states: "Citizens of the People's Republic of China enjoy freedom of speech, of the press, of assembly, of association, of procession, and of demonstration." But in practice, free speech is routinely restricted by China's authoritarian government. The U.S. Congressional-Executive Commission on China (or "CECC")—which Congress created in 2000 and which consists of nine U.S. senators, nine members of the House of Representatives, and five senior administration officials appointed by the president of the United States—concluded in its 2006 annual report that government censorship in China, "while not total, is pervasive and highly effective, and denies Chinese citizens the freedoms of speech and of the press guaranteed to them in the Chinese Constitution" (Congressional-Executive Commission on China 2006, sec. Va.).

In the United States, there is a longstanding presumption against prior restraint (government censorship before publication). This presumption has its roots in English common law dating back to 1695. In his 1931 opinion for the Supreme Court in *Near v. Minnesota*, Chief Justice Charles Evans Hughes reiterated that the "chief purpose" of the First Amendment to the U.S. Constitution had been "to prevent previous restraints on publication" (see *Near v. Minnesota*). Such a principle does not exist in China. Instead, China imposes a strict system of licensing. No book, newspaper, or magazine in China may be legally published without a government license. As the 2006 CECC Report observed, "Chinese authorities banned 79 newspapers and periodicals and seized 169 million publications in 2005. From 2003 to 2005, the government cancelled the registrations of 202 news bureaus and shut down 73 others." It also concluded that China's system of prior restraint does not conform to international standards for freedom of the press (such as article 19 of the Universal Declaration of Human Rights) (Congressional-Executive Commission on China 2006, sec. Va.). A 2007 report by the Committee to Protect Journalists noted that "China has led the world in the number of jailed journalists since 1999" (Committee to Protect Journalism 2007, preface).

China's reluctance to allow freedom of speech and of the press was highlighted during the 2008 Olympic Games in Beijing. Before the Olympics, Wang Wei, a senior Chinese Olympic official, promised that journalists covering the games would have "complete freedom to report when they come to China" (quoted in Magnay 2008). Toward that end, China announced that it would temporarily loosen restrictions on foreign journalists during the Olympics so that they could travel and conduct interviews without the government approval normally required (Yardley 2006, A6). Once they arrived in China, however, some foreign journalists complained that these freedoms did not extend beyond coverage of sporting events (Hadad 2008). They also found their access to websites blocked by the government.

Similarly, China initially promised to allow public protests during the Olympic Games inside three designated parks in Beijing as long as the demonstrators obtained permits and followed Chinese law with regard to demonstrations (Yardley 2008, A6). At first blush, this arrangement did not appear to be much different than protest zones at previous Olympic Games or, for that matter, at political events in the United States. Although such protest zones have come under fire in the United States and have prompted the American Civil Liberties Union to file lawsuits against their use, protesters routinely obtain permits and use such zones in the United States.

In contrast, China did not grant a single permit to demonstrate during the Olympic Games. The state-run Xinhua news service reported on August 18, 2008, that the government had received seventy-seven applications for permits to protest, but that seventy-four of those were resolved "by relevant authorities or departments through consultations," one was rejected because the request violated local laws, and two others were dismissed for lack of information. Human rights organizations and Western news media, however, reported that the Chinese government had arrested and harassed citizens who had applied for permits to demonstrate, including two elderly women who wanted to protest their eviction from their homes. Instead of being granted permits, the two women were ordered to serve one year of "reeducation-through-labor" (Ramzy 2008). Human Rights Watch detailed other examples of detention and harassment of those who applied for protest permits and argued that "Nobody should confuse the lack of protesters with lack of complaint" (*Human Rights Watch* 2008). Such stories, along with others focusing on alleged human rights infractions, lead to renewed criticism that China remains far from a true embrace of the rule of law.

Even if such criticisms are true, recognition must be given to the progress that has nonetheless been achieved by the Chinese legal system over the last thirty years. For example, there has been a tremendous increase in the use of litigation by ordinary citizens to secure rights. This is especially true with regard to labor disputes. The 1993 Labor Regulations and the 1994 Labor Law helped to lay the foundation for labor rights in China (Monnin 2007,

753). Reflecting the long tradition of Confucianism, these laws suggested mediation as the first step toward resolving labor disputes, but they also provided for arbitration as an alternative option, and for adjudication as a final step. Over the years, there has been a significant shift away from reliance on mediation to arbitration and adjudication. From 1996 to 2001, the number of labor disputes accepted for mediation fell from 118,732 to 6,374, while the number accepted for arbitration grew from 47,951 to 184,116, and the number accepted for adjudication grew from 28,285 to 100,923. By 2005, parties filed over 300,000 labor lawsuits (Monnin 2007, 760). The government now actually encourages people to use courts, and the old notion that it is a disgrace to be involved in a lawsuit seems to be fading.

Faced with increasing numbers of appeals in labor disputes, and confronted with sometimes ambiguous and contradictory labor laws, the Supreme People's Court stepped in and issued an interpretation of the Labor Law in 2006 that allowed certain claims to bypass mandatory arbitration and required courts to accept appeals. Although this interpretation technically exceeded the official authority of the Supreme People's Court, the Standing Committee of the National People's Congress did not interfere with the interpretation. This suggests that the powers of the Supreme People's Court are expanding, and that those expanded powers can—at least under some limited circumstances—be used to accelerate legal reform and expand rights (Monnin 2007, 753, 770–71).

Citizen action has also, in a limited way, been used to help achieve legal reform. As described in detail by Keith J. Hand, citizen action led to the dismantling of a controversial form of administrative detention in China known as "custody and repatriation" (a practice used primarily to manage the flow of migrant workers into urban areas, which is closely regulated through a residence regulation system known as *hukou*).[14] Official Chinese sources claimed that between 2001 and 2003 there were more than 700 custody and repatriation centers throughout China that detained at least one million people. Some sources have suggested that there may have been as many as 3.2 million detentions in just one year. Corruption led some local police to misuse the system by engaging in the use of unlawful detentions, the extortion of fees from families in return for the release of detainees, and the use of detainees as forced labor. Conditions within the detention centers were also bad, with reports of beatings, sexual abuse, and deaths of detainees (Hand 2007, 114–15, 120).

The death of one such detainee, Sun Zhigang, drew widespread attention in China in 2003. Sun came from a poor rural family in Hubei Province. He had attended the Wuhan Technical Institute and upon graduation from university moved to the city of Guangzhou to work for a clothing company. Shortly after his arrival there he was arrested outside an Internet café because police suspected that he was an illegal migrant. In fact, Sun had a valid identification card (which he had left at home that day), a place of residence in the city, and a registered work unit, though he had not yet obtained a temporary residence permit. He was not released, even when his roommate produced his identification card and provided money for bail. Sun was transferred to a custody and repatriation center where he died. The center claimed he had died of complications from heart disease, but an autopsy later revealed internal injuries caused by blunt trauma (Hand 2007, 119–21).

As discussed above, the media in China are tightly controlled by the state, but even the media have become somewhat more commercialized as a result of economic reform. Reports about local corruption have also become more common (probably, at least in part, because such reports sometimes serve the interests of the central government). The Internet, in particular, has become a vehicle for some degree of citizen action, despite the fact that China has developed one of the most sophisticated Internet filtering systems in the world. In addition to blocking access to controversial sites, the government also closely monitors who is online and what sites they visit. Chinese citizens who sign up for Internet service must register with the local police within thirty days, and patrons of Internet cafés must present an identification card which the café is required to keep on file for sixty days along with a detailed log of that person's online activity.[15]

Despite these restrictions, the Internet played a key role in publicizing the death of Sun Zhigang. Sun's family posted the story of his death online, along with a petition, and the local Guangzhou newspaper, the *Southern Metropolitan Daily*, followed up with a story and editorial warning readers that what happened to Sun could happen to anybody. Local authorities in Guangdong tried to crack down on the story by banning local newspapers from further coverage of the incident, but the central government allowed state-run media outlets to cover the story, which soon received widespread coverage throughout the country. This in turn prompted a deluge of Internet chatter about what had happened to Sun.

Legal reformers seized the opportunity to challenge the custody and repatriation system by filing petitions with the Standing Committee of the National People's Congress which, unlike China's courts, has the authority—in theory—to invalidate laws which conflict with the Constitution. Reformers hoped the petitions would prompt the Standing Committee to set a precedent for such review. In the end, the Standing Committee did not. Nonetheless, the petitions received widespread media coverage, and the publicity did lead to the trial and convictions of those involved in Sun's death. It also prompted the State Council to issue new regulations that repealed the old custody and repatriation measures. The reform undoubtedly occurred because it furthered the interests of the central government (and, of course, the reform was carefully constructed so as not to set a precedent for constitutional review). Still, it is unlikely that this reform would have happened when it did without the initial publicity generated by citizen action (Hand 2007, 123–30).[16]

Such action, however modest, would have been unthinkable thirty-five years ago, as would the remarkable development of China's legal system during that time span. At least some meaningful steps have been taken toward some of the basic elements of the rule of law. It would be unrealistic to expect China—a Communist, authoritarian state—to embrace all the elements that the Western liberal tradition expects of a full-fledged rule of law system (such as democracy, individual rights, and a well-developed civil society). But too much emphasis on China's very real shortcomings obscures the equally real progress that has been made. Structural and cultural impediments remain, but the possibility—even likelihood—of further progress is real.

NOTES

1. This figure is posted under "Facts and Figures" by *China Today* at www.chinatoday.com/law/a.htm.

2. The precise number of lawyers surviving in 1976 is difficult to determine. There were fewer than 3,000 before the Cultural Revolution (see Peerenboom 2002, 347). Jia Wuguang, general secretary of the All-China Lawyers Association, said in 2002 that the number may have dwindled to as few as 200 or so (quoted in "Number of Lawyer's Rapidly Rising in China," *People's Daily*, July 8, 2002, available at china.org.cn/english/Life/36430.htm).

3. See also "Facts and Figures," *China Today* at www.chinatoday.com/law/a.htm.

4. Peerenboom (2002) is a good example of this point of view.

5. See, for example, Ruwitch and Beck (2008). For a descriptions of the new Labor Contract Law, see Dickinson (2007) and Cha (2008, A01).

6. See, for example, the website of the group Human Rights in China (founded by Chinese students and scholars in March 1989), www.hrichina.org/public/. See also the website of the Congressional-Executive Commission on China, created by the U.S. Congress in October 2000 with the legislative mandate to monitor human rights and the development of the rule of law in China, www.cecc.gov/index.php?PHPSESSID=b259eb007028442ceeeebf8ad9c7de4c.

7. This is the classic English translation of the *Analects* by James Legge, first published in 1893 by Clarendon Press and available on several websites, including ebooks.adelaide.edu.au/c/confucius/c748a/.

8. In contrast to movies made in Shanghai during this period, movies made in Hong Kong—a British colony with a different legal system—portrayed lawyers in a much more favorable light.

9. The most common figure cited in the West is 30 million, based on research of population statistics by Judith Banister in the 1980s, but some suggest that the number may be far higher. For an overview of the question about how many died, see Becker (1996) chapter 18. See also Bannister (1987).

10. Translations vary slightly. One variant is: "The People's Republic of China practices ruling the country in accordance with the law and building a socialist country of law." See english.people.com.cn/constitution/constitution.html.

11. For an official description of the Three Represents, see www.idcpc.org.cn/english/policy/3represents.htm.

12. See also the transcript of a PBS NewsHour interview with O'Connor and Breyer on September 26, 2006, available online at www.pbs.org/newshour/bb/law/july-dec06/independence_09-26.html.

13. See www.ajs.org/cji/cji_task_force.asp.

14. This and subsequent discussion of the practice of "custody and repatriation" and the death of Sun Zhigang is drawn from Hand (2007, 114ff).

15. This paragraph is based on an interactive website, "China and Internet Censorship," hosted by CNN.com at www.cnn.com/interactive/world/0603/explainer.china.internet/frameset.exclude.html.

16. The central government had already considered reform of the custody and repatriation system, but had never acted on it. Publicity created a perfect climate for reform. The reform strengthened the power of the central government over local governments (a step that might have been more difficult without the publicity and strong public support for reform). Moreover, the reform came in the midst of a leadership transition in which Hu Jintao (the new party general secretary) and Wen Jiabao (the new premier of the State Council) were trying to consolidate their power by projecting themes of openness and appealing to marginalized groups in Chinese society (Hand 2007, 132–35, 142–43).

REFERENCES

Bannister, Judith. 1987. *China's Changing Population*. Berkeley, CA: Stanford University Press.

Becker, Jasper. 1996. *Hungry Ghosts: China's Secret Famine*. London: John Murray.

Cha, Ariana Eunjung. 2008. "New Law Gives Chinese Workers Power, Gives Businesses Nightmares." *Washington Post*, April 14.

Chow, Daniel C. K. 2003. *The Legal System of the People's Republic of China*. St. Paul, MN: Thomson/West.

Cohen, Jerome. 2007. "An Introduction to Law in China." *Vermont Journal of Environmental Law* 8 (Spring): 399.

Cohens v. Virginia. 19 U.S. (6 Wheat.) 264 (1821).

Committee to Protect Journalism. 2007. Preface. In *Falling Short: As the 2008 Olympics Approach, China Falters on Press Freedom*. Available online at www.cpj.org/Briefings/2007/Falling_Short/China/preface.html.

Congressional-Executive Commission on China. 2006. "Freedom of Expression." In *2006 Annual Report*, section Va, available at www.cecc.gov/pages/annualRpt/annualRpt06/Expression.php?PHPSESSID=3ffbd786e849f0215171ee985b9d1e65.

Conner, Alison W. 2007. "Chinese Lawyers on the Silver Screen." In *Cinema, Law, and the State in Asia*, ed. Corey K. Creekmur and Mark Sidel. New York: Palgrave Macmillan.

Dickinson, Steven M. 2007a. "Debunking Myths about China's Legal System." *Business Week*, November 29, online edition. www.businessweek.com/globalbiz/content/nov2007/gb20071129_851610.htm?chan=top+news_top+news+index_global+business.

———. 2007b. "Power to the People." *China International Business*, November. www.cibmagazine.com.cn/ShowAtl.asp?ID=257.

Dreyer, June Teufel. 2006. *China's Political System: Modernization and Tradition*. 5th ed. New York: Pearson/Longman.

Ducat, Craig R. 2009. *Constitutional Interpretation*. 9th ed. Boston: Wadsworth/Cengage.

Folsom, Ralph H., and John H. Minan. 1989. *Law in the People's Republic of China*. Boston: Martinus Nijhoff Publishers.

Goodman, David S. G. 1994. *Deng Xiaoping and the Chinese Revolution*. London: Routledge.

Hadad, Chuck. 2008. "China Falls Short on Olympic Promises, Critics Say." CNN.com, August 12. www.cnn.com/2008/WORLD/asiapcf/08/12/china.promises/.

Hamilton, Alexander. 2000. "Federalist No. 78." In *The Federalist: A Commentary on the Constitution of the United States*, ed. Robert Scigliano. New York: The Modern Library.

Hand, Keith J. 2007. "Using Law for a Righteous Purpose: The Sun Zhigang Incident and Evolving Forms of Citizen Action in the People's Republic of China." *Columbia Journal of Transnational Law* 45:116.

Huang, Philip C. C. 2006. "Court Mediation in China, Past and Present." *Modern China* 32 (July).

Human Rights Watch. 2008. "China: Police Detain Would-Be Olympic Protesters." Human Rights Watch press release, August 13. hrw.org/english/docs/2008/08/12/china19601.htm.

Hung, Melissa S. 2008. "Obstacles to Self-Actualization in Chinese Legal Practice." *Santa Clara Law Review* 48.

Kelly, Michael. 1997. "Judge Dread." *New Republic*, March 31.

Killion, M. Ulric. 2005. "China's Amended Constitution: Quest for Liberty and Independent Judicial Review." *Washington University Global Studies Law Review* 43 (4).

Kinkley, Jeffrey. 2000. *Chinese Justice, The Fiction: Law and Literature in Modern China*. Stanford, CA: Stanford University Press.

Li, Yuwen. 2000. "Lawyers in China: A 'Flourishing' Profession in a Rapidly Changing Society?" *China Perspectives* 27 (January–February). www.cefc.com.hk/uk/pc/articles/art_ligne.php?num_art_ligne=2702.

Lubman, Stanley. 2006. "Looking for Law in China." *Columbia Journal of Asian Law* 20 (Fall): 29.

MacFarquhar, Roderick. 1997. "The Succession to Mao and the End of Maoism, 1969–82." In *The Politics of China*, 2nd ed., ed. Roderick MacFarquhar. Cambridge: Cambridge University Press.

Magnay, Jacquelin. 2008. "Chinese Red Tape Redefines Freedom for the Press." *Syndney (Australia) Morning Herald*, July 12. www.smh.com.au/news/beijing2008/chinese-red-tape-redefines-freedom-for-the-press/2008/07/11/1215658131357.html.

Marbury v. Madison. 5 U.S. (1 Cranch) 137 (1803).
Martin v. Hunter's Lessee. 14 U.S. (1 Wheat.) 304 (1816).
Mauro, Tony. 2005. "O'Connor Fires Back on Judicial Independence." *Legal Times*, November 28. www.law.com/jsp/article.jsp?id=1132740311603.
———. 2006. "Roberts Gonzales Speak on Judicial Independence." *Legal Times*, October 2. www.law.com/jsp/article.jsp?id=1159567621347.
Monnin, Jill E. 2007. "Extending the Reach of Chinese Labor Law: How Does the Supreme People's Court's 2005 Interpretation Transform Labor Dispute Resolution?" *Pacific Rim Law & Policy* 16 (June): 761.
Nathan, Andrew J. 2006. "China's Constitutionalist Option." In *China's Deep Reform: Domestic Politics in Transition*, ed. Lowell Dittmer and Guoli Liu. Lanham, MD: Rowman & Littlefield.
Near v. Minnesota. 283 U.S. 697 (1931).
"Number of Lawyers Rapidly Rising in China." 2002. *People's Daily*, July 8. china.org.cn/english/Life/36430.htm.
Paine, Thomas. 1994. *Rights of Man*. New York: Everyman's Library/Knopf.
Peerenboom, Randall. 2002. *China's Long March toward Rule of Law*. Cambridge: Cambridge University Press.
Perkovich, Robert. 1996. "A Comparative Analysis of Community Mediation in the United States and the People's Republic of China." *Temple International and Comparative Law Journal* 10 (Fall): 315.
Provine, Doris Marie. 1986. *Judging Credentials: Nonlawyer Judges and the Politics of Professionalism*. Chicago: University of Chicago Press.
Qian, Yingyi. 2006. "The Process of China's Market Transition, 1978–1998." In *China's Deep Reform: Domestic Politics in Transition*, ed. Lowell Dittmer and Guoli Liu. Lanham, MD: Rowman & Littlefield.
Ramzy, Austin. 2008. "Would-Be Beijing Protesters Punished." *Time*, August 21. www.time.com/time/world/article/0,8599,1834474,00.html.
Ruwitch, John, and Lindsay Beck. 2008. "China Migrant Workers Learn the Law to Win Rights." *Reuters*, March 1. today.reuters.com/news/articlenews.aspx?type=reutersEdge&storyID=2008-03-02T002839Z_01_HKG280962_RTRUKOC_0_US-CHINA-MIGRANTS-LAWYERS.xml&pageNumber=0&imageid=&cap=&sz=13&WTModLoc=NewsArt-C1-ArticlePage3.
Shapiro, Martin. 1981. *Courts: A Comparative and Political Analysis*. Chicago: University of Chicago Press.
Song, Jianli. 2007. "China's Judiciary: Current Issues." *Maine Law Review* 59:141.
2004 Republican Party Platform, 84. www.gop.com/images/2004platform.pdf.
2008 Republican Platform, 53. www.gopplatform2008.com/2008Platform.pdf.
Yardley, Jim. 2005. "A Judge Tests China's Courts, Making History." *New York Times*, November 28.
———. 2006. "China Plans Temporary Easing of Curbs on Foreign Journalists." *New York Times*, December 2.
———. 2008. "3 Parks Set as Zones for Protest in Beijing." *New York Times*, July 24.
Zou, Keyuan. 2007. "Toward the Rule of Law." In *Interpreting China's Development*, ed. Wang Gungwu and John Wong. London: World Scientific.

6

China's Intellectual Property Rights Protection and Sino-U.S. Relations

Qingtang Kong

There are many factors influencing Sino-U.S. relations such as safety, ideology, economy, and trade. They interacted with each other, and they acted differently on Sino-U.S. relations in different historical stages. The Sino-U.S. economic and trade relations developed rapidly with changes of international situations, such as the disintegration of the Soviet Union, the performance of China's opening-up policy and the Sino-U.S. economic relations coming into focus. Today, China is the third largest trade partner and the fourth largest export market as well as the fastest-rising overseas market to the United States, while the United States is the second largest trade partner, the largest export market, and the second largest source of foreign capital for China. It's rare that the biggest developed country and the biggest developing country in the world could form such intimate economic and trade relations. However, the achievement of economic and trade achievements between the two powers could not cover the frictions, and sometimes the fierce scuffles in the process of contact, among which issues of intellectual property rights (IPR) are outstanding. In the 1990s only, three serious disputes about IPR happened between the two countries. The conflict has no tendency to ease following the increase of the economy and trade. Instead, the disagreements become more and more violent and even reach a point of lawsuit in the twenty-first century. The reasons for the United States attaching high importance to the issues of IPR are mainly due to the fact that the proportion of information and technology trades is getting larger and larger in the foreign trade of the United States. Only by giving effective protection to IPR can China keep ahead in international trade and fully maintain its own interests. The IPR and related protection policies have been a part of China's foreign strategy. The protection of IPR always takes top priority both in national legislation and in bilateral, multilateral negotiations with the United States. Following the rapid development of Sino-U.S. economic and trade relations during the 1980s, issues of IPR swiftly climbed into the schedule of bilateral relations and grew to be an important factor influencing the Sino-U.S. relationship.

THE ACHIEVEMENT IN PROTECTION OF IPR DURING THE LAST THIRTY YEARS IN CHINA

China was among the latecomers to the protection of IPR but they developed it fast. Since the implementation of the reform and opening-up policy at the end of the 1970s, Chinese government and people have had full realization of the importance of inventions and innovations to economic and social progress. They knew well the significance of the protection of IPR in Sino-U.S. relations. While adhering to the international protection principles of IPR, they determined the appropriate level of protection of IPR according to the national condition, strenuously balanced the interests among the creators, users of IPR, and the public, and actively promoted the work of IPR protection. All the work has already made great progress.

Efforts Are Being Made to Advance the Awareness of the General Public about IPR

Chinese government attaches great importance to publicity concerning IPR. Beginning in 2004, the state designated the week from April 20 to 26 each year as the "week for publicizing the importance of IPR protection." By making wide use of newspapers, magazines, television, radio, and the Internet, and through holding seminars and knowledge contests and making public-interest advertisements, the government carries out publicity and education among the general public regarding IPR protection. The aim is to create a social atmosphere in which labor, knowledge, talent, and creation are respected, and to advance the awareness of the general public regarding IPR.

A Relatively Complete System of Laws and Regulations that Covers a Wide Range of Subjects and Is in Line with Generally Accepted International Rules Has Been Established and Keeps Improving

Since the 1980s, the state has promulgated and put into effect a number of laws and regulations covering the major contents in IPR protection. These include the Patent Law of the People's Republic of China, Trademark Law of the People's Republic of China, Copyright Law of the People's Republic of China, Regulations on the Protection of Computer Software, Regulations on the Protection of Layout Designs of Integrated Circuits, Regulations on the Collective Management of Copyright, Regulations on the Management of Audio-Video Products, Regulations on the Protection of New Varieties of Plants, Regulations on the Protection of IPR by the Customs, Regulations on the Protection of Special Signs, and Regulations on the Protection of Olympic Logos. China has also promulgated a series of relevant rules for the implementation of these laws and regulations, and their legal interpretation. As a result, the system of laws and regulations on IPR protection in China has been continuously improved. In 2001, around the time when China was admitted to join the WTO, in order to provide effective legal protection to IPR, the country made comprehensive revisions to the laws and regulations regarding IPR protection and their legal interpretation. While more emphasis is given to promoting the progress of science and technology and innovation with regard to legislative intent, content of rights, standards of protection and means of legal remedy, the revisions brought the laws and regulations into conformity with the WTO's Agreement on Trade-Related Aspects of IPR and other international rules on IPR protection.

A Coordinated and Efficient Work System and a Law Enforcement Mechanism Have Been Established and Improved

In its practice of IPR protection, a two-way parallel protection mode, namely administrative and judicial protection, has emerged in China. Several departments in China are assigned with the duty to protect IPR. They include primarily the State Intellectual Property Office, State Administration for Industry and Commerce, Press and Publication General Administration, State Copyright Bureau, Ministry of Culture, Ministry of Agriculture, State Forestry Administration, Ministry of Public Security, General Administration of Customs, Supreme People's Court, and Supreme People's Procuratorate. For many years these departments have done effective work in their respective fields. To further strengthen IPR protection, in 2004 China established the State IPR Protection Work Team headed by a vice premier of the State Council, responsible for planning and coordinating the work regarding IPR protection throughout the country. Its office, located in the Ministry of Commerce, handles the routine work of the team.

In recent years, the state has increased work contacts between administrative law enforcement organs and public security organs and people's procuratorates with respect to IPR protection. In October 2000, the relevant departments jointly issued the Notice on Strengthening Cooperation and Coordination in the Work of Investigating and Dealing with Criminal Cases that Infringe IPR, which contains clear provisions on relevant issues. In July 2001, the State Council promulgated the Regulations on the Transfer of Suspected Criminal Cases by Administrative Law Enforcement

Organs, which includes clear provisions on how the administrative law enforcement organs should transfer suspected criminal cases to public security organs in a timely fashion. In March 2004, the relevant departments jointly issued the Opinions on Increasing Work Contacts between Administrative Law Enforcement Organs and Public Security Organs and People's Procuratorates. A work mechanism involving the coordination of administrative law enforcement and criminal law enforcement has been established, creating a joint power to deal with IPR infringements. This ensures that suspected criminal cases enter the judicial process promptly. In recent years, the judicial organs have adjudicated a large number of IPR infringement cases according to law. In civil cases, the infringed parties have received timely compensation for their financial losses, and IPR-related crimes have been effectively combated.

Administrative Law Enforcement Has Been Strengthened with Respect to IPR Protection

As gradual improvements are made in the legal system on IPR protection, China has shifted its focus from legislation to law enforcement. Administrative law enforcement has been enhanced through the combination of routine management and supervision with special crackdown campaigns. In August 2004, Chinese government decided to launch a special one-year campaign to protect IPR across the country from September 2004 to August 2005. It was decided at the national TV and telephone conference on rectification and standardization of the market economic order convened by the State Council on March 31, 2005, that the campaign was extended to the end of 2005. With unified planning, the relevant departments have investigated and dealt with major IPR infringement cases, focusing on major fields in the protection of trademark rights, copyrights, and patent rights, on major links in the import and export of goods, all types of exhibitions and wholesale markets of commodities, and on key places where producers and sellers of counterfeit goods were known to be concentrated. Their quick action and strict law enforcement efforts have dealt a blow on IPR offenders, achieving positive results.

Actively Fulfilling International Obligations to Protect IPR

China has taken an active approach to joining major international conventions and agreements on IPR protection. Following its accession to the World Intellectual Property Organization in 1980, China joined in succession more than ten international conventions, treaties, agreements, and protocols, such as the Paris Convention for the Protection of Industrial

Property, Patent Cooperation Treaty, Budapest Treaty on the International Recognition of the Deposit of Microorganisms for the Purposes of Patent Procedure, Locarno Agreement Establishing an International Classification for Industrial Designs, Madrid Agreement Concerning the International Registration of Marks, Nice Agreement Concerning the International Classification of Goods and Services for the Purpose of the Registration of Marks, Protocol Relating to the Madrid Agreement Concerning the International Registration of Marks, Agreement on Trade-Related Aspects of IPR, International Convention for the Protection of New Varieties of Plants, Berne Convention for the Protection of Literary and Artistic Works, Universal Copyright Convention, and Convention for the Protection of Producers of Phonograms Against Unauthorized Duplication.

While strictly executing its international obligations in IPR protection, China has devoted great efforts to adjust and improve international rules regarding IPR protection in order to let all countries of the world share the fruits and benefits brought about by the progress of science and technology. In recent years, China has held talks, and engaged in exchanges and cooperation with other countries, international organizations, and foreign-invested enterprises in the field of IPR. At the suggestion of the United States, starting in 2003, China and the United States have held a round-table conference on IPR every year, and reached agreement on many IPR-related issues at the two round-table conferences. In 2004, China and Europe held their first round of talks on IPR in Beijing. Initial agreement was reached between the two sides on matters of cooperation related to IPR. Relevant Chinese departments have established good cooperative relations with corresponding departments in several countries, and international organizations such as World Intellectual Property Organization and International Union for the Protection of New Varieties of Plants. In September 2003, a mechanism was established for regular contact and coordination between relevant Chinese departments and foreign-invested enterprises. Under the mechanism, a meeting is held every three months to solicit comments and suggestions from the foreign-invested enterprises on issues related to IPR protection.

We should say that the accomplishments that China has made in the protection of IPR are universally acknowledged. Dr. Arpad Bogsch, the former director general of World Intellectual Property Organization (WIPO), appreciated that "China had accomplished all this at a speed unmatched in the history of intellectual property protection." However, we can't ignore the existing problems. In conclusion, the population has a rather incomplete understanding of IPR and in some areas we do have infringements, even serious acts of tort. Especially repeated occurrences of software piracy and counterfeit trademark could not be stopped despite prohibitions.

DIFFERENCES ON ISSUES REGARDING IPR BETWEEN CHINA AND THE UNITED STATES

The continuous progress on the protection of IPR that China made is largely due to the built-in incentive of its reform and opening-up policy and implementation of the strategy of scientific and technological power. Moreover, the conflicts and cooperation focusing on the protection of IPR among developed countries including the United States during the process of economic trades accelerated the course of China's IPR protection to a certain extent. Objectively speaking, both China and the United States own the same aspiration to develop the two countries' trade relations and the unanimous purpose of promoting the standard of IPR protection. However, we can not deny and ignore that serious disagreements on some relevant principles of intellectual property protection do exist because of the differences of history and culture, political systems, and economic standards, which also are the main reasons why the two counties had conflicts on the issues of IPR.

The United States' Expectation and Stance Regarding China on Issues of IPR Protection

As the factor of IPR appears conspicuously following the development of Sino-U.S. economic and trade relations, the related international treaties on the protection of IPR have not become the standard of the two countries, as is quite evident from the numerous Sino-U.S. negotiations on IPR in the 1980s and 1990s. The United States not only required China to establish and improve an intellectual property system which could effectively protect its intellectual products regarding aspects of legislation, jurisdiction, and law enforcement in order to minimize the loss caused by China's ineffective protection of IPR, but also put the Chinese market under close supervision to test the commitments that China made in the Sino-U.S. negotiation. They even provided many concrete suggestions and measures on how to promote China to improve its standard of IPR protection. After China entered WTO, aiming at the unfavorable situation in protecting U.S. IPR in China, the Chamber of Commerce of the United States issued a study report named "Important Issues in Sino-U.S. Commerce Relations," which gave suggestions on the improvement of China's status of IPR protection from the following eight aspects: piracy on the internet, resource of law of enforcement, amendment of criminal laws, reinforcing the transparency of administration of law, of data, and of study, crackdown on fraudulent design patents, and patent imperative licensing system being consistent with TRIPS agreement. And it also analyzed the advantages of these suggestions to China. From the conflicts we can see that the United States attaches more importance to the results rather than how far China has gone to approach the aim.

The reason why the United States has this stance on and attitude to China's protection work of IPR is that the United States itself has a comparatively sophisticated intellectual property system. Its intellectual property system has a history as long as the history of the country and it always in the process of continuous improvement and perfection. In 1790, the United States made the first law and in 1820, the federal government set up a patent office. Furthermore, neither of the two world wars happened in the mainland of the United States and the protection of industrial property rights pushed the fast development of its science, technology, and economy. To value knowledge and talents is always the principle that the United States observes. Especially when the United States exploited the western states and after the Second World War, it attracted specialists extensively, which nearly made the United States the world's collecting and distributing center of all kinds of talented people. The long-existing stability and the considerable "liberty" assuredly provided certain condition for scientists and technologists to dive into scientific research. The collection of experts historically made successful law protection objectively necessary. It is the system that protects and promotes the technological creation and innovation. None of the geniuses from Edison to Bill Gates could create anything without the protection of IPR.

In settling disputes, the United States is accustomed to using revenge. As early as 1989, it put China on the list of the "observed countries," which was seen as having serious problems in this regard. One year later, it further put China on the list of "strictly observed countries." And then in 1991, it started the "special 301 survey" of China and had launched many "special 301 surveys" followed by retaliatory measures in the late 1990s. In the three disputes in the 1990s, the United States respectively required a 1.2 billion, a 2.8 billion, and 3.0 billion (U.S. dollars) revenge bill but ended up with the signing of a bilateral agreement. After China entered into the WTO, the United States paid closer attention to this aspect. In 2004, it questioned the momentum of IPR protection in China because of the infringement and piracy of songs on the Internet and sued the WTO against this.

The powerful means that the United States used to settle the disputes are relevant to the level of its economic development. Besides the economic trade, the United States became the top arms dealer in the world since the disintegration of the Soviet Union. The annual volume of arms trade reached about $15 billion and accounts for half of the total turnover of the global arms trade. In 1998, the United States' GDP was U.S.$7,677 trillion while China's was U.S.$959.6 billion. In 2000, the United States' economic scale was about $9 trillion dollars, which accounted for 27 percent of the total value of world production. By contrast, China's economic scale was about $1 trillion dollars, and only accounted for 3 percent of the total value of world production. In this sharp contrast of economic power, the United States can audaciously make "stakes" to threaten the trade partner with economic sanctions. When choosing the different policies, it usually decides its stakes' sizes based on the actual situation and what it needs.

China's Principled Stand on the Protection of IPR

IPR are new things for China. In regard to the IPR system, China consistently follows the principle of equality, mutual benefits, independence, and protection. It pays close attention to the combination of internalization and localization, and seeks the balance point between the improvement of the protection of IPR and the requirement of development. China should establish an intellectual property system that conforms to the country's national conditions abiding by the international convention and be dedicated to making the national IPR consistent with the related principles of the international convention. The legislative power has bearing on a country's sovereignty. China firmly opposes intervention in internal affairs by using IPR as an excuse. In its view, the United States refuses to take account of China's national conditions and stubbornly persists in its own criteria. This is violation of justice.

In impelling the process of the protection of IPR, China insists that the protection level need be in line with the level of economic development. From the perspective of China, the United States spent a long period in developing its own protection of IPR. Now the United States ignores what China has achieved in such a short term and made thoughtless comments unfairly and irresponsibly. The infringement of U.S. IPR in China is as common as the infringement of China's own IPR. However, the United States always disregarded the territoriality factor of IPR, took it for granted that the rights could be protected by its own IPR, required the same protection in China, and exaggerated the degree of the infringement of its IPR in some aspects.

As for disputes, China stands for settling them by negotiation and consultation in the spirit of mutual understanding and mutual accommodation rather than the oppressing means of trade sanction or threatening sanction, which is often used by the United States. It consistently believes that the commitment China made in the agreement of IPR between China and the United States is not a unilateral promise or made under the United States pressure but mainly in accordance with some conventions and common practices of international protection of IPR and it is good for the development of China's IPR system.

How Should We View the Controversy over IPR between China and the United States?

Issues on Sino-U.S. IPR are not unilateral but associated with factors such as the ideology and security of related countries that both influence and are influenced by the issues. And Sino-U.S. relations took different shapes at every different stage. Therefore, the politicization of issues on IPR becomes inevitable. Issues on Sino-U.S. IPR also reflect the interweaving contradiction in the United States between idealism and realism. Bearing the weight of historical humiliation because of foreign invasion and facing the historical responsibility of reform and opening-up and modernization, the Chinese nation should strike a balance to take full account of both national sentiments and the realistic situation. Therefore, issues on IPR must be viewed in the overall situation of Sino-U.S. relations, even of international relations.

IPR are the products of certain periods of social and economic development. The protection level of IPR should be compatible with the level of the country's economic development. China and the United States have different market economies: the United States has a highly developed market economy while China still has an immature marketing system. So it's common that the two countries have different standpoints and practices on range, time limit, and approaches of the protection of IPR. Actually, the United States' standard of IPR protection also went through a long time and reached the present level step by step following the history of its economic development. The system and standard that the United States wants to carry out in China are a little unrealistic and their extreme efforts of threatening with trade revenge can hardly achieve good results. What's more, we must notice that large quantities of Chinese products in the United States' market are labor-intensive while a mass of U.S. products in China's market need IPR protection. The reality is fated that the protection of IPR between the two countries could not move forward smoothly. As for the failure to stop software piracy despite repeated prohibition, we should think deeper. Besides the low purchase ability, another principal factor is the value orientation. China's present copyright regime is made on the basis of TRIPs Agreement and Nepal Convention, so it's not originated but imported. Although China had protection for authors' creative fruits in ancient times, in the long course of feudal society, the spontaneously established community under the self-subsistence peasant economic system formed the basis of personal existence with the influence of the ideal of "The land within four seas is my territory, while the hearts across the land belong to my majesty" and the social relations of an undeveloped commercial economy. The treasury relation under this social economic pattern is bound to be public-oriented and has little about "personal treasures." The formation and development of IPR in the nature of private rights is mainly required by China's modernization and the developed countries. The result of the combination of the external cause and the internal cause is that, with respect to the law, China's system of IPR protection has basically satisfied international criteria. But due to differences between the local and foreign legal culture there are still sharp conflicts over the cultural content of the law. This kind of conflict appears as: on the one hand, globalization makes foreign countries interested in urging China to override local law regarding the protection of IPR; on the other hand, the government's policy of intensifying its effort to protect IPR cannot be completely implemented in a short period of time among the common people.

CONFRONTING THE REALITY AND FACING THE FUTURE: THE COMMON TASK OF CHINA AND THE UNITED STATES

It is perfectly obvious that China had made great progress in IPR, even though the differences on the issues of IPR between China and the United States objectively do exist. How to reduce differences, increase common understanding, and impel the development of China's IPR work depends on the two sides' reasonable attitudes and common efforts.

Reinforcing Cultural Exchange, Mutual Understanding, and Mutual Trust between China and the United States

In order to settle the disputes on IPR between the two countries, first, we need to strengthen cultural exchange and mutual understanding. Only exchange and understanding could gradually disarm the hostility caused by innocence. Without exchange, there could not be real understanding and it could be hard to realize real dialogue and coordination, let alone mutual development. In July 1998, the Committee of 100 organized by Chinese and American leaders announced a white paper to appeal: the understanding that the American public has of China and the Chinese public of America should be deepened. Once there is dispute or difficulty, both sides need to consider not only one's own benefits but also the benefits of the other side. Harming others is unlikely to benefit oneself and it will go nowhere to impose one's own view on others. China should modestly acknowledge its shortage and the gap on the point of IPR and more importantly make unremitting efforts to take efficient actions to reduce its internal infringements. The United States also should review its mode of thinking, carefully consider the national conditions and status quo of China, and provide more understanding and less reproach for China's work in IPR protection.

Strengthen the Cooperation in the Fields of Economy and Trade and Creatively Settle Current Issues over IPR in the Course of China's Development

Issues on IPR between China and the United States are caused by Sino-U.S. economic and trade relations and are conversely influencing Sino-U.S. economic and trade relations, even the relation between the two countries. Today's Sino-U.S. economic and trade relations are interdependent and complementary. China's dependence on the American market, investment, and technology is self-evident: America is the principal trade partner in process of its economic development and modernization in the last thirty years; on the other hand, since the 1990s, the United States has been relying on China's economy more heavily under the circumstance of the consistently high growth of China's economy and the rapid development of Sino-U.S. economic and trade relations. From 1993 to 2005, the proportion of Sino-U.S. trade turnover in the GDP of America has increased from 0.61 percent to 2.36 percent and the percentage of export to China in the total export has increased from 1.89 percent to 4.69 percent. Moreover, the United States imports large quantities of good but cheap merchandise to help it control inflation. Without Chinese goods, the price index of the United States would rise by 2 percent. One research shows that, up to 2010, America's GDP will rise by 0.7 percent and its general prices will go down by 0.8 percent, which means that in 2005, every family's disposable income will increase by U.S.$500 and in 2010 it will increase by U.S.$1,000. This is just because China's entry into the WTO made America increase trade with and investment to China. Based on this fact, both China and the United States will lose a lot if a trade war caused by the issues on IPR breaks out between the two sides. There is an old saying in China: reconciliation benefits both while confrontation harms both. Former president of the United States Bill Clinton once pointed out that to draw back favored treatment of China would be to cut off Sino-U.S. economic relations and this "will push us back to the age of isolation and reproach" and will damage "the best means to advance the core benefit of the United States." The issues on IPR between China and the United States are in the process of the development of Sino-U.S. relations and should be settled by developments. The protection of IPR becomes more and more difficult following the development of the Internet and new communication techniques. Under such circumstances, the only wise choice is to open extensive cooperation between China and the United States and to settle the issues creatively. Clark T. Randt Jr., U.S. ambassador to China, stated that the American Embassy in China has regarded strengthening the protection of IPR as the major objective of interaction with governors responsible for the protection of IPR. We have seen the progress in many frontiers but a lot of work is still waiting for us. Jon W. Dudas, undersecretary of commerce for intellectual property and director of the United States Patent and Trademark Office, also expressed that both countries had much work to do in the aspect of cooperative protection of IPR. It's a gratifying phenomenon to hold a Sino-U.S. round-table meeting and a Sino-U.S. economic and trade joint conference every year. Conclusively, the exchange and cooperation between governments and industries become more and more urgent.

Quickening the Pace of Transforming IPR into a Practical Productive Force

In the age of knowledge economy, we have to vigorously promote the transformation of IPR into practical productive forces if we want a sustainable and steady development of our economy. Unconverted IPR are nominal rights. Only when they are translated into practical productive force can IPR play a positive role in the development of the society. The economic and technological development zones that have been established in China should play a leading and exemplary role in transforming IPR into practical productive forces. The Chinese government's policy on "Strengthening Technical Innovation Development, Development of High tech and Realization of Its Industrialization" strongly helps forward the process of transforming IPR into practical productive forces. Every year, the United States spends 20 percent of its GDP for the production and communication of culture, in which education takes 10 percent, training and in-service education takes 5 percent and research and exploitation takes 3 to 5 percent. The three basic elements of the scientific and technological policy of the federal government of the United States are: reinforce the management of IPR, support industrial research and exploitation, and provide funds for research in the field of science and energetic technology and the training of manpower. The lasting efforts that Washington made are critical to help the growth of America's economy. But an over-expanded protection area of IPR would bring some disadvantages to the development of social economy. The *Brookings Review* of the Brookings Institution once published an article that asked the question of "whether America's science polity will be in danger" and analyzed the United States' policy of science and technology and referred to the relation between patents and IPR. Over-extensive protection of IPR may strangle the next climax of commerce creativity. The typical example is that the right of patent of genius basically belongs to fundamental scientific patent right. Although this knowledge might be the basis for further study, the right of the first patentee would hamper further research and the use. Another urgent issue is the extensive commercialization of the Genome Project. Obviously, whereas profits are very important for the performance and industrialization of patents, the expansion of patent under protection becomes a double-edged sword.

Unceasingly Enhance Society's Awareness of IPR and Increase the Level of IPR Protection

The change of awareness can't be accomplished overnight or once and for all. We need to publicize IPR and make it sensible for the whole society that if we want to use the fruits, we must get the permission of the owner of the intellectual property right and pay compatible money according to the principle of market economy, and that the system of IPR is a mechanism to motivate the production, transmission, and application of knowledge so destruction of this system will not only damage the benefits of consumers but also interfere with the exportation and importation of technology as well as the international trade of the country. At the same time, in order to reduce infringements, we need to strengthen the popularization of IPR and set up the right awareness of IPR in the world of industry and commerce as well as in the world of science and technology in an effort to make the owners of IPR positively use legal weapons to protect their legal rights and interests and to make the users consciously gain the usage rights based on judicial proceedings. When increasing people's awareness of property rights, we should emphatically fight off local protectionism, strengthen the supervision of social opinion, bring the advertising ability of mass media into full play, and constantly improve laws and rules for the protection of IPR. When thoroughly protecting the legal interests of rights owners, we need to prevent them from abusing their rights to damage other interests.

As the process of economic globalization speeds up, China's market economic system is becoming gradually mature, the communication between China and America is continuously deepening, and the differences between China and the United States in IPR should reduce gradually, while consensus between the two countries will strengthen and widen. Thus, the future of trade relations and Sino-U.S. relations will be very bright.

III
INTEREST GROUPS AND THE POLICY PROCESS

7

Interests, Groups, and Information Aggregation

Scott H. Ainsworth and Ruoxi Li

PRELIMINARIES: A VIEW OF THE SOCIAL SCIENCES, PLURALISM, AND POLITICS IN THE UNITED STATES

It is immediately obvious that there are vast differences between the United States and China, affecting politics in the broadest sense as well as the standard views of interests and groups. Though acutely aware of their differences, we note that China and the United States are bound by some common characteristics. They each have large and diverse populations and encompass large bodies of land. The United States and China also both rely on local, regional, and national governing structures. These common elements allow us to focus on the most general findings related to politics, governance, and interest groups. Our goal, then, is to highlight the most fundamental, overarching models to offer insights into the most basic, broad-based problems and issues related to interest groups and governance in China and the United States.[1]

We organize this chapter around four topics. We begin with a discussion of interests and groups, detailing the place of pluralist studies in American political science. The earliest pluralists sought to "fashion a tool" to understand better the political world surrounding them. The earliest of the pluralists were realists first and foremost. To overlook or ignore groups would simply deny the foundations of social and political life. Second, we discuss the mobilization of interests into groups. For an important set of scholars following the early pluralists, groups remained important, but groups were not seen as the "automatic fruit" of interests (Salisbury 1969). Olson characterized the circumstances that made it so difficult for groups to form around interests (1965). In the third section we explore how political interest groups aggregate and communicate information. Every government relies on information related to the governed. To be certain, government bureaucracies can gather and aggregate information, but there are also nongovernmental sources. Elections, for instance, aggregate the voices of those who vote. Markets aggregate information about the demand and supply of goods and services. Political interest groups also aggregate information. The third section of this chapter contrasts the information aggregation characteristics of political interest groups, comparing and contrasting those characteristics with bureaucracies, elections, and markets.

The third section of this chapter also explores the conduits for information. If the government seeks information from bureaucracies, elections, markets, or interest groups, then there must be established channels for the information to flow. Government officials always have the upper hand in this regard because they are able to regulate the conduits for information. Channels for communication may be opened or closed. Of more interest is how a government can screen the flow of information, separating the "good" information from the "bad" information. Everyone recognizes that information from political interest groups, as well as bureaucracies, elections, and markets, may be faulty or biased. The faulty information must be screened out so that only the valuable information remains. The third section explores the means by which government officials can screen information from political interest groups. To the extent that governments can and do screen information from interest group communication, interest groups can become valuable entities for a state and its governance.

The fourth section considers some implications of this work for China in the future. China is rapidly changing economically and socially. Competing interests and groups are likely to play a prominent role in such a dynamic society. In the fifth section, we conclude the chapter.

UNDERSTANDING PLURALISM AND POLITICS IN THE UNITED STATES

In the United States, the earliest works in political science included no role for interest groups because groups were not constitutionally mandated institutions and most scholars adopted a legalistic, doctrinal view of politics and political science. Constitutionally mandated institutions were deemed appropriate subjects for study, but little else was of concern. Even as some scholars moved beyond traditional institutional analysis, there were still ties to governing bodies. For instance, liberal scholars of the nineteenth century often focused their work on individuals as much or more than on governing bodies; but a prominent concern of the liberal tradition of the late 1800s was the structuring of government to preserve individual rights and individual sovereignty. Whereas the liberal tradition was centered around individuals and placed considerable faith in the abilities of individuals to make reasoned choices, "[o]ne of the central thrusts of... pluralism had been to redefine democracy along group lines precisely to avoid the rationalist assumptions" of individual behavior (Garson 1978, 125). Early group theories evolved from the conservative tradition of the nineteenth century, which was more organic and more sensitive to the community as a whole (or at least large segments of the whole). Individuals existed first and foremost within classes or groups, however defined. Bentley argued the case particularly strongly. "The individual stated for himself, and invested with an extra social unity of his own, is a fiction" (1908, 215). Any truly individual concern or activity is "of trifling importance in interpreting society" (Bentley 1908, 215). Garson and others connected the disregard of the individual with a distrust of the individual. Pluralists deemed individuals "restless and immoderate" (Garson 1978, 125), but groups could be a moderating influence.

By the 1940s and 1950s, political scientists' focus was changing. Pluralism provided a welcome counter to the dry, legalistic institutionalism common in the early part of the century. The earliest of the pluralists wanted to turn scholars' focus away from the formal institutions and toward groups. Pluralists emphasized the multiplicity (or plurality) of interests in society and inspired scholars to become increasingly concerned about the political bargaining that occurred between groups themselves and between groups and government. Such bargaining occurred throughout the three branches of government, but pluralists often looked beyond the formal, constitutionally mandated institutions of Washington. Public policy was thought to be the product of the relative group pressures brought forth during the bargaining. Pluralists argued that the best way to understand the governmental process was by studying interest groups and the bargaining between interest groups, not legal doctrine. For the pluralists, the interest group system itself was central to the representation of individuals. Scholars more enamored of formal institutions and legal doctrine ignored interest groups because they were not a constitutionally mandated element of the government; but for the pluralists, groups were the most fundamental element of politics and the governmental process.

The single most important centerpiece for pluralist studies in the United States was the work of David B. Truman in the 1950s. Truman sought to establish fundamental social and political underpinnings that would explain the omnipresence of interest groups. Truman suggests that the group precedes the interest. Groups are a product of our social tendencies. To disavow groups is to disavow what makes us social beings. "Man is characteristically human only in association with other men" (Truman 1951, 15). For Truman, all of the defining features of human existence are group related. Regular social interactions at home provide the basis of the family unit or group. Ultimately, even for the family unit, the biological ties are less important than the daily social interactions. Regular association with individuals provides the basis for the natural establishment of groups in society. Groups emerge out of regular interactions at school, work, or play. The effect of any group on a member depends substantially on the frequency of the interactions. Given the importance of regular interactions for groups, Truman concludes that the family unit is the most important group in society. Different group affiliations provide different socialization, affecting how one views the world. In such fashion, group affiliations structure our ideology, education, recreation, network of friends, political preferences, and every other aspect of our human nature.

For Truman, there were important distinctions between different types of groups. Groups were distinct from interest groups, which in turn were distinct from political interest groups. A simple *group* emerges from regular interactions of individuals. *Interest groups* are groups with members who are prone to make demands on others, and *political interest groups* make demands upon others through government officials. That is, Truman distinguished interest groups and political interest groups from the primary social groups—such as one's family. For Truman, each of the following two conditions are necessary for an interest group and together they are sufficient for interest group formation.

Condition 1: Shared Attitudes
Condition 2: Claims upon Others

Shared attitudes lead to the common interests that are fundamental to interest groups. One might even equate interests with groups. That is, there could be no group without its interests, and no interest without its group (Bentley 1908, 211). Bentley considered them one and the same. For Truman, the second condition is also necessary for an interest group. The claims upon others make it clear that the groups pursue their narrow, self-interested goals even at the sake of others' well-being. Debtors and creditors and developers and environmentalists seldom view the world in the same fashion, and they frequently make costly demands or claims upon one another. Only when these claims upon others are made through governmental bodies are the interest groups truly *political* interest groups. Consider a modern day example. Residents in a highrise apartment constitute a group. If that group makes demands on the vendors at a nearby open market, then it becomes an interest group. For instance, the apartment residents and the vendors may need to negotiate solutions to crowding and congestion or the hours of operation for the market. There may be demands to move the market. An interest group becomes a *political interest group* when the demands of an interest group are made through a government official. If the residents and the vendors reach an impasse, government officials may be lobbied to seek a remedy. In this instance, the government determines how the costs of regulating or moving the market are distributed. The government could mandate that the apartment developer bear the costs of moving the market, or the government could mandate that the market organizers bear their own costs of moving. A third option might allow the market to operate unfettered and have the apartment dwellers bear the costs of crowding and congestion. In any event, the government is determining the distribution of social costs associated with the operation of the market.

The government's role in the distribution of the costs of various kinds of public projects has received wide attention since the pathbreaking work of Ronald Coase (1960). Coase was the first social scientist to study systematically the effects of property rights on social, political, and economic transactions.[2] If property rights are well established and negotiation costs are relatively low, then Coase (and now many others) suggest that the government has little role in resolving private disputes. Given the underdeveloped state of property rights in China today, it is inevitable that competing claims are brought to government officials to adjudicate. When legal, political, or economic rights are not well defined, there is a natural gravitation toward political or legal adjudication. Interest groups become political interest groups because rights are not well established and negotiation costs are high.[3] Political interest groups force the government to take an active role in the balancing of interests and the adjudication of conflicting claims.

What can allow competing interests to bypass government venues to pursue their claims? Well-established property rights play a role simply because they reduce transaction costs. If a set of rights are so well recognized that they are beyond dispute, then the subsequent negotiations over some sort of social cost are easier. Without recognized property rights, negotiation and transaction costs are higher. Aside from property rights, what else might lower transaction costs and allow for more negotiations prior to government involvement? In areas with strong nongovernmental institutions, well-established norms of behaviors, or well-established networks of relations, citizens might be able to resolve intricate disputes without involving the government. We see this sort of phenomenon reported in Chow's description of *guanxi* (2004, 19). *Guanxi*, the web or matrix of vertical and horizontal personal relations (*tiao/kuai guanxi*) affect all aspects of Chinese society. "*Guanxi* also serves to perform some of the functions that a legal system performs. Disputes can be settled through mediation under the system of *guanxi* without the need to settle in court" (Chow 2004, 78). Tsai makes a similar claim in her assessments of traditional, nongovernmental institutions in China (2007a; 2007b).

At this juncture, three points deserve attention. First, as construed by Truman, groups are a byproduct of our social existence. Second, interest groups may make demands upon others, but those demands need not be channeled through government officials. Individuals often negotiate solutions to everyday problems without reliance on the state. Finally, as construed by Truman, *groups*, *interest groups*, and *political interest groups* are relevant for every social and political system.

Pluralism and Normative Politics

Pluralism offered many avenues of study and seemed to mirror the dynamics of American politics. Scholars investigated group behavior and group interactions with governmental officials. Pluralism provided a new perspective on the bargaining, maneuvering, and stratagems that emerged in the absence of large, stable majorities with the brute force of numbers. Indeed, some scholars argued that the continual bargaining and ever-changing coalitions in a pluralist setting provided an element of stability that a permanent majority-minority division with set winners and losers might not provide (Miller 1983). Whenever there was no dominant and enduring majority, the pluralists' emphasis on coalitions of smaller groups and political bargaining seemed more and more relevant. For a large number of pluralists, the governmental process was best described as a balancing of the various interests expressed by groups and coalitions of groups (Truman 1951, xxv, xxxi).

Some scholars were so enamored of pluralism that they considered pluralism as an antidote for all sorts of societal ills. These scholars moved from *describing* politics from a pluralist perspective to *prescribing* pluralist solutions for societal ills.[4] For prescriptive pluralists, enhanced participation, especially from traditionally underrepresented groups, improved the governing process. Such pluralists were quick to recall Madison's admonitions in the tenth Federalist Paper about controlling the "tyranny of the majority." Pluralism, it was argued, ensured the dispersion of power among organized groups. The inclusion of more and more interests was deemed beneficial because it provided a brake on majority tyranny as well as other forms of concentrated power. To many pluralists, greater inclusion was considered a part of the natural process of political development. Greater inclusiveness broadened the negotiation process, which in and of itself was beneficial because the voicing of interests and concerns enhanced the deliberative process (e.g., Mansbridge 1992). The outcomes of the deliberating and bargaining processes often allowed groups to dominate certain policy areas where their interests were particularly strong.[5] Why should a society weigh all individuals' views on all issues equally if these same individuals themselves weigh the importance of issues very differently? Why not allow individuals more weight on matters of most concern to them? Pluralism seemed to allow for finely calibrated political inputs. Once again, pluralism seemed to be a natural process and a stabilizing influence. Elections and voting were suddenly appearing quite crude as measures of the public's opinions.

Critics of Pluralism

Most critics of pluralism were not opposed to studying groups, per se; but they did dispute the purported benefits of prescriptive pluralism. Some of these critics argued that the deliberations and bargains inherent to pluralism were really quite limited (see, e.g., Bachrach and Baratz 1962, 1963; Schattschneider 1960; Walker 1966). Seldom were all interests included in the deliberative process, and often deliberations addressed only minor issues.[6] At no time were issues about the fundamental nature of American politics addressed within the pluralist paradigm. Was American politics too elitist, too socialist oriented, or too enamored with the free market? These fundamental concerns about the nature of American politics and society did not arise within the pluralist paradigm. Perhaps attempts to secure broad-based input on minor or inconsequential issues were simply a ruse to avoid debating fundamental concerns about the nature and structure of government. In short, most critics were unconvinced by the purported inclusiveness of pluralism. Furthermore, they feared that the promises of prescriptive pluralism would never be fulfilled. Pluralism appeared elitist, and it favored the status quo. Rather than dispersing power, pluralism seemed better designed to concentrate it among the upper classes (Schattschneider 1960) and business interests (Lindblom 1977).

Some of the most trenchant criticisms of pluralism were made by E. E. Schattschneider. Schattschneider bemoaned the elitist elements of pluralism. In *Semisovereign People*, Schattschneider stated that the "flaw in the pluralist heaven is that the heavenly chorus sings with a strong upper class accent" (1960, 34–35). Although largely remembered for this one catchy phrase, Schattschneider's critique of pluralism was much more extensive. Yes, Schattschneider criticized the biases in the "heavenly chorus," but he also stated a concern about the *persistence* of the bias, which he ultimately connected to the political rules and structures that affected the mobilization of interests.[7] That is, biases in outcomes in our interest group society were inevitable because of the rules governing the political process. Schattschneider's work shows how the institutionalists' emphasis on rules and procedures have relevance to group theories of politics since the "mobilization of bias" was directly tied to the rules and procedures of the governing process (1960, 71). In a similar vein, Lindblom (1977) argues that businesses possess a privileged position because of the desire of any country to expand its economy.

In some ways, Schattschneider was not terribly explicit, but he did state that "conflict, competition, leadership, and organization are the essence of democratic politics" and that at "the root of all politics is the universal language of conflict" (1960, 139). Conflict occurs because "the winners get so much more than the losers" (Schattschneider 1942, 37). Conflict may occur among individuals with very different political tendencies or among individuals within the same organizations. Indeed, conflict and cooperation coexist in organizations because the individuals in them often have mixed motives. Even within organizations, where one might envision harmony and common purpose among like-minded individuals, Schattschneider still saw the opportunity for conflict. Within political organizations, "[a] thousand men want power for a thousand different reasons" (Schattschneider 1942, 36).[8] For Schattschneider, individuals were strategic and calculating because of the inherent conflict in politics. Indeed, Schattschneider favorably viewed "a little cool calculation" on the part of individuals maneuvering for greater influence (1942, 41). Clearly, Schattschneider's understanding of politics presumes strategic thinking on the part of individuals as they pursue their interests.

Applications to China

In every state there are concerns about the handling of the diversity of interests, whether those interests are articulated by groups or not does not always matter to pluralist scholars—or government officials. Consider, for instance, the early years of modern China. Instead of focusing on the development of different political and social interest groups, Mao promulgated the "Two hundreds" principle to promote diversity and competing schools of thought in the development of art and science. The "Two hundreds" principle was phrased as "Let a hundred kinds of flowers bloom, let a hundred schools of thoughts contend" (*Bai hua qi fang, bai jia zheng ming*). In his "On the Correct Handling of Contradictions among the People" (*Guan yu zheng que chu li ren ming nei bu mao dun de wen ti*) in 1957, Mao made it clear that he believed that only through free debate and discussion could the strengths and weaknesses reveal themselves in the development of the arts and sciences. Further, Mao was initially opposed to the use of administrative power either to promote or oppress a school of thought. Mao suggested that some contradictions were natural and readily handled through discussion. Others were "antagonistic" and rightly controlled, repressed, or destroyed. One could safely let "a hundred schools of thought contend," as long as the contradictions avoided becoming antagonistic. Mao intended to divert a problem seen in the former Soviet Union when official party doctrine in 1948 outlawed criticism of Trofim Lysenko's poorly structured studies of genetics. For over a quarter of a century, Lysenko used his official administrative powers to oppose and persecute geneticists who held scientific views different than his own. In time, all of the sciences as well as the arts in the Soviet Union were largely directed by party doctrine. Mao argued that the natural superiority of better ideas would gradually emerge—through careful analysis and comparisons. The use of administrative power to support one school of thoughts was, therefore, undesirable. As long as the different ideas were supporting socialism and the Communist Party rule, they would all be allowed to exist. Specifically, even Marxism would be considered as just one school of thought to be compared with other schools of thought. Due to its superior nature, Mao believed, Marxism would survive the careful assessments and gradually become the dominant ideology for Chinese people.

Distinguishing between the natural and the antagonistic contradictions quickly proved to be difficult. More and more schools of thought were seen as a threat to regime or party stability and by June of the same year, the anti-rightists campaign was in full swing. Adherence to Maoist doctrines was increasingly important for party members. Experimentation with open debate was over, and within a year China would attempt its Great Leap Forward, a set of policies linked to monumentally disastrous results. In the United States, critics of pluralism questioned whether all voices were heard (Schattschneider 1960) and whether the most fundamental questions related to society were being asked (Bachrach and Baratz 1962). That is, more interests and more questions might strengthen pluralism and improve governance. In Maoist China, handling and—if necessary—repressing conflicting interests was deemed more important than hearing all interests. In Maoist China, it was clear that some interests were not to be voiced and some questions were not to be raised. Competing interests and schools of thought were feared by Mao because the groups tied to those interests raised questions that Mao did not want to address.

INDIVIDUALS' ATTACHMENTS TO GROUPS AND COLLECTIVE EFFORTS

To suggest that individuals can ignore their basic group affiliations is to suggest that they can disavow all that makes them human. Groups in the United States and China are deep rooted and tied to regional, cultural, economic, and ethnic differences. Even with these deep roots, there is fluidity in the political interest group environment. The set of groups choosing to press claims does regularly change, and the set of groups that pursues relief through the government does regularly change. In addition, individuals' allegiances to their various groups change as circumstances change. Groups move in and out of the public sphere insuring that the array of interest groups staking their claims and seeking political adjudication is ever changing. Truman recognized that new groups were always emerging and that many groups faded away with time. Truman's disturbance theory tied changes in the group environment to social, economic, technological, or political disturbances. Technological change, for instance, affects the group environment by strengthening some groups and weakening others. In the United States, computer and printing technologies affected the labor unions representing lead typesetters and printers as well as the unions and trade associations in the computer and software industries. Truman argued that any fundamental disturbance that affected the interactions within or between groups led to the demise of some established groups and to the creation of completely new groups. Ultimately, as a society's social and economic interactions became more complex and more complicated, its group affiliations became more complex and complicated.

Olson's Freerider Problem

For Olson (1965), there was a fundamental contradiction in Truman's analysis. Recall Truman's second condition for interest groups—claims upon others. Obviously, interest groups are narrowly focused on their own well-being. The sense that "groups act to serve their interests presumably is based upon the assumption that the individuals in groups act out of self-interest. If the individuals in a group altruistically disregarded their personal welfare, it would not be very likely that collectively they would seek some selfish common or group objective" (Olson 1965, 1). In short, if groups pursue narrow self-interests, then certainly the individual members of the groups must be sensitive to their own narrow self-interests. Therefore, individual concerns and individual choice must be incorporated into the analysis of interest groups. Starting with this simple assumption, Olson proceeded deductively to develop his theory of collective action.

What sort of narrow self-interests might emerge as one considers whether or not to join a political interest group? Individuals pursuing their narrow self-interests might join a group depending on the sorts of benefits provided by the group. In the United States, many groups provide members with magazines, bumper stickers, and t-shirts while also conducting lobbying campaigns and public rallies. Olson carefully distinguished between the different kinds of benefits that groups provide in their attempts to attract individuals to join collective efforts. Group benefits are essentially either private or public goods. Private goods are characterized by two conditions: rivalrous consumption and excludability. Both conditions are straightforward. Rivalrous consumption precludes two or more people from using the good at the same time without there being some diminution in the value of the good. Excludability insures that one can prevent others from using or benefitting from the good. Your breakfast and the shirt on your back are private goods. In contrast, public goods have non-rivalrous consumption and are non-excludable. Many people can consume the same good without any depreciation in the value of the good because they are non-rivalrous. In addition, no one can be prevented from using or benefitting from the good because they are non-excludable. Freeriding allows one to benefit from the provision of a public good or collective effort even if he or she did not contribute any money or effort. There are many public goods all around us. National defense and clean air are public goods. Old-fashioned television broadcasts (as opposed to cable or pay-for-view) are public goods. My television reception of the Beijing Olympics was unaffected by millions of other viewers, and once I purchased a television I could not be prevented from watching network broadcasts.

Two common misperceptions about public and private goods deserve attention. First, the provider of the good does not determine whether or not the good is public or private. Certainly, governments do provide public goods, but they also provide many private goods in the form of contracts and entitlements. Consider the bidding process that takes place before any public roads, bridges, or airports can be built. The government's selection of a bid bestows a private good on the chosen construction company, even though the construction project itself may yield a public good. The government *contracts* for roads, bridges, or stadiums are themselves private goods. In addition, governments are not the only providers of public goods; individuals, private firms, interest groups, and other nongovernmental institutions also provide public goods. The gifted musician practicing in the courtyard provides a public good. The second misperception is that everyone values a public good. Analogous to the diverse demands for private goods, citizens have different preferences for the types of public goods provided as well as the level of any public good's provision.

What sort of public goods do groups provide? Keeping in mind that one may not value all public goods, groups provide a public good every time they affect public policy. Whether they lobby to pass, defeat, or amend legislation, groups are providing a non-excludable good with non-rivalrous consumption. For instance, the legislation that leads to cleaner air or water affects everyone, whether they have joined a group pushing for the legislation or not. Interest groups are vulnerable to freeriding because the public goods they provide are vulnerable to freeriding. We can still benefit from the group's provision of the public good whether we contribute or not. Given Olson's assumption about individuals' goal-oriented behavior, one inexorably runs head long into the freerider problem. For some critics, Olson's by-product theory seemed to belittle the grand concerns of collective efforts. Did not the existence of collective efforts indicate that people were inherently altruistic and community oriented? "[I]t is futile to try to determine whether men are stimulated politically by [self] interests or by [grand] ideas (Schattschneider 1942, 37). Individuals simply choose an alternative that is most likely to yield favorable results. Moral training cannot redirect demands for narrow interests because the pursuit of self-interest is "sown in the nature of man" (Madison 1961, 79). One can preach against self-interest or threaten penalties if self-interest is expressed, but cannot alter the presence of self-interest. Ironically, the very selfishness that many states associate with political interest groups also impedes the ability of those groups to form.

The freerider problem can be onerous, but it need not undermine all collective efforts. The question is how can one obviate the freerider problem? Olson considered numerous options, but here we highlight just two. Olson wrote of the effects of group size and coercion on the freerider problem. Olson argued that the freeriding would be most onerous for large rather than small groups. For instance, automobile manufacturers might avoid the freerider problem because they were so few in number. They could readily coordinate their actions and they could see the impact of their efforts because the benefits of their efforts were concentrated. In contrast, automobile consumers faced much greater obstacles in their collective efforts. Suppose, for instance, the manufacturers lobby for particular safety regulation standards. Millions of dollars are at stake for a small number of producers. Suppose consumers want safer cars. Although there are millions of consumers each of whom might value safer cars, the benefits are widely disbursed rather than concentrated. No single consumer is likely to see the impact of his or her collective efforts. Whenever collective benefits are concentrated, collective efforts are easier; and whenever benefits are widely disbursed, collective efforts are harder (see, e.g., Wilson 1973).

Coercion or social pressure, Olson argued, greatly affected individuals' decisions about joining. In the United States, labor and trade groups as well as professional societies often seek legal sanctions to make membership in their organizations all but mandatory. Unions seek closed shops, wherein union support is compulsory for all workers. The argument for a closed shop is straightforward. If unions fight for safer work conditions and a higher wage, then all workers benefit whether they are union members or not. The goods provided are public goods and thereby non-excludable. Since all benefit, all should be forced to support the collective efforts. Debates about the rectitude of open and closed shops are beyond the scope of this book, but such debates are enhanced by Olson's discussions of freeriding and collective efforts.

Professional societies have secured considerable influence over accreditation processes and licensing procedures, making membership all but necessary for one's professional standing. Many states require practicing lawyers to be members of the state's bar association.[9] The American Medical Association manages all school and hospital accreditation issues. Many of the most respected academic journals are published by groups. The American Medical Association's *JAMA* may be the most widely recognized, but it is hardly alone. Professional associations of economists, political scientists, and sociologists publish the best journals in their fields as well. In exchange for modest dues, one may secure a highly professional publication or a simple newsletter. China's social and professional associations maintain close affiliations with the government, mainly because most of these associations, such as the All-China Women's Federation and the China Law Society, were initially created by government agencies. These associations serve important consulting purposes to governmental affairs; they provide research information as well as expertise related administration and legislation. For example, in 1996 the China Law Society was a primary source for suggestions on how to modify China's Criminal Code. The China Law Society was composed mainly by law experts and legal scholars in universities and other institutions, which enables the association to provide professional legal advice from a jurisprudence point of view. It also has branches at different local government levels, which enables the association to gather enforcement and feedback information related to the Criminal Code implementation at the local level. This information offered by the association is indispensable to the governing process, and the government agencies made the information accessible by creating professional associations to serve this purpose. In both China and the United States, nongovernmental organizations (NGOs) and government-organized nongovernmental organizations (GONGOs) are used to manage the accreditation and licensing issues related to numerous professions. These NGOs and GONGOs typically coordinate their activities with associated government agencies. The state/group relations are sometimes so tight in China that there appears to be two labels for one organization (*yitao jigou, liangkuai paizi*).

Concluding this section, let us consider the Great Leap Forward and the concept of *gong jia* (publicly owned) properties. The entire rural economy was restructured during the Great Leap Forward. In August of 1958, the "peoples communes" (*renmin gongshe*) were established. Cooperatives were organized around village units, and the communes might include as many as twenty to thirty cooperatives. Some communes had as many as twenty thousand workers. The entire structure relied on common efforts and corvee labor. The communes were "too large to link rewards closely with labor" (Lieberthal 1995, 105). Clans and villages were swept away in favor of the large units. The reforms were both socially and economically disruptive. Worsening matters, local officials used wildly inflated production figures, establishing such a culture of self-promotion and exaggeration that many statistical figures of that era remain suspect. "[C]entral officials lived in substantial ignorance of actual conditions in the countryside" (Lieberthal 1995, 106). Aside from the official reports, there were no other means to evaluate the conditions in the countryside. The failures of the Great Leap Forward were not minor or technical shortcomings. Peasants were to undertake tremendous new efforts and responsibilities without consideration of "technical" issues. Is the freerider problem a technical issue? One cannot engineer a solution to the freerider problem. The best one can do is to restructure the incentives to minimize it, but one cannot simply will it away or pretend it does not exist. By some counts, twenty to thirty million people starved during the first two years of the new decade. The three hard years (1959–1961) were a result of many factors including poor weather and reduced Soviet support, but the greatest, preventable failures were a product of the Great Leap itself. The Great Leap failed to recognize that individuals are motivated by clear connections between their efforts and their rewards. Work points were tallied for individual workers, but rewards were based on team efforts. When those connections were severed, productivity fell. Disjunctures between labor or effort and reward can lead to freeriding and socially inefficient outcomes. It must be stressed that socially efficient outcomes are not always compatible with individual rationality. Coercing behavior—corvee labor—does not yield efficient outcomes. By 1962, the units were downsized to more closely resemble the smaller, earlier units. By the late 1970s, reports indicated that units averaged fewer than two hundred workers (O'Leary and Watson 1982–1983). There are now clearer usufruct rights and some lend/lease opportunities for peasants.

The freeriding problem also reveals itself in the abuses of *gong jia* (publicly owned) properties. The concept of commonly owned property is a cornerstone of socialism in China. State-owned and collective-owned properties are *gong jia* properties, which imply a common resource as well as a common responsibility. The relationship between shares of the resources and shares of the responsibilities make the *gong jia* properties akin to common pool resources. Common pool resources, like public goods, are non-excludable and, like private goods, have rivalrous consumption. Not surprisingly, people tend to maximize their share of the common resource by personalizing the benefits as much as possible while trying to avoid the responsibilities and costs of maintaining the commonly owned resource. For instance, cloth manufacturing workers, every now and then, might bring home "free" cloth from their workplace for family use. Civil servants' children might enjoy a regular supply of stationery from their parents' offices. Taking advantage of *gong jia* properties fell into the grey area of behavior. It was not considered something to be proud of, yet it was commonly practiced by almost everyone who worked in state-owned or collective-owned enterprises or bureaucracies. Taking advantage of *gong jia* property allowed individuals to secure narrow benefits while spreading the costs of their actions across the entire public. Narrowly focused benefits and broadly distributed costs create the incentives for the widespread adoption of *zhan gong jia de pian yi*, the taking advantage of commonly owned property. In this scenario, freeriding behavior is not the absence of a contribution, but the presence of *zhan gong jia de pian yi*. In other words, workers and civil servants should make their contribution by refraining from taking advantage of the commonly owned properties; failure to do so indicates a freeriding problem.

INFORMATION AGGREGATION

Central governments often fail to control all regions and all levels of their own countries. Consider a classic view of the U.S. in the late 1800s.

> Sovereignty was to be shared between the new central government and the old regional units of government, which retained their revolutionary designation as "states." Constitutional federalism inhibited the penetration of central power throughout the nation by ensuring the integrity of these states, each with its own institutional organization, legal code, and law enforcement apparatus. The unity of the American legal order rested on the vaguely worded constitutional prerogatives of the national government . . . to intervene as the final authority. (Skowronek 1982, 22)

Skowronek argues that in the United States political parties allowed for the penetration and reach of the central government. "[P]arties were less notable for their programs than for this procedural unity they lent the state" (Skowronek 1982, 26). The lack of information and reliable statistics related to the peripheries of the nation exacerbated the lack of penetration and reach of the central government. "The need for significant series of political statistics is a vital need in a free democratic society which requires the holders of political power to be responsive to their constituencies. Not only the academic specialist, therefore, but the man in the street has a stake in good political statistics" (Latham 1948, 637).

Unfortunately, states sometimes avoid collecting data and political debates often swirl around both the collection and appropriate measurement of concepts (Desrosieres 1998). Before and during the Great Depression in the United States, national unemployment measures were seldom collected. Attitudes toward unemployment and its correct measure divided the two main political parties. Both Herbert Hoover and Franklin Delano Roosevelt questioned the validity of unemployment measures. Should one collect and publish the number of unemployed or the rate of unemployment? What should be included in the numerator: those unemployed, those actively looking for work, those immediately available for work? How should one measure underemployment, the intermittently employed, or the infirmed? Should the denominator include the total population or the economically active population over a set age? "If realism of the measurement . . . was debatable, that of its variations was less so, once the conventions of recording were stabilized" (Desrosieres 1998, 204). In the end, the actual measure was less important than changes in that measure, but numerous political officials had fought strenuously over those very measurement issues.

States need information to govern effectively, but they do not always possess it. Official state data may simply not exist or it may be terribly skewed. We argue that there are several channels for information transmission to the central government, including bureaucracies and local-level officials, markets, elections and public opinion polls, and interest group activity—including the activity of non-registered groups. We also argue that information revelation problems exist with each source. Typically, information revelation problems arise when individuals have incentives to withhold or contort information.

Bureaucracies and Information

Bureaucrats are typically charged with meeting certain goals, and often they are rewarded based on their ability to meet or surpass those goals. A narrow focus on those assigned goals may cause bureaucrats to lose sight of the larger purposes behind their agency. Goal displacement is inherent in all bureaucracies (Downs 1967; Knott and Miller 1987). For instance, an agency charged with making roadways may emphasize the number or length of roadways and show little regard to the width of the lanes or the quality of the pavement. The larger, overarching goals, navigability and connectivity, are lost. Of course, in this example it would be easy for a central government to create clearer standards, but it is impossible to create a set of standards that prevents all goal displacement. Information from a bureaucrat may be skewed for two reasons. First, a bureaucrat has strong incentives to exaggerate his successes. Of course, the best bureaucrats would never falsify reports, but human frailties do not disappear when one enters into government service. Second, the inevitability of some amount of goal displacement insures that the measures of navigability and connectivity will themselves be flawed. In our roadway example, the crude proxies measuring the number of kilometers paved overlook the width of the lanes, the quality of the pavement, the efficiency of the entrance and exit ramps, the sharpness of the turns, and the steepness of the grade. All of those measures affect navigability too.

Groups and Information

Cai (2008) nicely condenses the traditional view of popular movements in strictly centralized or authoritarian regimes. Cai notes that "authoritarian governments may face serious uncertainties in dealing with popular resistance. Making concessions tends to trigger more resistance . . . , but reliance on repression damages the regime's legitimacy" (411). Under either circumstance, the regime may be severely undermined. We suggest that one should view popular movements entirely differently. Rather than focusing on how to "control" the event, government officials should instead consider what the movement signals. Suppose long-haul truck drivers form a group and protest in front of a regional government building. Their presence and their claims are informative. They could be protesting against long hours and low pay or they could be protesting against unsafe roadway conditions and poor navigability. In the latter instance, the truck drivers are offering a different perspective on the "official" information related to navigability. Information from the group provides a check on the information from the bureaucrats. Is the group information without flaws? Absolutely not. The group has an incentive to exaggerate the problem and hide or fail to reveal some information. For instance, the truck drivers have no incentives to reveal information related to their unsafe driving practices.

Markets and Information

Citizens operate in both the public and private spheres, and readily move back and forth between them. For instance, parents might form a political interest group to demand better schools for their children, or parents might hire private tutors for their children. In each instance, the concerns motivating the actions are similar: a better education for one's child. But one action occurs in the public sphere and one in the private sphere. What information does the market for private tutoring provide the government? The mere presence of the market may provide information about the quality of the public schools, the rigors of college admissions, or the anxieties of parents about their children's futures. The demand and supply data can be very helpful if it is linked to other issues. If there is a surfeit of tutors, then perhaps the economy is unable to handle each new year of college graduates. As people move into and out of a market and as prices shift upward or downward, government officials can glean important information.

Markets seldom work perfectly. Almost every market has some sort of imperfection. Ironically, some markets are structured in a way that limits their capacities to provide information. In the 1990s, China experimented with a dual price system, issuing an official state price for a certain amount of production and allowing a market price to prevail for any additional production. The state creates two difficulties with a dual price system. First, buyers seek the state market and sellers desire the private market. Second, the true market price is lower than the existing private market price and higher than the state plan price. Sometimes people in positions of political power are given privileged positions yielding economic power in newly created markets. For instance, support for various property reforms is sometimes secured by allowing family members of party officials to engage in profiteering. Some of the most prominent property developers along coastal China or in other special administrative regions (SARs) are relatives of party officials. Lieberthal notes a further problem: "The money made by corruption is not being put to use to integrate the polity. . . . [T]he big-city political machines in the United States . . . worked hard to win people's votes by solving problems that . . . citizens faced" (1995, 269).

Elections and Public Opinion and Information

More and more governments and government officials rely on public opinion polls. Some polls contain a wealth of information, but they are not devoid of problems. Polls presume salience. That is, respondents can only answer the questions they are asked—whether those questions are salient to them or not. When political interest groups mobilize, there are fewer questions of salience. The choice to mobilize indicates salience. Polls also rely heavily on average responses and provide less information about the distribution of responses. Upon reflection, the interpretation of polls is never straightforward. Dissatisfaction seen in Chinese public opinion surveys is sometimes difficult to assess. For instance, changes from 1992 to 1999 in satisfaction with the government may be tied to concerns about market reforms or excitement tied to the fiftieth anniversary (Tang 2001). Indeed, as Chinese citizens feel freer to express themselves, one might, ironically, measure declines in satisfaction. Here again, is a situation exemplifying the difficulties associated with the collection and evaluation of information.

Elections provide regular feedback to governing officials, thereby enhancing their abilities to shift policies as circumstances change. Elections indirectly yield another benefit. Adsera, Boix, and Payne (2003) explore corruption across nations and across the American states. They find that corruption is reduced in those settings where there are regular elections and well-informed citizens. "[P]olitically active, well-informed, [and] sophisticated electorates" lead to less corruption and greater governing efficiency (Adsera, Boix, and Payne 2003, 480). China has recently shown more interest in elections (see chapter 3 in this volume). One reason to experiment with more local-level elections in China is to facilitate citizens' monitoring of local-level officials.

There are many sources for information for a state, but each of the four sources we evaluated here had shortcomings. Sometimes the state actually has too much information to evaluate. Whenever there is a cacophony of demands, states must use audits, screening devices, and reputations to separate the good information from the bad information. So far, we have discussed audits, suggesting that each source of information is an unofficial audit of the other sources. The costliness of an action can create a screening effect. The costliness of an action can sometimes be used to assess salience. Traveling to a regional office to press claims is costlier than focusing on local-level officials. The costliness of an action provides some prima facie validity. Those claimants unwilling to bear such costs may still have concerns, but those concerns are not so great as to warrant the costs of action. Central government authorities can also structure their interactions with various sources of information in such a way that those sources value their reputations for accuracy.

CHINA IN THE FUTURE

Prior to concluding, we introduce four issues to consider related to China's future. For each issue, we predict that GONGOs, NGOs, and independent interest groups will carve out central roles for themselves. That is, regardless of how closely the groups or organizations are tied to the government and regardless of whether the groups or organizations are officially recognized by the government, they will find ways to establish themselves. Each of these issues as well as others will once again be on the world stage when Shanghai hosts the 2010 World Expo.

Country-to-City Migration

The greatest migration of people in the history of the world is currently underway, and it is the migration from the countryside to the cities. Such a massive movement of people affects every aspect of life in the countryside. As people leave the countryside, their children and farms are often left in the care of the children's grandparents. Economic, social, and familial connections are strained. As we noted in reference to Truman's work, disturbances lead to the creation of new interests and demands for new groups and organizations to represent those interests. Some of the demands of those new potential groups are likely to aim directly at local, regional, and national government officials.

The massive influx of workers into the cities can create another whole set of disturbances. Even as the urban dwellers benefit from rapid economic expansion, they may not warmly welcome the presence of hundreds or thousands of workers from the countryside. Many workers from the countryside may not possess residency cards or work permits, making it difficult for the government to adjust policies related to the influx of workers.

Technological Changes

The whole world is now connected via phone systems and the Internet. Some developing countries have been able to leapfrog over older communication infrastructures, bypassing the landlines and moving directly to cell phones and other wireless technologies. These new technologies enhance communication networks and allow for the rapid spread of information. How are communication networks and information related to groups? Information spread by cell phones or over the Internet can enhance governmental transparency. Consider the recent Sichuan earthquake. Any citizen with a cell phone could snap a photo or send a text message relaying information about the current conditions, the government response, or the construction failures of some schools. In addition to enhancing transparency, new communication technologies also facilitate the mobilization of collective efforts. Citizens from around China as well as those residing abroad learned of the disaster and contributed to the relief effort in unprecedented numbers.

Increased transparency can improve citizens' faith in their governing officials and also increase the ability of central government authorities to monitor lower-level authorities. With new technologies, central authorities can use official reports from lower-level officials as well as unofficial "reports" from regular citizens. Each source of information acts as a check on the other. Increased transparency also enhances the ability of different government agencies, across different levels of government and in different regions of the country, to coordinate their own efforts.

Wealth Disparities

Economic markets do not solve all problems, and markets intertwined with governmental institutions or connected to strong cultural traditions may have particularly onerous problems. For instance, *guanxi*, which can facilitate smooth negotiations, is also tied to issues of cronyism and nepotism. Entrenched interests in a government may secure privileged positions in the market.

Environmental Concerns

Environmental degradation is a growing concern across China (see chapter 8 in this volume). Poorly defined property rights are especially problematic when individuals and groups make competing environmental claims. For instance, peasants with usufruct rights to raise fish in lakes or rivers may see those rights jeopardized when manufacturers pollute the same water.

As the commonly owned resource has greater and greater demands placed on it, conflicts are inevitable. As air or water resources become particularly strained, citizens will find ways to communicate their concerns to all levels of government about clean water and clean air. Environmental activists can be safely ignored if they are single malcontents, but the presence of activists often signals greater overall concern among citizens (see, e.g., Ainsworth and Sened 1993). If the presence of activists can be linked to greater overall concern among citizens, then central government authorities should value such information.

CONCLUSION

All regimes and all governing systems require constant renewal. Consider Mencius, the ancient Chinese philosopher (c. 372–289 BCE), who traveled his country and offered advice to rulers. For Mencius, "royal blood did not constitute a continuing basis of political legitimacy. The Mandate of Heaven was subject to change (*tianming feichang*), and required constant renewal required through public support" (Perry 2008, 39). Hsun Tzu (300–230 BCE), though very different from Mencius, also argued that a governing system required regular renewal. "Legitimacy and survival of the ruler rest upon the support of his people: he is a boat, they the water which may bear him up or capsize him as they choose. No claims of hereditary right or iron discipline can hold out forever in the face of popular indifference or anger" (Watson 1967, 7). Legitimacy required a constant monitoring of conditions followed by an appropriate adjustment in policies. Simply put, legitimacy requires information about conditions and information about the impact of policies. Indeed, some scholars are so enamored of the possibility that this notion of legitimacy is so fundamental to governing that they have explored whether at the macro-economic level democracies and non-democracies have similar public policies. Mulligan, Gil, and Sala-i-Martin (2004) suggest that there are few differences across governing systems when one examines economic and social policies. If legitimacy requires freedom from deprivation, then all types of leaders will pursue policies to strengthen social and economic well-being. Going a step further than Mulligan and his coauthors, Mertha (2008) explores a single policy in much greater depth and explicitly considers citizens' reactions to policy proposals. Mertha's conclusions dovetail with the Mulligan et al. work. Even when one looks carefully at a single policy area, hydropower in this case, Mertha sees greater similarities than differences across regime types. Moreover, across regime types Mertha sees similar strategies among those citizens seeking to alter policy.

One way to insure constant renewal is to maintain free flows of information between the governed and the governors so that policies can be regularly adjusted to maximize benefits. Deng argued that one must find "truth from facts." The sources of those facts should not matter, but as we have seen perfect information revelation simply is not compatible with individuals' incentives. Given the information revelation problems that exist with all typical sources of information, the state is best off relying on a multiplicity of sources, so that each source acts as an audit of the others. That some information from interest groups might be biased is readily understood. What is less well appreciated is that all sources of politically sensitive or economically important information are likely to be biased. However, central authorities can use multiple sources of information, with each source acting as an audit of the others. When viewed as valuable sources of information, political interest groups can be seen as beneficial to both citizens and governments.

NOTES

1. There are numerous sources for further reading related to models in political science. A good place to start is Clarke and Primo (2007).

2. Volumes of work have addressed these issues. Other excellent readings on this subject include Eggertsson (1990), Posner (1977), and Sened (1997). Also see Bates (1997).

3. It is important to note that Truman also writes of the "inevitable" gravitation of groups toward government. Truman argues that groups seek to supplement their power and resources with the support of larger, more encompassing institutions. Governments are the quintessential "encompassing institution." See Truman (1951, 104–6).

4. The distinctions between descriptive and prescriptive pluralism are made by Berry (1997).

5. This process is seen in Dahl (1961).

6. In *Who Governs* (1961), Dahl examined various local, community organizations. Some critics wondered whether Dahl's conclusions about a local PTA (Parent Teacher Association) offered meaningful insights into other issues or other, larger, more powerful organizations. Could a study of the local PTA offer insights into the governmental process?

7. Dahl also recognized the importance of rules. "Constitutional rules are mainly significant because they help to determine what particular groups are to be given advantages or handicaps in the political struggle" (1956, 137).

8. In his criticism of the nineteenth-century conservative Edmund Burke, Schattschneider argued that no political party was "an association of men who have agreed on some principle" (1942, 37).

9. Associations themselves used to restrict accreditation or certification to members, but as Walker notes: "a decision by the Supreme Court in 1978 [largely] pre-

vented the practice" (Walker 1983, 397). Walker refers to Supreme Court decision *National Society of Professional Engineers v. U.S.*, 435 U.S. 679, 98 S. Ct. 1355, 55 L. Ed. 2 637, 1978.

REFERENCES

Adsera, Alicia, Carles Boix, and Mark Payne. 2003. "Are you Being Served? Political Accountability and Governmental Performance." *Journal of Law Economics and Organization* 19:445–80.

Ainsworth, Scott H., and Itai Sened. 1993. "Interest Group Entrepreneurs: Entrepreneurs with Two Audiences." *American Journal of Political Science* 37:834–66.

Bachrach, Peter, and Morton S. Baratz. 1962. "The Two Faces of Power." *American Political Science Review* 56:947–52.

———. 1963. "Decisions and Nondecisions." *American Political Science Review* 57:632–42.

Bates, Robert H. 1997. "Social Dilemmas and Rational Individuals." In *The New Institutional Economics and Third World Development*, ed. John Harriss, Janet Hunter, and Colin M. Lewis. London: Routledge.

Bentley, Arthur F. 1908. *The Process of Government*. Chicago: University of Chicago Press.

Berry, Jeffrey M. 1997. *The Interest Group Society*. 3rd ed. New York: Longman.

Cai, Yongshun. 2008. "Power Structure and Regime Resilience: Contentious Politics in China." *British Journal of Political Science* 38:411–32.

Chow, Gregory C. 2004. *Knowing China*. River Edge, NJ: World Scientific.

Clarke, Kevin A., and David M. Primo. 2007. "Modernizing Political Science: A Model-Based Approach." *Perspectives on Politics* 5:741.

Coase, Ronald H. 1960. "The Problem of Social Cost." *Journal of Law and Economics* 3:1–44.

Dahl, Robert A. 1956. *A Preface to Democratic Theory*. Chicago: University of Chicago Press.

———. 1961. *Who Governs*. New Haven, CT: Yale University Press.

Desrosieres, Alain. 1998. *The Politics of Large Numbers: A History of Statistical Reasoning*. Cambridge, MA: Harvard University Press.

Downs, Anthony. 1967. *Inside Bureaucracy*. Boston: Little, Brown.

Eggertsson, Thrainn. 1990. *Economic Behavior and Institutions*. Cambridge: Cambridge University Press.

Garson, G. David. 1978. *Group Theories of Politics*. Beverly Hills, CA: Sage.

Knott, Jack H., and Gary J. Miller. 1987. *Reforming Bureaucracy: The Politics of Institutional Choice*. Englewood Cliffs, NJ: Prentice-Hall.

Latham, Earl. 1948. "Political Statistics." *Journal of Politics* 10:636–58.

Lieberthal, Kenneth. 1995. *Governing China: From Revolution to Reform*. New York: W. W. Norton.

Lindblom, Charles E. 1980. *Politics and Markets*. New York: Basic Books.

Madison, James. 1961. "Federalist No. 10." In *The Federalist Papers*, ed. Clinton Rossiter. New York: New American Library.

Mansbridge, Jane. 1992. "A Deliberative Theory of Interest Representation." In *The Politics of Interests*, ed. Mark P. Petracca. Boulder, CO: Westview Press.

Mertha, Andrew C. 2008. *China's Water Warriors: Citizen Action and Policy Change*. Cornell, NY: Cornell University Press.

Miller, Nicholas R. 1983. "Pluralism and Social Choice." *American Political Science Review* 77:734–47.

Mulligan, Casey B., Ricard Gil, and Xavier Sala-i-Martin. 2004. "Do Democracies Have Different Public Policies than Nondemocracies?" *Journal of Economic Perspectives* 18:51–74.

Ogden, Suzanne. 2002. *Inklings of Democracy in China*. Cambridge, MA: Harvard East Asian Monographs.

O'Leary, Greg, and Andrew Watson. 1982–1983. "The Role of the People's Commune in Rural Development in China." *Pacific Affairs* 55:593–612.

Olson, Mancur. 1965. *The Logic of Collective Action*. Cambridge, MA: Harvard University Press.

Perry, Elizabeth J. 2008. "Chinese Conceptions of 'Rights': From Mencius to Mao—and Now." *Perspectives on Politics* 6:37–50.

Posner, Richard A. 1977. *Economic Analysis and the Law*. 2nd Ed. Boston: Little, Brown.

Salisbury, Robert H. 1969. "An Exchange Theory of Interest Groups." *Midwest Journal of Political Science* 13:1–32.

Schattschneider, E. E. 1942. *Party Government*. New York: Holt, Rinehart & Winston.

———. 1960. *The Semisovereign People*. New York: Holt, Rinehart & Winston.

———. 1969. *Two Hundred Million Americans in Search of a Government*. New York: Holt, Rinehart & Winston.

Sened, Itai. 1997. *The Political Institution of Private Property*. Cambridge: Cambridge University Press.

Skowronek, Stephen. 1982. *Building a New American State: The Expansion of National Administrative Capacities: 1877–1920*. New York: Cambridge University Press.

Tang, Wenfang. 2001. "Political and Social Trends in the Post-Deng Urban China: Crisis or Stability?" *The China Quarterly* 168:890–909.

Truman, David B. 1951. *The Governmental Process*. New York: Knopf.

Tsai, Lily L. 2007a. "Solidary Groups, Informal Accountability, and Local Public Goods Provision in Rural China." *American Political Science Review* 101:355–72.

———. 2007b. *Accountability Without Democracy: Solidary Groups and Public Goods Provision in Rural China*. Cambridge: Cambridge University Press.

Walker, Jack L., Jr. 1966. "A Critique of the Elitist Theory of Democracy." *American Political Science Review* 60:285–95.

———. 1983. "The Origins and Maintenance of Interest Groups in America." *American Political Science Review* 77:390–406.

Watson, Burton. 1967. *Basic Writings of Mo Tzu, Hsun Tzu, and Han Fei Tzu*. New York: Columbia University Press.

Wilson, James Q. 1973. *Political Organizations*. New York: Basic Books.

8

China's Environmental Protection and Sino-U.S. Cooperation

Shan Ningzhen

THE ENVIRONMENTAL ISSUES OF CHINA

The Environmental Situation in China

The "China's environmental situation bulletin in 2006" published in 2007 shows that national environmental quality was stable given that China's GDP grew 10.7 percent over the previous year and total energy consumption increased 9.3 percent over the previous year in 2006. The quality of the Pearl River and Yangtze River were good, the Songhua River, Yellow River, and Huai River were moderately polluted, and the Liaohe and Haihe were severely polluted. The centralized source of drinking water in key cities is qualified in general: the coastal water quality of the South China Sea and Yellow Sea maintain good water quality, the seashore of the Bo Sea and East China Sea shore were mildly and moderately polluted, while the far sea water quality is good overall. National urban air quality has improved over the previous year and air quality of key urban areas remained stable. The regions affected by acid rain, which are mainly located in the south of the Yangtze River and east of Sichuan and Yunnan, remain stable. The acoustic environment quality and radiation environmental quality of national urban areas are good. In the first three quarters of 2007, the total emissions of two major pollutants both declined for the first time.

Although the Chinese have made positive progress in environmental protection, the environmental situation is still grim. The data from "China's Environmental Situation Bulletin in 2006" shows that sulfuric dioxide emissions increased by 27.8 percent from 2000 and chemical oxygen demand was reduced by only 2.1 percent which doesn't reach the reduction objective of 10 percent. The management task of key regional watersheds such as the Huai River, Hai River, Liao River, Taihu Lake, Chaohu Lake, and Dianchi Lake (hereafter referred to as the "three rivers and three lakes") complete only about 60 percent of the goal.

Pollution is serious because emissions of main pollutants exceeded environmental capacity. Out of the national state-controlled surface water section (the state's key monitoring target), 26 percent is inferior to Class V standards of water environment, 62 percent of the cross-section hasn't reached Class III standards; 90 percent of river areas are subject to different degrees of pollution, 75 percent of the lakes have eutrophication, the quality of drinking water sources in 30 percent of major cities can't reach Class III water quality standards. One cannot be optimistic about coastal waters' environmental quality; the air quality of 46 percent of cities is less than Class II, the number of Ash Haze days of some large- and medium-sized cities has increased and the degree of acid rain pollution has not been reduced.

China has 1.61 million square kilometers of water erosion areas, 1.74 million square kilometers of land desertification, more than 90 percent natural grassland degradation; water ecological functions of many rivers have been seriously degraded; biodiversity reduced, the economic losses caused by invasive alien species is serious, and the ecological performance of important Ecological Functions Districts has degraded as well. The rural environment problem is notable and soil pollution is becoming increasingly serious. Pollution from hazardous waste, automobile exhaust, and persistent organic pollutants continue to increase. The situation involved with climate change is grim and the task of addressing it is arduous.

The development of China's economy that took the short span of thirty years to accomplish took one hundred years for the developed countries, and this growth will be maintained. The environmental problems faced by China are complex and acute because of the process of rapid economic development. It can be said that environmental problems that were phased in during the industrialization process in the developed countries over one hundred years have emerged in China in just thirty years. China has entered a period of multiple incidents of pollution and prominent contradictions. In the historical process of building a well-off society and realizing the objective of modernization, environmental protection has become the most significant issue.

Handling the Relationship between Environmental Protection and Economic Development Properly

The relationship between economic development and the environment has increasingly become the focus of the whole society. Practice has proven that economic development and environmental protection are closely linked, economic development is bound by environmental resources, and the improvement of environment quality cannot be separated from economic development. As a developing country, China is now confronted with the multifaceted task of developing the economy and protecting the environment. The Chinese government has recognized that in order to fundamentally solve China's current environment problem, it must use scientific methods to understand in a profound way the mutual relations between economic development and environmental protection. On March 2, 2008, at the China Development Forum, Zhou Shengxian, the minister of environmental protection, said that determining how to correctly handle the relationship between economic development and environmental protection is vital for the Chinese government. If it cannot successfully handle the relationship between them, China will face significant environmental risks, and national environmental safety will be threatened.

In the sixth meeting of the National Environmental Protection Conference in China, Premier Wen Jiabao offered an in-depth and incisive exposition of the relationship between economic development and environmental protection and proposed that speeding up the realization of the Three Changes is necessary to properly handle this relationship. First, from stressing economic growth and belittling environmental protection, China must now stress both economic growth and environmental protection. Second, while environmental protection lagged behind economic development, environmental protection and economic development had to be addressed in a synchronic fashion. This means studying environmental issues and economic problems at the same time and raising the issue of environmental protection to an unprecedented level. Third, protecting the environment must be shifted gradually from mainly relying on an administrative approach as in the past to relying on legal, economic, and technological policy. This is also the most important political idea and guiding ideology of the current Chinese government on environmental issues.

A Brief Analysis of Environmental Problems in China

Recalling the development of China in the past several decades, China to some extent takes the same approach the Western developed countries did, namely, developing the economy at the expense of resources and the environment. While creating significant economic achievements, China exacerbated damage to the environment. The major reason is that environmental management relies much more on administrative measures and less on economic and legal means. The implementation of environment policy often requires government agencies to forcibly intervene through administrative means. Excessive reliance on administrative means has weaknesses such as short-term instability and rent-seeking. Administrative means don't fundamentally address the underlying political problem: the overwhelming majority of local governments and enterprises promote economic development over protection of the environment. Their policies may to a certain extent also weaken or detract from the existing system of environmental policies and regulations. Therefore, as soon as the environmental economic policy system is adjusted to the reality of industrialization, urbanization, and internationalization, the interest demands of different market participants such as the government, enterprises, and the public can be fully expressed and policies addressing the multiple needs of economic development and environmental protection can be effectively coordinated. The fundamental way to solve China's environmental problems and address future important issues related to environmental protection is to promote environmental protection action at the enterprise level arising from unfettered development to conscious development through the integration of economic policy and law (Sun 2007).

At present, China is in the crucial period of building a comprehensive well-off society, and the resulting economic and social development puts great pressure on population, resources, and the environment. Therefore, environmental protection is facing immeasurable opportunities and challenges. The Chinese Government attaches great importance to environmental protection and has made overall arrangements on environmental protection work in the new era. In 2007, the report of the Chinese government at the 17th National Congress proposed to firmly establish the concept of an ecological civilization and basically create an industrial structure, mode of growth, and consumption patterns designed to conserve energy resources and protect the ecological environment for the whole society. The report indicates that environmental protection has become an expression of national will and environmental protection as a basic national policy has really entered the mainstream of national economic and social life. In 2008, the establishment of an Environmental Protection Department, which was approved in the 11th National People's Congress, realized the dream of generations of environmental protection advocates and once again fully reflected the Chinese government's great determination to strengthen environmental protection.

THE GUIDELINES AND PRINCIPLES OF ENVIRONMENTAL POLICY IN CHINA

The Guidelines of Environmental Policy

Environmental protection work in China began in the early 1970s. A national conference on environmental protection in 1973 established the thirty-two-part guideline with respect to "comprehensive planning, rational distribution, comprehensive utilization, benefiting victims, relying on the masses, protecting the environment, benefiting the people." The second national environmental protection conference held in 1983 claimed that environmental protection is a strategic task and the basic national policy of modernization construction in China. Under the guidance of the thirty-two-part guideline, national and local governments began to formulate environmental protection policies, regulations, and standards, and gradually formed the environmental protection policy system with Chinese characteristics.

The Principles of Environmental Policy

The principles of environmental policy proposed in the "State Environmental Protection Standards Planning During the 11th Five-Year Plan" in China are: coordinated development with mutual benefits and a win-win situation. China will address the relations between environmental protection and economic development and social progress. It will protect the environment during development and promote development alongside environmental protection. China will adhere to conservation development, safe development, clean development, and scientific development with sustainability to achieve GDP per capita quadrupling from 2000 to 2020.

China Will Strengthen the Rule of Law with Comprehensive Controls.

It will adhere to administration according to law, continuously improve environmental laws and regulations, and strictly enforce these laws and regulations. China will use integrated decision-making on environmental protection and development and principles of scientific planning focusing on prevention of environmental harm. It will prevent and control pollution and ecological destruction from the relevant sources. It will employ comprehensive means such as laws, as well as economic, technical, and necessary administrative methods to address environmental problems.

Incur No New Environmental Debts and Pay Back as Many Old Debts as Possible.

China will strictly control the total emissions of pollutants. All new and expanded projects must meet the requirements for environmental protection with increased output but no pollution. China will strive for more output with less pollution and actively address the environmental problems left in the past.

Depend on Scientific and Technological Innovation.

China will vigorously develop environmental science and technology and facilitate the addressing of environmental problems by technical innovation. It will set up a diversity input mechanism from the government, industry, and social groups, and a commercialized mechanism for some pollution treatment facilities. China will improve environmental protection institutions and establish a unified, coordinated, and efficient environmental supervision system.

Classified Guidance and Focused Work.

According to local conditions, China will develop a plan for each region and make overall arrangements for urban and rural development and address environmental problems that constrain economic development and allow strong public input at every stage. China will improve the environmental quality of key river basins, regions, sea areas, and cities.

THE MAIN CONTENTS OF ENVIRONMENTAL POLICY IN CHINA

After thirty years of effort, China has initially formed a relatively complete system of environmental laws, policies, systems, and standards.

The Environmental Protection Laws and Regulations in China

So far, the National People's Congress and the State Council have issued a total of eight environmental protection laws, fourteen natural resource management laws, and thirty-four environmental protection regulations. The Environmental Protection Department issued more than 90 national environmental regulations and over 1,020 local environmental protection laws and regulations. So the environmental legal systems are maturing.

In 1989, the first Environmental Protection Law was formally promulgated. After the United Nations Conference on Environment and Development in 1992, China was one of the countries to formulate and implement a strategy of sustainable development. In 1993, the Environmental Resources Committee of the NPC Standing Committee was officially established. During the eleventh Five-Year Plan, China will develop four laws relating to nature reserves including the Nature Reserve Act (Central Government Website, accessed July 27, 2005).

Environmental Protection Policies in China

The environmental policy system includes economic policy, technology policy, management policies, and industrial policies.

Since 2008, a number of environmental-economic policies including green credit, green insurance, and ecological compensation have been introduced. These policies began an exploration designed to establish long-term mechanisms to solve China's environmental problems. State environmental protection departments promote strategic environmental protection, which closely combined environmental protection and economic and social construction. They have implemented an environmental economic policy of green credits to promote a sustainable development strategy that provides strong tools for strengthening macro-control by the state. In 2007, "On the Implementation of Environmental Policies and Regulations to Prevent the Views of Credit Risk" was jointly promulgated by the State Environmental Protection Administration, the People's Bank of China, and the China Banking Regulatory Commission, and imposed credit controls on enterprises and projects that do not conform to the industrial policy and environmental law but instead blindly expand high energy-consuming and high-pollution industries.

China's Main Points of Environmental Policies in the New Era

Zhou Shengxian, the minister of the State Environmental Protection Department, pointed out that China must accomplish four tasks to achieve historical changes in environmental protection in China. The following are the main points of China's environmental policies in the new era.

Establish a Comprehensive Pollution Prevention and Control System.

Environmental protection should be extended from production to exchange, distribution, and consumption and expanded from investment to foreign trade. China should implement exchange in a way conducive to environmental protection, govern transport pollution such as railway and water transportation, secure the security of transport and storage of dangerous chemicals, restrict the trade of high-polluting products, and establish clean and safe modern exchange systems. China implemented environmental labeling, environmental certification, green procurement, and extended producer responsibility systems and established green and conservation-oriented consumer systems. According to the national targets—optimized development, key development, restricted development, and prohibited development—China identified the environment access threshold of different regions and developed a corresponding industrial policy.

Strictly Enforce Environmental Law.

China amended water and air pollution laws and enacted a nature reserve act; it resolutely cracked down on environmental crimes using judicial means. In order to improve its environmental monitoring capacity, China built an advanced environmental monitoring and pre-warning system and a complete law enforcement supervision system.

Perfect Environmental Economic Policy.

China gradually increased the environmental crime standards for industrial enterprises and built their incentive mechanisms for protecting the environment and reducing pollution emissions. China implemented full penalties for improperly disposing urban sewage and waste; established a new mechanism for protecting the environment in mining areas and for ecological restoration; and it actively explored mechanisms for pricing emission rights.

Mobilize All Social Forces to Protect the Environment.

China strengthened environmental protection training for local government decision-makers, leaders of key enterprises, it publicized information on environmental quality, environmental management, and corporate environmental behavior, and insisted on the public's right to know about the environment and to participate and supervise. The Chinese government listens to public views and accepts accountability through mass media, public hearings, feasibility studies, and publicity for development planning and construction projects involving the public environmental interest (Zhou 2006).

THE EFFECT AND PROBLEM OF ENVIRONMENT POLICY IN CHINA

Achievements in China's Environment Policy

After thirty years of reform and opening, the government of China has taken environment protection to be basic national policy and sustainable development as a major strategic goal. It launched a large-scale pollution prevention and ecological environment protection program across the country as part of the process of modernization.

While China's GDP grows an average annual rate of around 10 percent, the basic quality of the environment has not experienced a corresponding deterioration. This shows that the policy of coordinating economic, social, and environmental development has been effective.

The major achievements are as follows: first, environmental protection objectives have been made clear. The government takes environmental protection as a basic national policy and it initially established an environment policy in accordance with national conditions and sustainable development. It played a role in guiding and controlling actual practice and made environmental protection work the right direction. The World Bank noted in "Clear Water and Blue Sky of China's 2020 Environment" that while many countries are often commited only to vague environmental goals, China has formulated a series of specific goals (Zhang n.d.).

Second, funds for environmental protection increased. Over the past two years, the country invested a total of 556 billion yuan in environmental protection, accounting for 1.24 percent of GDP over the same period. The central financial authorities set up pollution abatement special funds and activated the project of building emissions-reduction capacity, with a total investment of 3.2 billion yuan for the construction of pollution emission reduction and monitoring and evaluation systems (Zhou 2008; source: Wen Wei Po).

Third, the government uses various comprehensive means to protect the environment, including legal means, economic means, and administrative means. This involves paying attention to the role of the law of value of the market system, the supply and demand mechanism, and the price mechanism.

Fourth, the government has improved the environmental awareness of citizens through public environmental education. For example, in accordance with the "notice of restricting to produce and use plastic shopping bags" issued by the Office of the State Council, since June 1, 2008, merchandise retail outlets such as supermarkets, shopping malls, and country markets have implemented a fee system for the use of plastic shopping bags and will not be allowed to provide free plastic shopping bags. The purpose of this notice did not only restrict, but also changed people's habits by reducing the use of disposable plastic products. Thus an awareness of environmental protection can be created, ultimately achieving the objective of reducing white pollution. In addition, the activities of local environmental protection are increasing. The role of Chinese environmental NGOs is also growing ("Strategic Restructuring" 2007, 133–34).

Fifth, a major breakthrough was achieved in international environmental cooperation. The Chinese government has projected the image of firm confidence in strengthening environmental protection as a responsible major country, and this has won praise from the international community.

The Difficulties Facing Environmental Policy

China faced two fundamental constraints of reality in the choice of environmental policy. First, China has never and will not have the resources and environmental capacity enjoyed by the developed countries in the process of industrialization. Second, in China, the world's largest developing country, there is a contradiction between the rapid and stable economy growth in demand with very limited resources and environmental support capacity. Therefore, China's current environmental policy is facing some practical difficulties.

First, environmental policies are out of line with regional economic development policies. The implementation of certain specific environmental policies is affected by many factors at the regional level, which is still difficult to incorporate into national macro-related development strategies and the integrated decision-making processes of regional development. Thus, it can't be effective because of intervening socioeconomic activities. It can be said that the key to China's environmental protection is to combine environmental protection with a national economic development plan.

Second, the current environmental management system isn't conducive to the implementation of a regionally differentiated environmental policy. One of the important characteristics of environmental problems is that they are regional. Environmental issues exhibit a strong externality in that local environmental pollution will affect the surrounding areas, often beyond the border of administrative divisions. But China's environmental management system is dependent on administrative divisions, the local Environmental Protection Bureau affiliated with the local government. This fragments an organically whole system.

This local protectionism phenomenon happens frequently as the local government damages other regional interests and hinders environmental management in the interest of development. At the same time, due to poor coordination between departments, interregional environmental law enforcement becomes more difficult. On the other hand, depending on the impact of geographical location, climatic conditions, natural resources, socioeconomic development level, as well as the other conditions, environmental problems of different regions do exhibit different characteristics, so environmental management should reflect their respective characteristics. In the current environmental management system, regionally differentiated environmental policy is difficult to implement and not easily coordinated with the main functions of the district.

Third, coordination between the various environmental policies should be strengthened. China has established a relatively complete system of environmental policy, but the connection between the various environmental policies still needs to be strengthened.

Fourth, the compensation policy related to the promotion of ecological and environmental protection, rehabilitation, and construction is imperfect (Sun and Gao 2007).

Fifth, the implementation of environmental policy needs to be improved. The "China Environmental Performance Assessment" report submitted by the Organization for Economic Cooperation and Development (OECD) Environmental Council in 2007 recommended that the government should strengthen environmental protection policies, especially the implementation and enforcement efforts of the weak links in the enforcement chain.

OECD Deputy Secretary-General Mario Amanoa argues that one of the reasons for China's environmental problems is that "the intensity of the implementation of government agencies is soft." Although the Chinese State Council and the Environmental Protection Administration and other departments have formulated a series of laws and regulations, the implementation effectiveness of these policies is low (*Economical Observation Newspaper*, July 22, 2007).

OVERVIEW OF INTERNATIONAL COOPERATION IN ENVIRONMENTAL PROTECTION IN CHINA

China has always claimed that economic development must be coordinated with environmental protection and the protection of the environment is the common mission of all mankind, but developed countries have a greater responsibility. Strengthening international cooperation should be based on respect for national sovereignty, and the protection of the environment and development need peace and stability in the world. Attempts to deal with environmental issues should take into account both the national interests of each country and the long-term interests of the world.

While China adopted a series of measures to solve its environmental problems, it has also participated positively and pragmatically in international cooperation in the field of environmental protection and has made unceasing efforts to protect the global environment, which is the common cause of mankind. China has supported and actively participated in the environmental affairs launched by the United Nations. China, which is a member of United Nations Environment Program (UNEP), has had fruitful cooperation with UNEP. China joined UNEP's "Global Environment Monitoring Network," "Potential Toxic Chemicals International Registration Centers," and the "International Environmental Sources of Intelligence Information Inquiry System" in 1979.

In 1987, the United Nations Environment Program established headquarters of "international training center for desertification control and research" in Lanzhou, China. Under the organization of UNEP, China transfers the experience and technology of desertification prevention and construction of ecological agriculture to many countries. By 1996, China already had eighteen units and individuals who were awarded "Global 500" titles by the United Nations Environment Program. China has established a good record of cooperation with the United Nations Development Program, the World Bank, the Asian Development Bank, and other international organizations.

Now, China has established an effective model of cooperation with the Multilateral Fund with respect to the loan use and management of ozone depleting substances, the Montreal Protocol, the Global Environment Fund, the World Bank, and the Asian Development Bank which played a positive role in pushing forward China's pollution prevention and environmental management capacity-building. China is a member of the United Nations Commission on Sustainable Development, established in 1993, where it has been playing a constructive role in this high-level political forum on global environment and development.

China has maintained close cooperative relations with the United Nations and other organizations of the Economic and Social Commission for Asia and the Pacific (ESCAP) and made contributions to the environment and development of the Asia-Pacific region's environment through participation in regional environmental cooperation in Northeast Asia, the Northwest Pacific Action Plan, and the East Asian Seas Action Plan coordinating body. The world's largest plant diversity conservation organization, Botanic Gardens Conservation International Union (BGCI), set up offices for the first time in China on June 5, 2008.

China has actively developed bilateral cooperation in the field of environmental protection. During the last ten years, China has signed bilateral environmental protection cooperation agreements or memoranda of understanding with the United States, Canada, India, South Korea, Japan, Mongolia, Russia, Germany, Australia, and other countries, and has had exchanges and cooperation in environmental planning and management, global environmental issues, pollution control and prevention, forest and wildlife protection, marine environment, climate change, air pollution, acid rain, sewage treatment, and other aspects where there have been some important achievements. China has also participated in the Global Environment Conducive to Learning and Observation Plan activities initiated by the United States.

China established the "China Environment and Development International Cooperation Committee" to further strengthen international cooperation in the environment and development field in April 1992. The Committee, which is composed of more than forty leading Chinese and foreign experts and social celebrities, was responsible for advising and formulating recommendations for the Chinese government. The committee has put forward concrete and valuable suggestions on the energy and environment, biodiversity protection, ecological agriculture, construction, resources accounting and pricing system, public participation, and environmental laws and regulations which gained the Chinese government's attention and response.

SINO-U.S. ENVIRONMENTAL COOPERATION

Overview of Sino-U.S. Environmental Cooperation

The United States is one of the most important countries with which China cooperates in the area of environment protection. Since the "Agreement on Cooperation in Environmental Protection Technology," signed in 1980, environmental cooperation between the two countries has achieved significant achievements under Sino-U.S. government support. In 2000, the two governments signed the "Sino-US Environment and Development Cooperation Joint Statement," reflecting the high degree of concern shown by the leaders of the two countries. Environmental issues have been an important part of the Sino-U.S. strategic economic dialog. The Environmental Protection Agencies of China and the United States launched a pragmatic, effective, and mutually beneficial cooperation. At present five contracts totaling US$72 million have been signed as part of the Sino-U.S. economic and trade cooperation projects for environmental protection (Q. Wang 2007).

The Necessity for Sino-U.S. Environmental Cooperation

As the largest developing and developed countries, respectively, China and the United States have a significant impact in global affairs, share extensive common interests, have a common responsibility in environmental matters, and share a common desire to solve the global environmental problems. Strengthening Sino-U.S. environmental cooperation is beneficial not only for the two countries, but also for sustainable global development.

As with all developing countries of the world, China faces domestic and global environmental problems that come with a growing economy. In response, China has put forward the slogan of a green economy, and takes the sustainable development path of integrating economic and environmental protection. The United States is a major economic power with its own environmental problems. Meanwhile, the United States has better environmental policies, regulations, and standards and has a higher level of environmental protection technology, while China has a huge demand for environmental protection and pollution control and has a vast market for environmental protection. Both China and the United States have great potential for cooperation on ecological and environmental protection.

The Main Areas of Sino-U.S. Environmental Cooperation

Since the 1990s, the two countries have strengthened cooperation on environmental technology, environmental policy, energy, and other areas, implemented practical projects such as the Sino-U.S. environmental education project, Yangtze River Delta regional environmental cooperation, Sino-U.S. environmental legal training, and environmental monitoring technology. These have all played a good role in improving China's ability to formulate environment policy and use environmental technology. At the same time, the two sides communicate repeatedly on coastal zone management, land-based sources of pollution, alien species invasion, sand storms and land planning, and have expressed the wish to strengthen cooperation as well (Q. Wang 2007). On December 2007, in the second Sino-U.S. Joint Commission on Environmental Cooperation, the two countries signed the "Environmental Legislation and Supervision over Law Enforcement Cooperation in the New Annex" and further broadened cooperation in the field of the environment.

"China and the United States Issued the 13th Joint Release on the Third Sino-U.S. Strategic Economic Dialogue," released by China's Xinhua News Agency on December 13, 2007, claimed that in view of the urgency of environmental challenges, China and the United States will hold talks in 2008 and jointly work to eliminate or reduce appropriately tariff and non-tariff barriers to environmental products and services under the WTO framework as soon as possible.

Since the Sino-U.S. cooperation in forest health demonstration projects launched in 2002, the first pilot completed a total of 1,216 hectares of artificial forestation and 920 hectares of low-efficiency forest transformation. The quality of the forest in the demonstration zone improved remarkably and the ecological environment improved significantly.

In addition, the two sides will expand cooperation to develop a specific plan of low fuel vulcanization which will gradually reduce the sulfur composition of vehicle fuel to 50 ppm or less and introduce advanced technology to control motor vehicle–related pollution in combination with China's twelfth Five-Year Plan.

The two sides have also reached a cooperation agreement on sulfur dioxide emissions trading, illegal logging, and management of water pollution. China committed to developing and implementing national sulfur dioxide emissions trading projects (emissions trading) in the power industry. However, the United States agreed that it will provide technical support for infrastructure and institutional capacity-building which is essential to implementing the project. The memorandum signed by China and the United States, which includes terms concerning the fight against illegal logging and related trade, is also groundbreaking in that it is the first time that the two sides recognized the importance of the issue of illicit trade in natural resources such as timber. According to the memorandum, the two sides will establish a bilateral forum, share information on timber trading from now on, strengthen law enforcement against illegal acts, and encourage cooperation with the private sector to promote sustainable forest management. The memorandum will lay the foundation for reaching bilateral agreement negotiations on illegal logging and related trade issues.

In addition, the United States will provide technical support for basic water management projects to help China achieve good control and management of water pollution, including emissions rights, technology-based emission standards, monitoring, implementation of compulsory and voluntary approaches, and so on (Y. Wang 2007).

The Differences between Chinese and U.S. Policies

U.S. environmental policy has two prominent characteristics. First, it motivates local governments and enterprises by stressing the diversity, innovation, and flexibility of environmental protection measures. Second, basically, it is an economic development policy that emphasizes the development of new technologies and new products instead of changing lifestyles to achieve environmental protection and sustainable economic development. As a result, there is no change in the high efficiency of production and the large amount of inefficient energy consumption (Su 2005). The source of environmental laws in United States is extensive. In addition to the basic federal and local constitutional provisions, there are administrative regulations, treaties signed by the president and ratified by the Senate, and executive orders. In addition, the adjudication in the U.S. courts at all levels and the management experience of a mature market economy are also important sources of environmental laws and regulations.

China's environmental legal source is unitary in that a large part of the original laws and regulations have come from the executive branch's internal regulations and executive orders. The nature of administrative control of environmental legislation decides its effectiveness and functional limitations.

The law enforcement system of the United States is sound. The EPA (United States Environmental Protection Agency) is the most important environmental protection agency in the United States. Its purpose is to protect citizen health and improve the quality of the environment. It has more punitive power than most common federal agencies and has close contact with various states. The Office of State Environmental Protection, whose power is directly commissioned by the EPA, is a major law enforcement agency of the United States. Penalty judgments on the environment made by court are executed by the EPA or local environmental departments, which significantly ensures independent and impartial law enforcement.

China's courts and environmental protection departments have not established a relatively complete system and mechanisms for law enforcement cooperation. Problems with law enforcement often occur because judgments made by the court cannot be supported by environmental protection departments. Compulsory enforcement and fixed penalties are the most frequently used forms of enforcement by the United States courts.

The form of China's environmental enforcement is also special in that monetary penalties are the most important form of enforcement. The United States has established a complete environmental legal system which allows individuals, environmental groups, and companies to institute legal proceedings to protect their own rights and interests in suitable circumstances relating to environmental issues. When the accused involved are U.S. government agencies, individuals and companies can handle the legal proceedings related to the environment.

One of the more distinctive characteristics of the U.S. system is that when the punishment determined by the EPA or a U.S. government department is deemed improper and is found to have caused damage to those punished, these public agencies will face legal proceedings at any time and the court will make fair judgment based on law.

This sound litigation system not only provides weapons to curb environmental pollution for U.S. citizens, organizations, and companies, but also provides a legal basis for environmental legislation by the U.S. Congress. In contrast, China's environmental legal system is not perfect. For a long time, environmental problems and disputes between individuals largely depended on the intervention and mediation of the executive branch and the court played a limited role in this regard. When individual interests regarding the environment conflict with administrative departments, their legitimate rights and interests often cannot be guaranteed (Zhiyuan: president of the Federation of Chinese Students and scholar at Texas Southern University).

Although there are striking differences between China and the United States, they have the common goal of protecting the environment. The advanced practice and experience of the United States in this regard deserves consideration in future legislation on environmental protection and law enforcement in order to better protect environmental resources for the benefit of the Chinese people.

Environmental Cooperation Channels

Sino-U.S. environmental cooperation has governmental cooperation and civil cooperation channels. On November 8, 2005, the first Sino-U.S. Joint Commission on Environmental Cooperation Conference was held in Washington. This meeting discussed the priority areas for future Sino-U.S. cooperation and approved the new annex in the Sino-U.S. environmental cooperation memorandum—hazardous waste management and water and toxic substances under annex 2 of the cooperation strategy. After the meeting, China's State Environmental Protection Administration Secretary Xie Zhenhua and the United States Environmental Protection Bureau's Stephen Johnson signed the "Sino-U.S. Joint Commission on Environmental Cooperation Joint Declaration." At the same time, environmental protection is an important part of the Sino-U.S. strategic economic dialog. China's International Cooperation Association for the Promotion of Civil Society Organizations and the United States Environmental Protection Association signed a memorandum of cooperation on Sino-U.S. nongovernmental environmental protection, forming a strategic partnership. The signing of the memorandum indicates that after the environmental associations of the United States successfully carry out an "emissions trading" project in China, they will cooperate with China's environmental nongovernmental organizations in more areas and advise China concerning sustainable development.

The Prospects for Sino-U.S. Environmental Cooperation

Sino-U.S. relations are one of the world's most important bilateral relations; China and the United States have cooperated extensively on bilateral, regional, and global environmental issues. Sino-U.S. strategic economic dialog provides a good opportunity for Sino-U.S. environmental cooperation. One of the important achievements of the third Sino-U.S. strategic economic dialog is the Decade Planning of Energy and Environment Cooperation, which was signed in December 2007. It is important to maintain the continuity of this dialog. In addition, cooperation to prevent water pollution, sulfur dioxide emissions trading, air pollution control, waste disposal, and other areas of cooperation between the two parties have excellent prospects. For example, after Hurricane Katrina in the United States in 2005 and the May 12, 2008, earthquake in China, the two parties can strengthen cooperation in environmental disaster prevention and management.

REFERENCES

"The Strategic Restructuring of Chinese Environment and Development." 2007. *Chinese Environmental Press*, 133–34.

Su, Yang. 2005. "China and the U.S., Whose Environmental Protection Is Better?" People's Net.

Sun, Fuling. 2007. "Construction of Environmental Policy System Is Currently One of the Fundamental Questions of Environmental Protection." The 12th Forum of Green China, China Environmental Culture Promotion Association, September 21.

Sun, Zhiyan, and Gao Shiji. 2007. "The Environmental Policy Issues and Adjust Ideas." The Marxist Research Network.

Wang, Qianjun. 2007. "The Issue of International Environmental Cooperation." *China Environmental Science Press* 147.

Wang, Yichao. 2007. "Environment of Chinese and American Strategy Economy Dialogue Achievement Analysis." *Finance and Economics* network version, December 13.

Zhang, Kunmin. n.d. "The Environmental Challenges and Countermeasures China Has Faced in the Twenty-first Century." The Research Center of Economic and Human Development in Peking University.

Zhou, Shengxian. 2006. "Chinese and Foreign Environmental Protection Work Together to Promote the Historical Changes in China, the Chinese Environment and Development for International Cooperation on Three of Five Meetings." Xinhua Net, November 13.

———. 2008. "2008, Chinese Environmental Protection Critical Year." February 13.

9

The Development of the Public Service in China

Chen Xingbo

This chapter covers the following subjects. First, public service is the backbone of the modern governmental management. Second, regarding public service the key issue for China is how the government can provide highly effective and diversified public service. Only by solving this problem will the government perform well and promote its efficiency. Last, in light of globalization, this is a universal issue.

It is clear from international experience that public service plays a basic role in guaranteeing a country's smooth economic development and maintaining a stable society. According to the developed world the building of a civil service is a developing process that accompanies rapid improvements both in the economy and people's everyday lives. In this process, some developed countries have undertaken a long-term path toward growth and development and have reached new heights. Others have restricted their own national and local economies, kept their societies from harmonious development, and have made their economies stagnate and their societies unstable. Both these experiences could offer useful inspiration to developing countries.

Since the reform and the opening-up policy was initiated in 1978, China has been the center of enormous economic development and has made great economic strides with the average annual rate of growth up to 9.7 percent through 2007. But at the same time social development in China is still backward, which, to some extent, has hampered the comprehensive and sustainable development of the whole society. Currently, China has entered a crucial time when it will be challenged by many new situations, new problems, new conflicts, and new dissension. According to the experience gained by most countries, reinforcing the public service is an important impetus to the economic development. Thus China must learn from human experience and progress and thus greatly advance the development of public service in order to create a good environment for the harmonious development of the whole society.

THE HISTORY OF THE DEVELOPMENT OF THE PUBLIC SERVICE CONSTRUCTION

Generally speaking foreign countries, especially the developed ones, pay a lot of attention to the development of their public service, each producing a system of public service with its own characteristics.

For the sixty years after the creation of the New China, its public service has undergone a hard but productive course of development, from the very beginning to the current period. In the early 1950s, during the course of the economic recovery and development and during the socialistic construction, the new government invested a lot in the social sectors such as education, technology, culture, and sanitation, which greatly increased the overall scale of the public service and social undertakings and laid a foundation for the public service system.

Since 1978, the government has diverted its focus to economic construction, and concentrated its efforts on freeing and developing the country's productivity. All this has promoted thirty years of rapid economic growth, which has provided a material basis for the public service development. Meanwhile, the government has combined the establishment of a public service, the transformation of government functions, and the development of an administration management system that offers a stable basis and strong support for the development of the public service. The 1998 reform of the clerical management system explicitly placed substantial government functions under macro-control, civil management, and the public service. With these developments, the government gave a great boost to public service construction. It took significant and effective measures to reform and develop the public service system, such as the promulgation of a series of laws and policies concerning compulsory education, public medical treatment, social security, and public employment. The World Bank pointed out in its 2003 report "China: Economic Growth to Promote Justice" that such indices as average life expectancy and the mortality rate of newly born babies and children under five are better than that of medium- to lower-income countries.

In the twenty-first century, with China's historic transition from a society trying to solve the problem of providing basic food and clothing to a well-off society, the people's demand for public services is increasing sharply. Besides, the inconsistency between economic and social development and the unequal development of the social market economy and the construction of the public service make the problem of a backward public service construction more prominent. The 16th Chinese Communist Party (CCP) Congress proposed that China should advance the government's role in economic regulation, market supervision, and public service, which indicates that the government has achieved greater recognition of the need to consolidate the public service function and the construction of the public service system and produce policies in this direction that are more vigorous and whose achievements are more noteworthy.

THE STATUS OF CHINESE PUBLIC SERVICE CONSTRUCTION

In the industrial age, with the continuously improved systematization of the American society, more and more social activities have been brought under the influence of administration and the scale and number of civil servants are increasing, at the same time bringing considerable pressure on the theory of administration. Past public service theory and practice find themselves in a situation in which knowledge can't guide action, theory lacks the power to interpret reality, and management techniques can't adapt to actual practice.

In order to face up to this problem and go beyond a situation in which public service is left weak and out of touch, public service reform is imperative. The core of a postindustrial society is service for people, careers, and technology. Thus the aim of most economic activities in the postindustrial society is to provide service relating to education, sanitation, recreation, and so on. The most important function of the government is no longer to control but to provide service.

The fundamental tenet of proletarian parties is to serve the people, heart and soul. The Chinese government wished to launch civil service construction, raise the standards of the basic civil service, and enlarge the scope of the civil service. For example, by the end of 2007, GNP equaled 24,660 billion yuan and the population with insurance for the aged, medical care, unemployment, job injury, and fertility had increased by an average of 7 percent. By the end of 2007, 201 million people had basic unemployment insurance and 220 million had basic medical insurance. The level of every kind of social insurance increases year by year. The basic retirement pension in enterprises has risen from an average of 615 yuan in 2002 to 963 yuan in 2007 per person. And workers' compensation insurance and unemployment insurance have improved as well.

In rural areas more than 2.9 million peasants can enjoy welfare protection. By late 2007, the average population helped out of poverty came to over 130 million, while more than 50 million people are regularly helped. The new system of cooperative medical care in rural areas has covered 86 percent of all the nation's counties (cities), with the number of peasants who have such insurance reaching 730 million. The experiment with basic medical insurance for urban residents has spread nationwide, with the covered population amounting to 40.68 million. There are already nearly 180 million urban workers who have basic medical insurance.

Nowadays, public service is progressing rapidly. This has played a great role in ensuring for people a basic level of financial security, enhancing the welfare of China's citizens, maintaining social stability, advancing the social development, and helping to realize social justice.

THE CHARACTER OF PUBLIC SERVICE CONSTRUCTION IN CHINA

The Different Historic Background of the West

Since the mid-nineteenth century, the various conflicts in capitalist societies have become more and more serious, and the gap between the rich and the poor has grown. The Great Depression of the 1930s, which was a disastrous crisis for the U.S. economy, put American society on the verge of collapse. Accordingly, President Franklin Roosevelt adopted Keynes's proposal that government functions should expand. This seems to be a great violation of individualism, but it was really a practical way to avoid the total collapse of the American economic structure. Roosevelt thought that effective governmental management required expanding the power of the federal government and thus enhancing its role in the country. Hence the traditional role of "night watchman" for the government was discarded and replaced by national intervention based on Keynes's economic theory. The U.S. government has set up a system of national intervention since the end of World War II and built a complete welfare system in which every individual is influenced by government from birth to death.

The Different Approaches to Providing Public Service

When it provides public service, the U.S. government pays considerable attention to strengthening the relationships among government, market, and society, coordinating the market and social mechanisms, and practicing various forms of public service as contracting, agreements between governments, licensing business, voluntary service, and so on. A majority of the services sponsored by government are provided by the both private for-profit and nonprofit organizations, including social services, employment and training services, housing and community development, medical care, the arts, and culture.

In order to provide some public goods and public service, the government has reached widely into many areas where the market can't work. State governments have also developed social service functions. And the private services own large amounts of capital. All these have formed a mature mechanism that can enhance the efficiency of public service provision. All provide good vehicles for reforming the way public service is offered. Public service that in the past was provided by the government is now provided by other organizations.

The trend toward privately owned organizations in the United States indicates that the government and private managers (including those in the for-profit and nonprofit sectors) sign contracts with the government to engage in public business. In general, however, the first way for the government to provide public service is still internal production, and external contracting is the second way.

There are various kinds of contractors providing public service by contracting with the U.S. government. Those that provided service only for private organizations have now started to serve the federal government, while some others that provided services for the government have now changed their focus to private organizations. Nonprofit organizations including universities and other nongovernmental entities are also supported by the federal government and sign contracts with the governments.

In order to eliminate certain sources of instability and solve social problems, the U.S. government is undertaking social reforms and systematic modifications in areas such as tax policy, medicine, sanitation, housing, relief and insurance, social service, and the labor-capital relationship. At the same time, the government relies on a wide net of social organizations, such as nonprofit social service and relief organizations, various charities, voluntary organizations, the clergy and churches, and media, to erase or eliminate social conflicts between labor and capital, over race, and over the gap between the poor and the rich.

THE DIFFERENT LEVEL OF EQUALITY IN THE PUBLIC SERVICE

The governments of the developed countries have cast the public service net widely, trying to enlarge the coverage of their public services, continually raise the level of public service, and make public service the main function of the government. Equality in the provision of public service has made it a welfare system in the United States in which people can enjoy basic insurance. It is estimated that the proportion of total federal expenditures on education, social service, medical care, and social insurance has risen from 43.7 percent in 1940 to 63 percent in 2006. Taking the level of current basic insurance as the standard, the United States has realized basic equality of the public service.

Since the 1850s, the United States has offered free public education to its citizens. By the 1960s, middle school enrollment had reached 95 percent. The United States adopted compulsory education up to age twelve, in reality up to age thirteen. Children can enjoy free education from preschool education starting at age five until age eighteen. Public school students need not pay tuition and their books and basic supplies are all offered by the government. Moreover, the government provides special services for those children living in remote and rural areas.

Disabled children can go to special schools to receive education or get their education through correspondence teaching. But educational standards are always rising. Take America's compulsory education as an example. Given the education enrollment of every child as the standard, the United States has already realized equality of the compulsory education. However, with the goal of "realizing educational achievements equally" proposed by President Bush, the American educational system still has a long way to go.

For China, the disparity between urban and rural areas is comparatively large and so it is appropriate for the goal of public service equality to be more distant. It is more reasonable for China to take as its immediate goal solving the problem of providing lower-level groups with basic insurance.

Public service construction in China is incomplete, and obviously there is unequal development of urban and rural areas. For example, in 2000 the sanitation fee for every urban citizen was about 3.8 times that for rural citizens, and it increased to 4.2 times in 2004. Public service in other areas is also unequal. For instance, in the western areas, the proportion of the population receiving rural social endowment insurance is less than 20 percent of the total for the whole nation, while only 5 percent of the rural population is covered, which is only half the national level. The large floating population hasn't enjoyed reasonable social insurance, and the social insurance level for laid-off workers is comparatively low.

THE DIFFERENCE BETWEEN THE U.S. AND CHINESE GOVERNMENTS' CONTROL OF PUBLIC SERVICE

In the public service sectors that are crucial to people's lives, there will be social conflicts and disturbances if the market is out of control. Thus we need the tangible hand of the government to make macroscopic readjustments and exert control in order to fix some of the bugs created by market development. The U.S. government, on the one hand, permits and encourages private entities (enterprises) to invest in public service, and on the other hand the government itself has become the biggest investor in those sectors in which private entities are unwilling to invest or those programs where the required amount of investment is large, the production cycle is long, and profits are low.

The government has also created a good market environment. Private entities invest in private schools and other public organizations, thereby introducing the discipline of the market's competitive mechanism. This introduction of market forces is supported by preferential policies of the government. For example, every year America's private universities receive substantial governmental funds through different channels. Indeed, the U.S. Carnegie Fund takes the amount of scientific and research funding as one of the basic criteria for categorizing schools as research universities. In fact without the government's help, most private universities would find it quite difficult to survive.

Currently, compared with China's economic development, public service funding is insufficient, the supply imperfect, basic bread-and-butter issues are still prominent, and the government public service functions are weak. Those are all inconvenient factors restraining China's economic and social development. They are a bottleneck for the country that must be addressed through the reform of the administrative and management system.

DIFFERENCES IN THE PUBLIC FUNDING SYSTEMS OF THE UNITED STATES AND CHINA

In the three-level U.S. political system the relationship between social rights and the financial structure is quite clear. The income of the federal government mainly comes from the individual income tax. The biggest program financially is the compulsory national social welfare program, including income support and medical care for the elderly, children, the handicapped, and those living under the poverty line. The primary source of income for state governments is the sales tax and the income tax. One of the biggest expenditures is for education provided by the local government. Two of the main income sources for the local government are the real estate tax and allocations from state government. The main expenditure is for local public service programs, including middle and primary education.

The ability of China's local governments to provide public services is still meager and this is directly connected with the weak coordination of social and financial rights and the low proportion of funds invested in public service. China therefore should first aim at realizing a basic equality of "ability" and then equality of "opportunity."

Funds for compulsory education in the United States come from the income tax levied by the federal government and from the budget of the state government. The education budget is derived from consumption taxes, education taxes, and property taxes levied by school communities or municipalities. State government finance is the biggest source of funds for compulsory education. In the state's budget and in actual investment, education is always given preferential treatment. The middle and primary school education payout in states occupies 35.5 percent of the budget, sometimes up to 40 percent. Take Minnesota as an example. In 2005 the state government's investment in school education was 69.5 percent, individual property tax provided 14.6 percent, the local government provided 9.1 percent, and the federal government 6.8 percent.

Though in the United States the federal government is not in direct charge of the basic management of public service, the federal contribution has not only equalized the financial capacities of state governments but also increased the individual financial capacity. What is more important, federal involvement enhances the government's macro-control and the guidance of the federal government regarding this nationwide basic public service.

In the United States, in order to ensure a minimum standard for national public services, the federal government offers state governments substantial special payments and transfers based on specific programs or plans. Every special program involving transfer payments by the federal government is accompanied by special regulations whose purpose is to tailor the use of the transfer and increase the efficiency with which it is used. The special fund is managed and inspected by the department allocating the fund, mainly through audits and reports.

Nowadays, the investment in public service in China is still low. Using World Bank criteria, China ranks among the middle-low income countries. In 2006, education expenditures took up 3.01 percent of China's GDP. According to the "World Development Indicators in 2005" of the World Bank, world public education amounted to 4.4 percent of total GDP. The average level of the medium-low income countries is 3.5 percent and that of the high-income countries 5.5 percent or so. Besides, because China hasn't had effective regulations of the payment transfer system and its bureaucratic management is still not sufficiently scientific, some transfer funds haven't produced fully adequate results.

China should not copy the U.S. tax system. But it is necessary for it to reform its tax system. Reform will provide stable income sources for basic public services. Currently, China should involve the poor groups in society in the insurance component of the public service system and ensure them the basic rights of living and development by providing basic and guaranteed public goods. Also, China should increase legal protections for disadvantaged groups.

What is particularly worthy of note is legislation related to state-owned enterprise reform, social insurance, agricultural reform, employment, and income distribution. Much of this development is still a matter of policy and lacks full implementation through legal regulation. When China frames local laws and regulations, they should be based on local-level economic development and the practical situation of the disadvantaged groups, give full recognition of local characteristics, and enhance the ability of disadvantaged groups to have their interests legally protected. The social insurance system should be developed and perfected, including endowment insurance, unemployment insurance, and social relief and social welfare, and coverage of social insurance should be gradually enlarged.

Moreover, China should construct a new urban-rural social relief system and focus on guaranteeing the well-being of low-income people in both areas. It should adjust properly the current distribution of income and actively help the poor families solve practical difficulties in their everyday lives such as going to the hospital, finding housing, and schooling their children. This can be accomplished through such measures as increasing public welfare and transfer payments. These measures will reduce conflicts of interest and keep society stable.

THE MAIN TASKS FACING PUBLIC SERVICE DEVELOPMENT IN CHINA

The main impetus for further reform of governmental departments should be that public service involves a people-orientation and public policies should try to meet the public's basic needs in providing public goods. Since 1992, local government in the United States has progressed to the point where there is a basic rational orientation in the government's basic function. The aim of the administration is to allow the government's entire constituency and its taxpayers to share fairly in the enjoyment of public goods and services. Whether a government can provide people the service and opportunities to develop their own quality of life or not is how the staff is expected to gauge its work for the government.

The basic U.S. administrative system reform called "Reinventing Government" started in the 1980s and, according to U.S. expert Michael Hammer, "reinventing" means a thorough rethinking of the organization process and fundamentally redesigning it in order to bring about major improvements in organization performance. The administrative expert Paul Light of Yale University pointed out in his book *The Reform Trend* that the real meaning of Reinventing Government seems close to but in fact is different than earlier measures such as Administration Reform, Civil Service Reform, Public Service Reform, and Government Reform. The main purpose of Reinventing Government is to "transfer" but not "renew." That is to say, the purpose of "Reinventing Government" is to change the deep-layer construction of government, which government always took for granted, rather than the more superficial step of reshuffling the management of administrative resources. Simply put, "Reinventing Government" is a wholesale change and systematic revolution in government.

THE FINANCIAL SYSTEM OF THE PUBLIC SERVICE

With the economic development and increase of government's financial capability, it is the common practice and experience for every nation to increase its investment in public service. In current times, expenditures on public service have become the main component of expenditures by developed countries' governments. According to the statistics from the World Bank, expenditures by high-income nations on public education accounted for 5.5 percent of GDP, public health 6.6 percent, and social insurance above 25 percent. In 2003, the public subsidies and other social welfare expenditures accounted for 60 percent of the total budgets of central governments in the high-income nations.

The Social Security law enacted by the United States in 1935 was the first nationwide legislation concerning the problems of the old and unemployed in which the government assumed responsibility. After many amendments, the kind of insurance increased, the level of payments increased, and the social insurance system progressed from bad to good. Medical assistance for poor families and children provided by the U.S. government reached 18 billion dollars in 2005 and 19.36 billion dollars this year. There are also other relief programs and plans to help disadvantaged groups, such as the food stamp program and other programs allowing the poor to buy food at low prices or for free.

The U.S. "Employment Training Cooperation Law" has explicitly encouraged states and local governments to cooperate with private institutions to provide intensified education and technological training for the unemployed. Every year the federal government allocates about $7 billion to ensure the smooth implementation of the training plan.

The U.S. federal government has passed a great deal of legislation to assure that buildings are handicap accessible, children with special needs receive educational assistance, and more generally U.S. law strives to take good care of the handicapped with respect to their education, employment, welfare, and well-being. Considering social insurance broadly, private sources account for 57 percent of money provided, national and other official sources provide 35 percent, and state agencies and institutions provide 8 percent. Also, one important source of money is fundraising through charity provided by community and social organizations.

With respect to the final allocation of the burden across the nation, employers and employees have taken on the major part, about 70 percent to 80 percent of the social insurance fund. In the 1990s, the crisis faced by the elderly put heavy financial pressure on the social insurance system. The federal government designed a "trinity" consisting of a compulsory government management system, compulsory private management system, and private voluntary contribution insurance system. The social insurance system is constituted in such a way that private insurance is the foundation and government insurance assists. The individual takes part voluntarily in the form of personal saving, reallocation from other spending, and self-insurance.

A social insurance system has formed which combines governmental and private management, and mixes compulsion and choice. In addition, nonprofit civic organizations, charity groups, and individuals have played key roles in helping disadvantaged groups and have thereby reduced the pressure on government.

COOPERATION BETWEEN CHINA AND THE UNITED STATES

Taking into account each country's domestic situation and its specific stage of economic and social development, the need to study and communicate internationally about the development of the public service sector is important and indeed has become an objective imperative. The foundation for China's development in this area is quite weak. Accordingly, there have been many problems in public service and social development. So China should assure that there is a material foundation for its public service development and we must push development further.

At the same time, China must recognize that the foundation for its public service programs are still weak. Its task is to make a strong effort to modernize its social welfare system, and there still exist many difficulties and problems to solve. China must learn from the advanced experience and beneficial practice of other nations including the United States in order to continuously push the development of its public service programs.

CONCLUSION

There is no doubt that in developed countries the level of economic development is high, investment in the public service is substantial, the level of the public service provision is high, and public service capacity is strong. But developed countries have formed different public service systems with their own characteristics. For example, in the United States the public service system is part of a free market economic system. In Germany, the public service is governed under a social market economic system.

So an important lesson from international experience is that China should proceed based on its own national situation and learn from other nations' advanced experience and beneficial practice according to its own level of development, the social situation, its political and economical system, and its own history and culture.

Furthermore, China should proceed scientifically and construct its own public service system. Concretely speaking, it should speed up the development of the public service financial system in order to reform the way in which investments in the social system are made. It should apply the principle of an open society and respond to the specific requirements of the public service function, changing from a closed administrative system to an open and transparent one.

Finally, China should change its complex and overlapping administrative system into a uniform and focused one. It should simplify public service institutions and aim for a highly efficient form of government. Because the socialization of the public service and industrialization have not been fully completed, the provision of public goods is inefficient. China should "socialize" rather than privatize the provision public service. This will help provide adequate staffing for the public service and increase its quality.

IV
INTERNATIONAL RELATIONS

10

Reciprocity and Adaptation in Post–Cold War U.S.-China Foreign Policy Interactions

Xiaojun Li

Former Chinese ambassador to the United States Li Zhaoxing once commented in a retrospective on his years of service that "U.S.-China relations in the foreseeable future will not become better, nor will it become worse."[1] His view may only represent an experienced diplomat's perspective; nonetheless, scholars and policy analysts from both countries generally agree that Sino-American relations are complex, with the United States and the People's Republic of China (PRC) being neither allies nor enemies.

The end of the Cold War wrapped up twenty years of rapprochement between the two countries that began with Kissinger's historic visit to China and ushered in a period of volatility in Sino-American relations. Following the Chinese authorities' suppression of demonstrators in June 1989, the U.S. government suspended high-level official exchanges, imposed economic sanctions, and enacted a number of laws directed against the PRC. These strains on the bilateral relations were exacerbated in May 1995 when the United States permitted Lee Teng-hui, president of Taiwan, to make a public address at Cornell University. Fearful that such a move would portend a shift of U.S. policy toward Taiwan, Beijing launched a series of military demonstrations in the Taiwan Strait in late 1995 and early 1996 to deter both Taipei and Washington and later to intimidate the Republic of China (ROC) electorate before the pending presidential elections. The United States in turn moved two aircraft carrier battle groups to the seas off Taiwan to illustrate its continuing commitment to the island's security. Many observers regarded this Taiwan Strait Crisis[2] as the lowest point in Sino-U.S. relations and the closest the two countries would come to a direct military confrontation over Taiwan since the 1960s (Harding 1997).

When tensions in the Taiwan Strait diminished, relations between the United States and the PRC began to improve with increased high-level exchanges and progress on numerous bilateral issues. This culminated in President Jiang Zemin's visit to the United States in the fall of 1997 and the agreement to work toward a "constructive strategic partnership." However, this new partnership was soon put to a severe test when NATO bombed the Chinese embassy in Belgrade in May 1999. It was not until the end of 1999 that relations began to gradually improve.

Sino-U.S. relations were again tested when President George W. Bush assumed office. The new administration favored a U.S. security policy in East Asia that regarded China as a "rival" or "competitor" rather than a "partner." Tensions soon rose when Bush tightened the American relation with Taiwan and planned to authorize arms sales to the island. However, the biggest challenge facing the two governments occurred in April 2001. The mid-air collision between a U.S. EP-3 reconnaissance aircraft and a PRC J-8 fighter jet in the South China Sea triggered a sharp confrontation which was only resolved after eleven days of extensive negotiations and two carefully worded letters of apology from the United States.

The terrorist strikes of September 11 and the reordering of American priorities opened a timely opportunity for the two countries to salvage their deteriorating relationship. The two governments have since resumed regular high-level visits and exchanges of officials, cooperated on anti-terror initiatives, and worked closely on the Six Party Summit to restrain and eliminate North Korea's nuclear weapons activities. Despite fitful quarrels over a wide range of issues such as intellectual property, trade, and human rights, a recent Congress Research Service Report described U.S.-China relations during much of the George W. Bush Administration as "smoother than they had been at any time since the Tiananmen Square crackdown in 1989" (Dumbaugh 2008, 1).

What does the history of U.S.-China foreign policy interactions inform us about the future relationship between the most powerful country and the largest and fastest-growing developing country? To what extent do the two countries respond to each other's foreign policy decision-making? Is there any adaptive pattern in the foreign policy behavior between the two countries? These questions are particularly relevant as it is widely acknowledged that the nature and direction of Sino-American relations will be a major factor in determining the peace and security of the East Asian region and even the entire world in the twenty-first century.

In answering these questions, scholars who study foreign policy and Chinese politics have produced impressive research and in-depth case studies on various periods of China-U.S. relations using firsthand materials such as memoirs, speeches, and interviews, as well as declassified government documents pertaining to the formulation and implementation of U.S. policies toward the PRC (see, for instance, Harding 1992; Ross 1998; Kueh and Bridges 2001; Lampton 2001; Myers et al. 2001; A. Goldstein 2005; Hao and Su 2005). This chapter intends to contribute to this large and growing body of literature from a different approach that employs sophisticated statistical techniques to analyze a new and rich dataset on U.S. and China foreign policy interactions. I derive hypotheses from systemic explanations of foreign policy decision-making focusing on the state and domestic levels. I then test reciprocity and other alternative models of foreign policy interactions in a Vector Autoregressive (VAR) intervention model that captures specific shocks in the evolution of U.S.-China relations such as the EP-3 spy plane collision incident.

This study also contributes to the body of scholarly work that uses quantitative events data for foreign policy analysis. Most of the previous studies focus on Cold War interactions between status quo powers, that is, the United States and the Soviet Union (Dixon 1983; J. S. Goldstein 1991; Goldstein and Freeman 1991; McGinnis and Williams 1989; Rajmaira and Ward 1990; Williams and McGinnis 1988). With the end of the Cold War and the decline of Russia, China is now often depicted by policymakers and the media alike as the "emerging power" that would pose the greatest threat to the United States—the only great power in today's world.

Despite the policy salience and relevance of U.S.-China relations today, quantitative work on the foreign policy interactions between the two countries in the post–Cold War era are almost nonexistent. This paper intends to fill this gap by focusing on bilateral events involving China and the United States from 1990 to 2004. The results will shed light on the broader debate in the power transition theory regarding whether today's China should be characterized as an offensive realism/revisionist state or a defensive realism/status quo state and whether U.S. policy toward China is misguided in that regard. The results in general will also provide policy implications for U.S.-China relations in the future.

DATA

Data used for this study are drawn from Virtual Research Associates' (VRA) "10 Million International Dyadic Events" (King and Lowe 2003). These data are machine coded from Reuters News Briefings between 1990 and 2004. Each International Dyadic Event (IDEA) represents an event in the form of "Actor A does something to Actor B," with Actors A and B covering about 450 countries and "does something to" coded in a typology of about 200 types of actions. Examples include *Empathize* ("Express condolences, offer sympathy; includes attending funerals and other similar ceremonial events"), *Denounce* ("Disparage, vilify, defame, denigrate, condemn and name-calling") and *Threaten Military Attack* ("Explicit threat to use armed forces in a military attack or invasion"). Based on the IDEA scheme, actions are then assigned a numerical value according to the Goldstein Cooperation Scale (J. S. Goldstein 1992). This scale weights the IDEA categories according to how cooperative or conflictual they are. Actions are given scores that range from negative 10 (*Military Attack*, which represents extreme conflict) to 8.3 (*Extend Military Assistance*, which indicates extreme cooperation).[3] A total of 6,621 events for both the China-U.S. and U.S.-China dyads are recorded in this dataset.

For each month,[4] VRA generates a cumulative tally of all cooperative actions directed by one country toward the other (i.e., all events with a Goldstein weighting of zero and above), as well as a weighted total of cooperation that is the sum of Goldstein scores for all events coded as cooperative. The same procedure is used with events that are conflict-oriented. Since I am interested in accounting for the relative level of cooperation and conflict between China and the United States, I choose to focus on the weighted totals for both types of actions. In addition, I calculate an aggregate behavior score by subtracting the weighted monthly conflict score from the weighted monthly cooperation score. The result is a continuous variable for both dyads, with positive values representing the intensity of cooperation that increases with value, and negative scores representing the intensity of conflict-oriented actions that increases as values become more negative.

One potential criticism often leveled against the use of event data concerns the biases introduced by relying on one particular media source. I argue that this should not confound the data in this analysis. First, to the extent that event data coded from one country under study may systematically undercount the conflict events emanating from that country, the use of Reuters, a UK-based news agency, should lower the magnitude of this type of bias than the use of either the *New York Times* or the *People's Daily*. Second, the assumption in many of the event-coding schemes is that using one source rather than combining a number of sources is more consistent and the changes in the patterns of interaction will be more evident (Schrodt 1994, 19). Third, Joshua Goldstein (1991) suggests that potential bias in the media is not fatal for analyses of the interactions between states since an undercount of total events would not generally bias the reciprocity coefficient even if the undercount were nonrandom (197). In other words, any potential biases that may be present in a given news source will tend to produce "conservative" and consistent estimates (J. S. Goldstein 1991, 201). This in effect biases against finding a significant effect.

Figure 10.1 shows the time series for both dyads from 1990 to 2004. Several trends are immediately apparent. In both series, there is greater variability in the behavior scores in the post–Cold War era, indicating an in-

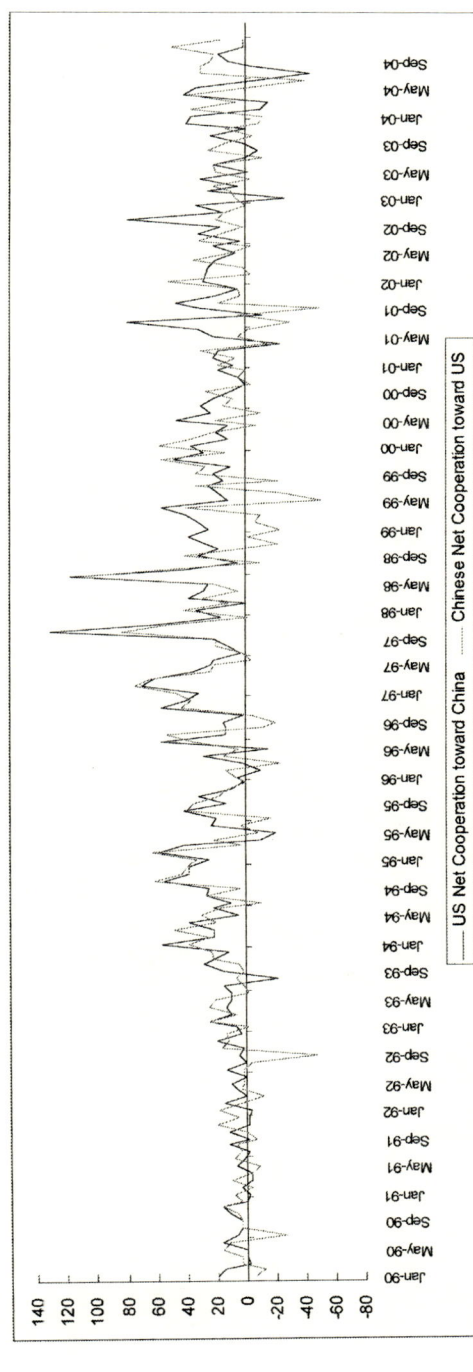

Figure 10.1. U.S.-China Foreign Policy Interactions
Source: Gary King and Will Lowe (2003) "10 Million International Dyadic Events"

creasing amount of volatility in the interactions between the two countries. The spikes in both series in 1997 and 1998 correspond to Jiang Zemin's visit to the United States and President Clinton's visit to China. Conversely, the two biggest dips in the China-U.S. dyad correspond to the bombing of the Chinese embassy in former Yugoslavia in 1999 and the EP-3 spy plane collision incident in 2001.

U.S.-CHINA RELATIONS IN THE POST–COLD WAR WORLD

Given the wide variability in U.S.-China Relations in the post–Cold War years, what explains foreign policy decision-making within the two countries? In the following subsection, I present potential explanations from system-, state-, and domestic-level perspectives and draw on this extant literature to generate *ex ante* expectations about foreign policy decision-making and interactions between the United States and China.

Power-Based Approaches

Approaches in foreign policy analysis based on the structural perspective suggest that a country's foreign policy is formed by its position in the international system and its relative material power capabilities. During the Cold War, U.S.-China relations were part of the larger bipolar competition between Washington and Moscow. U.S. policies toward China were formulated primarily as a counterbalance to Beijing's relationship with Moscow, friendly or hostile. With the end of the Cold War and the collapse of the Soviet Union, the United States became the only superpower in the world system. Since then, the declared objective of U.S. grand strategy has been to consolidate and extend American hegemony in the international system and to prevent the emergence of new great power rivals.[5] It is hardly surprising, therefore, that the increasing economic and political clout of China coupled with the decline of other leading powers has prompted policymakers and scholars in the United States to view China as Washington's next strategic competitor and the biggest threat to U.S. supremacy in world affairs (Bernstein and Munro 1997).

U.S.-China policy in the context of this grand strategy revolves around two major themes: containment and engagement. The containment policy reflects one analytic framework often applied to the evolving bilateral relations in American policy and intellectual circles, namely, the Power Transition Theory. First proposed by A. F. K. Organski, the theory predicts that conflicts and war are most likely to break out when a rising power dissatisfied with the international status quo (the revisionist challenger) catches up with a dominant power in decline—the two World Wars being the prime examples (Organski and Kugler 1980). The reigning power, therefore, needs to retain its power and hedge against any potential adversaries. The idea is rooted in offensive realism which posits that in the anarchic world with no central authority the best way for a state to survive is "to become the most powerful state in the system" (Mearsheimer 2001, 33). In the context of U.S.-China relations, the containment policy requires the use of American military power, and in extreme cases preventative wars, to rein in China's ambitions and compel Beijing to adhere to Washington's rules in issues such as arms control, trade, and human rights.

On the other hand, some scholars argue that peaceful power transitions may also occur when both states are democracies or when the emerging state is satisfied with the status quo (the status quo power) (Tamman et al. 2000; Chan 2008). This argument furnished the theoretical foundation for the engagement policy that suggests that by enmeshing Beijing in the global economy and various multilateral institutional frameworks, China will be socialized, and its rise to great-power status can therefore be managed. This idea is based on the liberal institutional tradition, which holds that, as China's contacts with the outside world grow, its exposure to western political and cultural values will result in evolutionary political change within China, which will in turn reduce the possibility of conflict between the two countries (the democratic peace theory).

It is obvious that the potential clash between the incumbent power and the challenger rests on two premises: the occurrence of a power transition and the challenger's dissatisfaction with the status quo.

The claim that China has become a major global power is little contested today, but the question of if and when China will eventually overtake the United States (i.e., the power transition) is still debated depending on the definition of power and the way power is measured. One study suggests that China's economy will surpass that of the United States in terms of GDP as early as 2015 (Tamman et al. 2000).[6] But economic wealth is only one source of power. When other measures such as military capability, technology, and human capital are considered, China still has a long way to go before catching up with the United States (Chan 2005). In addition, China is currently facing a number of critical domestic issues such as environment degradation and social inequality, which will likely prevent Beijing from engaging in full-scale power building.

To answer the question of whether China is satisfied with the status quo, we need to take into consideration Beijing's priorities regarding domestic prosperity and stability. On the one hand, after thirty years of opening up and marketization, China has been increasingly integrated into the current international system and Beijing has realized the importance of a global free-trade regime for its economic development. To some, Beijing's gradual

	Revisionist China	Status Quo China
Containment	Status quo	Conflict
Engagement	Conflict	Improvement

Figure 10.2. Four Outcomes of U.S.-China Relations

embrace of existing international norms suggests that it is on the right track of a peaceful rise, the ultimate goal of the engagement policy.

On the other hand, Beijing frequently expresses discontent over U.S. intervention in its human rights, weapon proliferation, and sovereignty issues, which it believes would threaten the rule of the central government. These episodes of tension confirm the so-called "China threat theory" in the United States and furnish evidence for calls to contain China's supposed quest for world domination. Nevertheless, barring a more dramatic shift in circumstances (Taiwan's declaration of independence, for instance), Beijing's basic foreign policy line is that economic development is essential to China's rise, and that efforts to foster the peaceful environment necessary for it are the top national priority (A. Goldstein 2005), which is reflected in its view of Sino-U.S. relations as a "strategic partnership."

Depending on the choice of U.S. policy toward China and the nature of China's foreign policy ambition, four potential outcomes in U.S.-China relations are summarized in figure 10.2.

In the scenario of the upper left box, the status quo in U.S.-China relations is preserved when the United States effectively contains Beijing's efforts to seek opportunities to challenge the U.S. position in East Asia. In the scenario of the lower right corner, we are likely to see the improvement of relations with increasing cooperation between the two countries. The off-diagonal columns represent two scenarios in which there is a mismatch between the U.S. and China's foreign policy agendas. Both scenarios will likely lead to instability in the relations between the two countries. U.S. containment policy applied to a status quo China will confirm Beijing's fear of American "hegemonic aspirations" and may lead to further mutual skepticism and an arms buildup. Conversely, U.S. engagement policy applied to a revisionist China will embolden Beijing, which may lead to a military showdown between the two countries over Taiwan.

Bureaucratic Politics Approach

The bureaucratic politics approach to foreign policy analysis is derived from an agency-based perspective. This approach suggests that the bureaucratic processes through which policy is enacted significantly influence states' foreign policy decision-making (Allison 1971). In other words, foreign policy decisions in both countries can be regarded as the product of a series of interagency negotiations within the bureaucracy and represent the convergence and/or compromise among a number of players.

The durability of these foreign policy decisions is a function of the size of the bureaucracy and the number of players whose views will be factored into the final outcome. The democratic nature of the U.S. government suggests that a greater number of actors are involved in the bureaucratic processes of foreign policy decision-making, which in turn constrains the ability of the various negotiators to achieve significant departures from the foreign policy equilibrium. In comparison, foreign policy-making in China is concentrated in a handful of people, making it easier to bargain and renegotiate over part or all of the existing policies.

Domestic Politics Approach

Since the publication of Putnam's (1998) seminal work on the two-level game, a substantial body of literature has examined the interaction between domestic politics and international relations, examining the role of interest groups and domestic institutions (see Gourevitch 2002). In post–Cold War U.S.-China relations, domestic factors in foreign policy-making are especially prominent in U.S. policy toward China (Ross 1998).

The authoritarian nature of China's political system suggests that it gives the public relatively little input into foreign policy-making (Roy 1998). While recent signs suggest that various societal forces have been increasingly active and influential in the formulation of foreign policy, foreign policy decision-making is still highly centralized in China (Hao and Su 2005). In the absence of open and public elections, Chinese leaders only need to maintain the support of key elites or the "selectorate" to remain in office (Shirk 1993; Bueno de Mesquita et al., 1999), and hence have far more latitude in their foreign policy decision-making.

By comparison, the making of U.S. foreign policy is a complex process of contention and struggle between the executive branch and the Congress which is heavily influenced by pluralist interest and lobbying groups (see table 10.1 for a sample of these lobbying groups). Neither a single president nor the Congress alone can determine the course of the country's foreign policy. In a simplistic version, U.S.-China policy-making can be summarized in the flow chart in figure 10.3.

At the decision-making level, while the president and the executive branch still take the central role of drafting the grand picture of U.S. policy toward China, Congress has also been active in airing its opposition to the administration when it sees the president going too far in placating China.

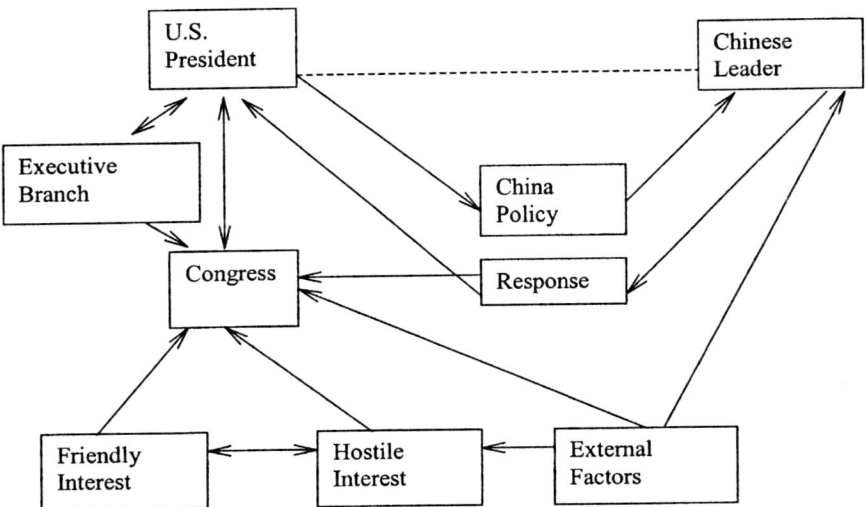

Figure 10.3. Flowchart of U.S.-China Policy-Making

The subsequent policy induces responses from the Chinese government, which in turn result in the reevaluation and reformulation of the policy. At the domestic level, both friendly and hostile interest groups strive to exert their influence on China policy by lobbying Congress. The effects of these groups sometimes cancel each other out. External factors such as the bombing of the embassy often dramatically change the views and preferences of both the interest groups and members of Congress toward China and can alter the subsequent policy-making of the administration in the most unexpected way (e.g., sudden, unprovoked hostility).

RECIPROCITY, ROUTINE, AND RATIONAL EXPECTATION IN FOREIGN POLICY INTERACTION

Three models of interaction can be found in the literature of quantitative foreign policy analyses using events data: the rational expectations model, the reciprocity (action-reaction) model, and the policy inertia (bureaucratic routine) model.

The reciprocity (action-reaction) model assumes that the past actions of a given state condition the current behavior of another state (Dixon 1983; 1986; J. S. Goldstein 1991; Ward 1982). States are presumed to be incapable of forming consistent expectations and/or reliable forecasts of the other state's behavior due to either information asymmetry or the dynamic nature of the relationship between them. Consequently, instead of forming

Table 10.1. Examples of Interest and Lobby Groups Active in the Making of China Policy

Interest/Lobby Groups		Focus	Example
Hostile	Taiwan Lobby	Taiwan independence, international organization membership for Taiwan, arms sale	Taiwan International Alliance
	Tibet Lobby	Tibet independence	Tibet Information Network
	Human Rights	One Child Policy, forced abortion, workers' rights, prisoner labor, etc.	Human Rights Watch, Amnesty International
	Religious Rights	Freedom of religion in China	Family Research Council
	Nonproliferation groups	Concern over China's selling of weapons to unfriendly countries	Carnegie Endowment for International Peace
Friendly	Business Groups	Granting MFN status to China, providing information and guard interests for U.S. companies in China	U.S.-China Business Council, Business Coalition of U.S.-China Trade
Middle-of-the-Way	NGO/Think Tank/Policy Research	Independent research on a variety of issue areas, provide counsel and policy suggestions to the administration	Committee on U.S.-China Relations, U.S.-China Policy Foundation, The Brookings Institute

Source: Adapted from Dumbaugh (2001), appendix.

expectations of the other state's behavior, nature, or intention, a state uses the past behavior of the other state to derive its response toward that other state. This is similar to the *quid pro quo* model in diplomacy hypothesizing that states will respond in kind to hostility or cooperative behavior from the other state. The state's memory of the other actor's past behavior is assumed to be long term (Lebo and Moore, 2003), often operationalized as a finite number of lags. Dixon (1983), for instance, found that "the action-reaction model provides a rather powerful explanation of foreign policy affect [between the United States and the Soviet Union]" (Dixon 1983, 847).

In contrast to the reciprocity model, the rational expectations model posits that actors "respond not to the actual behaviors of other powers but to rational expectations of others' future policies or to departures from these expected policies" (Goldstein and Freeman 1991, 17). In the rational expectations literature, the information environment is assumed to be quite "rich" (Williams and McGinnis 1988, 973). States are assumed to have sufficient information about the other state through previous interactions, and are able to discern norms of behavior, or expectations of the other state's future behavior (Ward 1981, 231). In this model, states have a priori knowledge of the other state's type and thus "will be excellent at predicting its behavior and will only take note of it when it deviates [substantially] from the expected pattern" (Moore 1995, 135). Williams and McGinnis (1988), and later McGinnis and Williams (1989), for instance, found evidence that rational expectations in the interactions of the United States and Soviet Union were a powerful predictor of military expenditures (1988; 1989) and diplomatic hostilities (1989).

The bureaucratic routine model on the other hand is more concerned with the policy inertia of a given state, or its "short term" memory (Ward 1982). Policy inertia is the notion that "countries tend to keep doing the same things that they themselves have been doing in the recent past" (Goldstein and Freeman 1990, 23). According to this model, what determine the state's behavior in the present are its own past behaviors.

It is apparent that while these models all attempt to explain and predict relations among states, the reciprocity and rational expectations models are dynamic in nature, since they both incorporate the notion of strategic interaction among actors. However, the key difference between the two models is how they assume that interactions shape behavior. In contrast, the bureaucratic routine model is static. Despite the differences in the mechanism, the three models are not necessarily mutually exclusive, as evidenced by the results from the previous literature. Goldstein and Freeman (1991) found that a mix of bureaucratic routine and reciprocity offered the best explanation for the trilateral interactions of the superpowers during the Cold War (28). Moore (1995) also found evidence of reciprocity, rational expectations, as well as policy inertia in the interactions between the nationalists and the Rhodesian regime.

Hypotheses and Specifications

The three models in foreign policy behaviors discussed earlier will be tested across a pair of directed dyadic interactions between United States and China from 1990 to 2004 in the following system of equations:

$$Dyad_{US\text{->}China,t} = \alpha_1 + \sum_{i=1}^{m} \beta_{1i} Dyad_{US\text{->}China,t-i} + \sum_{j=1}^{n} \gamma_{1j} Dyad_{China\text{->}US,t-j} + \delta_1 I_t + \epsilon_1 \quad (1)$$

$$Dyad_{China\text{->}US,t} = \alpha_2 + \sum_{i=1}^{m} \beta_{2i} Dyad_{China\text{->}US,t-i} + \sum_{j=1}^{n} \gamma_{2j} Dyad_{US\text{->}China,t-j} + \delta_2 I_t + \epsilon_2 \quad (2)$$

Each directed dyad measures the net cooperation score from one state toward the other at month t. The α's are the constants that represent the level of hostility or cooperation one country would exhibit toward the other in the absence of all three mechanisms of foreign policy interactions. The β's are the magnitude of policy inertia/routine in bureaucratic processes such as standard operating procedures or budget maximization (Lebo and Moore 2003, 15). The γ's are the reciprocity coefficients that measure the extent to which either country's foreign policy behavior varies in response to the contemporaneous or past behaviors of the other country. The I_t is the intervention/impulse response that represent shocks at month t. The two impulse dummies (interventions) included in the model correspond to the U.S.-led NATO bombing of the Chinese embassy in the former Yugoslavia in May 1999 and the other is the EP-3 spy plane collision incident in April 2001. There are three propositions related to equation 2 (similar propositions are true for equation 1 since the two equations are symmetric):

H1: The past behavior of the United States toward China ($Dyad_{US\text{->}China,t-j}$) is correlated with the contemporaneous behavior of China toward the United States in that dyad ($Dyad_{China\text{->}US,t}$).

Hypothesis 1 corresponds to the reciprocity (action-reaction) model. If a reciprocity relationship is borne out by the data, we would expect to see that past behavior by one state would yield a response (either increase or decrease in net cooperation) in the behavior by the other state in the dyad, and vice-versa. For instance, if some or all of γ_{2j} in equation 1 are found to be significantly greater than zero, we could conclude that China is engaging in the norm of tit-for-tat in dealing with the United States. On the other hand, if some or all of γ_{2j} are found to be negative, we could conclude that China responds to increased conflict (cooperation) from the United States with increased cooperation (conflict), exploiting U.S. cooperation and retreating in the face of resistance. Confirmation of the reciprocity model would also offer some evidence that China's foreign policy is not seeking overtly expansionist or revisionist goals (i.e., systematic conflictual behaviors toward the United States).

H2: The past behavior of the United States toward China in the dyad ($Dyad_{US\text{->}China, t-j}$) is not correlated with the contemporaneous behavior of China toward the United States in that dyad ($Dyad_{China\text{->}US, t}$).

Hypothesis 2 speaks to the rational expectation model and is the flip side of hypothesis 1 (i.e., the null hypothesis of hypothesis 1). If the coefficients γ in a given equation are not significantly different from zero ($H2$), then it could be regarded as tentative evidence for the rational expectations model. Given that China is regarded as the next potential threat in the U.S. grand strategy, I expect that the rational expectations model will hold for the U.S. dyad. Confirmation of the model on the Chinese side may also suggest that this emerging power is not satisfied with the status quo and is conducting its foreign policy within the offensive realism paradigm.

H3: The past behavior of China toward the United States in the dyad ($Dyad_{China\text{->}US, t-i}$) will be positively correlated with its contemporaneous behavior toward the United States in the dyad ($Dyad_{China\text{->}US, t}$).

Hypothesis 3 tests the bureaucratic routine model. If this hypothesis is not rejected, we would expect to find significant, positive parameter estimates for the β's, suggesting that a country's contemporaneous foreign policy behavior is positively correlated with its behavior in the previous time periods.

Estimation and Results

Table 10.2 shows the coefficient estimates for the VAR(4) intervention model.[7] In the first lagged period, the reciprocal relationship is evident in China's foreign policy reactions toward the United States. The statistically significant coefficient of 0.174 on the $Cooperation_{US\text{->}China, t-1}$ variable suggests that China reciprocates friendly behavior by the United States with behavior that will on average be about one-fifth as friendly as U.S. behavior. To use a concrete example, if the United States promises material support to China (a Goldstein score of 5.2), China is likely to send a note or meet officials from the United States (a Goldstein score of 1.0) in the following month. Conversely, if the United States threatens China with specific negative nonmilitary sanction (a Goldstein score of -5.8), China is expected to make an informal complaint (a Goldstein score of -1.9) in the following month. Similarly, $Cooperation_{US\text{->}China, t-3}$ is also statistically significant, suggesting that China reciprocates U.S. foreign policy behaviors toward China conducted three months before. In addition, a Granger causality test on the null hypothesis that past U.S. behaviors do not cause Chinese behaviors is rejected. These results, in combination, show that China's foreign policy is defensive-realism oriented and that China is interested in keeping the status quo.

Table 10.2. Estimates from VAR(4) Model on Foreign Policy Reciprocity

	$Cooperation_{China \rightarrow US,t}$	$Cooperation_{US \rightarrow China,t}$
Lagged Endogenous Term		
$Cooperation_{China \rightarrow US, t-1}$	0.206**	0.094
	(0.088)	(0.09)
$Cooperation_{US \rightarrow China, t-1}$	0.174**	0.272**
	(0.086)	(0.088)
$Cooperation_{China \rightarrow US, t-2}$	0.106	0.083
	(0.088)	(0.09)
$Cooperation_{US \rightarrow China, t-2}$	−0.013	0.14*
	(−0.089)	(0.091)
$Cooperation_{China \rightarrow US, t-3}$	0.03	−0.125
	(0.088)	(−0.09)
$Cooperation_{US \rightarrow China, t-3}$	0.259**	0.14*
	(0.089)	(0.091)
$Cooperation_{China \rightarrow US, t-4}$	−0.109	−0.042
	(−0.089)	(−0.09)
$Cooperation_{US \rightarrow China, t-4}$	0.012	0.242
	(−0.088)	(−0.09)
Deterministic Variables		
Embassy	−77.694**	−24.396
	(23.754)	(24.259)
ep3	−28.069	−38.299
	(23.078)	(23.569)

Note: T = 164, Log Likelihood: −1.46e+03, **p<0.05, *p<0.1 two-tailed test
Determinant (Cov): 1.95e+05, Breusch-Godfrey test for autocorrelation: p-value=0.4682, Jacque-Bera Test for normality: p(u1)<0.001, p(u2)<0.001. ARCH-LM test: p(u1)=0.1887, p(u2)=0.5261. VARCHLM test statistic: p-value=0.4375.

On the other hand, U.S. foreign policy behaviors toward China are largely independent of Chinese behaviors. This is also confirmed by the Granger causality test. Cooperative behaviors from China will not in general elicit similar responses from the United States. Nor will hostile behaviors from the Chinese side alone result in a downward spiral in U.S.-China relations.

However, this does not mean that the United States does not reciprocate at all in its foreign policy interactions with China. The test of Granger Causality on the null hypothesis that there is no contemporaneous causality in foreign policy behaviors between China and the United States is rejected at alpha < 0.001 level (with a test statistic of 30.77). This is understandable since both countries should be actively engaged in short-term diplomatic quid-pro-quos—issuing communiqués, informal protests, and so on. Since my data is aggregated at the monthly level, many of these interactions are likely missed. On the other hand, the insignificant coefficients of past Chinese behaviors toward the United States do suggest that the United States is acting according to rational expectations theory, that is, the United States is not updating its belief about China's "type" (a threat is a threat), at least over the immediate time horizon.

The bureaucratic routine hypothesis is also supported by the data. Both countries' contemporaneous foreign policy behaviors are positively correlated with their behavior in the previous time periods. This bureaucratic inertia is more evident on the U.S. side, with its effect spanning over three lag periods. On the Chinese side, effects of past foreign policy behaviors only pertain to the month immediately before the current one.

The two impulse dummy variables perform in the expected direction, although the one corresponding to Chinese behaviors toward the United States after the bombing of the embassy is the only one that is significant at conventional levels. However, this negative response does not persist. Replacing the impulse dummies with longer shifts ranging from six months to four years does not produce any statistically significant results. Combined with the previous results, this indicates that both countries are trying to maintain the status quo in their relationship.

In sum, the results show that all three models are borne out by the data generating process of the bivariate time series. Specifically, China is reciprocating both current and past U.S. behavior toward China, while the United States is only responding to current Chinese behavior toward the United States. This is consistent with the expectation of the power transition theory. As the emerging power, Beijing is wise in responding and reassuring Washington that it has limited goals and peaceful intentions to avoid instigating a premature confrontation with the still-dominant hegemon. This also helps China to further improve its bargaining position as time goes on. On the U.S. side, Washington's policy toward China is formulated in the context of the United States' grand strategy. Cooperative and conflictual behavior from China does not seem to resonate with similar behavior from the United States.

Domestic Politics and U.S.-China Relations

If reciprocity is present in the contemporaneous foreign policy behaviors between China and the U.S., shouldn't it lead to ever-increasing cooperation (or conflict) *in the long run*? Why then do we see ups and downs instead of an upward or downward trend in the history of U.S.-China relations? Most previous studies that found reciprocity in the foreign policy behavior between two or more countries have sidestepped this important question. It is therefore important to make sense of those departures from reciprocity (e.g., unprovoked conflict) that characterizes the pattern often found in those event series.

Reciprocity and Adaptation 209

To understand fully the foreign policy interaction between states, we need to incorporate domestic factors into the equation of foreign policy interaction. In the current case, it is therefore important to recognize the role of Congress and interest groups in the decision-making processes of U.S. China policies.

There is an interesting pattern in U.S. foreign policy toward China since Nixon. During the beginning of his term, the president usually takes a firm stance and seeks to carry out strong policies toward China so as to accommodate the hostile atmosphere accumulated in the Congress at the end of the previous presidency, usually the effect of a combination of domestic and international circumstances. This induces the friendly voice to rise. For during the course of his term, the president gradually realizes the cost of the deteriorating U.S.-China relationship and steps back from the precipice to halt the decline and move in more productive directions. Congress, on the other hand, backed by unfriendly domestic interest groups, now feels that the administration is overreaching or too "engaged" with its "strategic competitor." As a consequence, hostile sentiments become more vocal. The two contending voices can be best illustrated by the friendly and hostile bills put forward in the Congress. Evidence of this tug-of-war between the executive and the legislative branch in the making of the United States' China policy can be found in figure 10.4, which summarizes a content analysis of 787 Congressional bills concerning China from 1973 to 2003.

Interestingly enough, when this zigzag pattern is superimposed on the annual conflict-cooperation score in the event dataset for overlapping years,

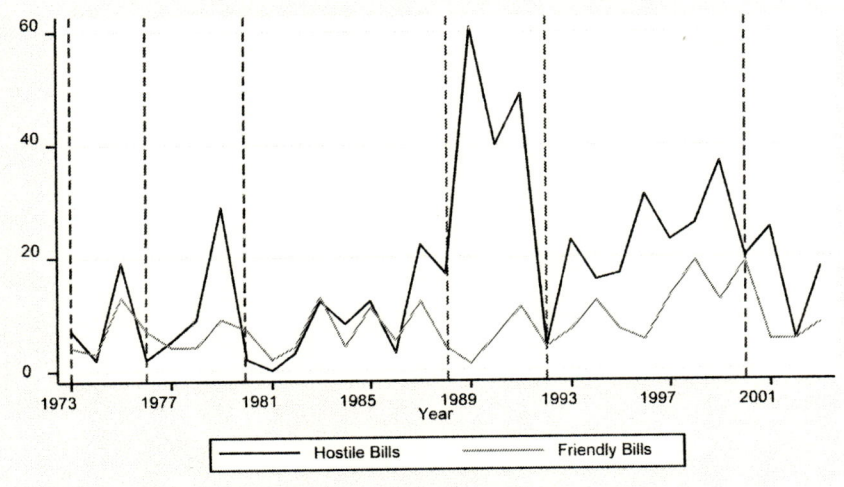

Figure 10.4. Content Analysis of Congressional Bills Concurring China from 1973 to 2003
Note: Data obtained from "Thomas: Legislative Information on the Internet."

a striking similarity emerges (see figure 10.5). The line for U.S. cooperation behavior toward China is almost the exact replica of the line for the friendly bills, only one year apart. The two lines converge after 2001. The line for conflictual behavior behaves the same way as the hostile bill series, except for the year 1991. In both cases, the shift in the number of friendly/hostile bills precede the change in the amount of cooperation and conflict events by approximately twelve months. Clearly, there is a connection.

To test whether this domestic component of foreign policy-making accounts for the turning points in an overall pattern of reciprocity in the foreign policy interaction between the United States and China, it would be ideal if one could measure the strength and activities of all relevant interest and lobbying groups that have a stake in the making of China policy. For the purpose of this paper, however, I propose to use the monthly trade volume between the United States and China as a proxy to represent two of the most powerful domestic interest groups that lobby in Washington—the pro-China, export-competing industries and the protectionist, import-competing industries. There are two reasons for this choice. First, monthly trade data is relatively easy to obtain. Second, the saliency of these industries makes the case a good candidate for a plausible probe.

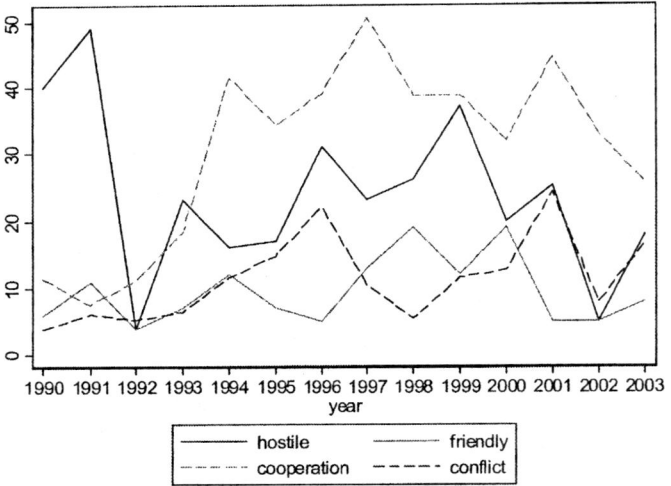

Figure 10.5. U.S. Congress Bills versus Conflict-Cooperation Score
Notes: The conflict and cooperation scores are aggregated from the monthly data.
1. Data obtained from "Thomas: Legislative Information on the Internet" (thomas.loc.gov) at the Library of Congress.
2. A total of 787 bills are analyzed in this study. They include House/Senate Bills, Resolutions, Concurrent Resolutions, Joint Resolutions, and Amendments.
3. Friendly bills are mainly in the economic sphere, including the extension of MFN to China, relaxation of import and export restrictions, and so on. Hostile bills span problems of abortion, human rights, prison labor, Chinese dissidents, nuclear and missile nonproliferation, international broadcasting, Tibet, Taiwan, Hong Kong, espionage, and religious freedom. See appendix for examples of both type of bills.

Two more series—one representing exports from the United States to China and the other from China to the United States—are included in the model. The hypotheses are:

H4a: The increase in $Export_{China->US,lag}$ will reduce $Cooperation_{US->China,t}$, but increase $Cooperation_{China->US,t}$.

H5b: The increase in $Export_{US->China,lag}$ will reduce $Cooperation_{China->US,t}$, but increase $Cooperation_{US->China,t}$.

The increase in exports from China and the ever-expanding trade deficit is a perennial debate on Capitol Hill. Firms and workers that are disadvantaged by increased competition and the inflow of goods from China will lobby the Congress to press for hard-line policies toward China. On the other hand, more exports from the United States to China will lead to more cooperative behavior since export-competing industries have a great stake in keeping the Chinese market open and hence will call for more engagement policies. The same logic holds for the Chinese side, although industries generally have little influence on foreign policy decision-making in China.

Results from table 10.3 suggest that both *H5a* and *H4b* are supported. In particular, a one-standard-deviation increase in imports from China results in a 4.79-point decrease (e.g., demand compliance) in $Cooperation_{US->China,t}$ in the following month and a 4-point increase (e.g., promise of future support) in $Cooperation_{China->US,t}$ in two months. Similarly, a one-standard-deviation increase in exports to China leads to a 4.63-point decrease in $Cooperation_{China->US,t}$. However, none of the twelve lags in $Cooperation_{US->China,t}$ is significant. This may reflect the fact that export-competing industries often face collective action problems when mobilizing due to the diffuse nature of the benefit brought by free trade. Note that both the reciprocity and bureaucratic routine theories are supported by the VAR(12) model. These results are also consistent with the Granger causality test.

Table 10.3. Condensed Results from the VAR(12) Model on Trade and Foreign Policy

	$Cooperation_{China->US,t}$	$Cooperation_{US->China,t}$
$Cooperation_{China->US,lag}$	L1(+), L2(+), L12(-)	L9(+), L12(-)
$Cooperation_{US->China,lag}$	L1(+), L3(+), L6(+), L8 (+)	L4(+), L6(+), L8(+), L9(+)
$Export_{China->US,lag}$	L1(-), L2(-), L3(-), L5(-), L7(-), L10(-)	None
$Export_{US->China,lag}$	L2(+), L4(+), L5(+), L6(+), L9(+), L10(+), L12 (+)	L1(-), L7(-), L11(-)

Note: L(i) denotes the ith lagged value of the endogenous variable. All variables in this table are statistically significant at a <0.01 level. (+) denotes a positive sign for the coefficient and (-) denotes a negative sign. The Export variables are first differenced due to their having a unit root. The other two columns are omitted due to space.

CONCLUSION

The previous analyses provide answers to two general questions regarding U.S.-China relations. Is there is reciprocity in foreign policy interactions between China and the United States? And if so, does such reciprocity lead to cooperation between the two states in the long run? The results of the VAR intervention model confirm that there is in fact strong reciprocity between the two countries in their foreign policy behavior, especially on the Chinese side. This offers some evidence that China's foreign policy is not pursuing overtly expansionist or revisionist strategies.

The second part of the paper shows that reciprocity does not necessarily lead to cooperation (or conflict) in the long run. The pendulous pattern of U.S.-China relations we have seen so far may be largely a function of the preferences and bargaining of domestic political interests, which dictates the turning points in an overall pattern of reciprocity. Curiously, these results suggest that it is often the United States that intentionally or unintentionally gets to determine the future of the relationship between two of the most important countries in world. However, with its foreign policy decision-making increasingly decentralized, China may no longer always be the one who follows suit.

The quantitative analysis also highlights the fact that understanding the impact of domestic factors on U.S. and Chinese foreign policy-making is crucial in the study of U.S.-China relations and the prospects for peace and stability in both East Asia and the world. Future research needs to focus more on the dynamics between domestic politics and foreign policy-making in China, particularly regarding issues such as trade and Taiwan.

U.S.-China relations have never been smooth sailing. Yet both countries have been through enough to tacitly understand the importance of maintaining the current equilibrium. Both should take the initiative to prevent this delicate balance from tipping over to a point of no return. The future is not that gloomy, and we could even entertain a good deal of guarded optimism. The system has proven to be resilient in the past three decades, so it should still work reasonably well in the foreseeable future.

APPENDIX: SELECTED U.S. CONGRESS BILLS CONCERNING CHINA

Friendly Bills

S.1287: A bill to extend diplomatic privileges and immunities to the Liaison Office of the People's Republic of China and to members thereof.

S.3285: A bill to extend most-favored-nation treatment to products of the People's Republic of China.

Reciprocity and Adaptation 213

> H.R.3488: Declares that exports to the People's Republic of China should be subject to no greater restriction under the Export Administration Act than exports to any friendly nonaligned country.
>
> S.2345: Removes the People's Republic of China and Tibet from the list of communist countries that are prohibited from receiving foreign assistance funds.
>
> H.RES.510: Providing for further consideration of the bill (H.R. 4444) to authorize extension of nondiscriminatory treatment (normal trade relations treatment) to the People's Republic of China.
>
> H.R.577: To encourage the People's Republic of China to join the World Trade Organization by removing China from Title IV of the Trade Act of 1974 upon its accession to the World Trade Organization.
>
> H.R.4444: To authorize extension of nondiscriminatory treatment (normal trade relations treatment) to the People's Republic of China, and to establish a framework for relations between the United States and the People's Republic of China.
>
> S.2522: To make available certain environmental assistance funds for the People's Republic of China.
>
> H.CON.RES.365: Recognizing the thirtieth anniversary of the historic visit of President Richard Nixon to China, and commending President George W. Bush for his effort to continue to advance a political, cultural, and economic relationship between the United States and China.

Hostile Bills

> H.CON.RES.16: Concurrent resolution providing for continued close relations with the Republic of China.
>
> H.J.RES.652: A joint resolution to prohibit the proposed export to the People's Republic of China of commercial communications satellites.
>
> S.CON.RES.73: A concurrent resolution calling on the president to place the Chinese human rights situation on the agenda of the UN Commission on Human Rights.
>
> H.J.RES.578: Disapproving the extension of nondiscriminatory treatment (most-favored-nation [MFN] treatment) to the products of the People's Republic of China.
>
> H.R.2759: To condition the extension of nondiscriminatory (MFN) treatment to China in 1992 upon the determination that the government of that country does not support or administer programs of coercive abortion or involuntary sterilization.
>
> S.1366: A bill to prohibit the entry into the United States of items produced, grown, or manufactured in the People's Republic of China with the use of forced labor.

H.CON.RES.148: Relating to the Republic of China on Taiwan's participation in the United Nations.

H.RES.188: To express the sense of the House of Representatives that the Olympics in the year 2000 should not be held in Beijing or elsewhere in the People's Republic of China.

H.CON.RES.33: Expressing the sense of the Congress regarding a private visit by President Lee Teng-hui of the Republic of China on Taiwan to the United States.

H.RES.347: Expressing the sense of the House of Representatives concerning the human rights situation in China and Tibet and encouraging the United States to sponsor and press for the enactment of a resolution condemning the human rights situation in China and Tibet at the annual meeting of the United Nations Commission on Human Rights.

S.AMDT.5062: To state the sense of the Senate on the delivery by the People's Republic of China of cruise missiles to Iran.

H.R.2611: Concerning democracy and human rights in the People's Republic of China and Tibet.

H.R.2613: To suspend most-favored-nation treatment for the products of the People's Republic of China and to suspend further operations by the Overseas Private Investment Corporation (OPIC) in the People's Republic of China until that country recognizes and protects fundamental human rights.

NOTES

1. The comment was made in an address to the faculty and students of the Foreign Affairs College before he became the minister of Foreign Affairs in 2003.

2. This is the fourth of five Taiwan Strait crises since the early 1950s.

3. For a full discussion of the weighting scheme, see Joshua Goldstein (1992). There has been some criticism of the weighting scale, as it was generated by a panel of five assistant professors, two associate professors, and one full professor at the School of International Relations at the University of Southern California. Still, the scale is the most widely accepted weighting scale in the events data literature.

4. Earlier work (e.g., Goldstein 1991) uses weekly or even daily events. However, the VRA dataset is only available in monthly intervals.

5. See, for instance, the Pentagon's *Defense Planning Guidance (DPG)* for Fiscal Years 1994–1999, which stated that "[the United States] must maintain the mechanisms for deterring potential competitors from even aspiring to a larger regional or global role."

6. Even then, the per capita GDP of China will still be about one fifth of that of the United States.

7. The VAR(4) model is the preferred model by the HC criterion. AIC suggests VAR(8) and SB suggests VAR(1). Both of these alternative models plus a handful of others were tried, all yielding similar results, at least in the first lag period.

REFERENCES

Allison, Graham T. 1971. *Essence of Decision: Explaining the Cuban Missile Crisis.* Boston: Little, Brown and Company.
Bernstein, Richard, and Ross H. Munro. 1997. "The Coming Conflict with America." *Foreign Affairs* 76 (2): 18–32.
Bueno de Mesquita, Bruce, James D. Morrow, Randolph M. Siverson, and Alastair Smith. 1999. "An Institutional Explanation of the Democratic Peace." *American Political Science Review* 93 (4): 791–807.
Chan, Steve. 2004. "Exploring Some Puzzles in Power-Transition Theory: Some Implications for Sino-American Relations." *Security Studies* 13 (3): 103–41.
———. 2005. "Is There a Power Transition between the U.S. and China? The Different Faces of Power." *Asian Survey* 45 (5): 687–701.
———. 2008. *China, the U.S., and the Power-Transition Theory.* New York: Routledge.
Christensen, Thomas J. 2001. "Posing Problems without Catching Up: China's Rise and Challenges for U.S. Security Policy." *International Security* 25 (4): 5–40.
Dixon, William J. 1983. "Measuring Interstate Affect." *American Journal of Political Science* 27:828–51.
———. 1986. "Reciprocity in United States–Soviet Relations: Multiple Symmetry or Issue Linkage?" *American Journal of Political Science* 30 (2): 421–45.
Dumbaugh, Kerry. 2001. "Interest Groups: Growing Influence." In *Making China Policy: Lessons from the Bush and Clinton Administrations,* ed. Ramon H. Myers, Michel C. Oksenberg, and David Shambaugh. Lanham, MD: Rowman & Littlefield.
———. 2008. *China-U.S. Relations: Current Issues and Implications for U.S. Policy.* CRS Report for Congress, March 17. Washington, DC: Congressional Research Service.
Goldstein, Avery. 2005. *Rising to the Challenge: China's Grand Strategy and International Security.* Stanford, CA: Stanford University Press.
Goldstein, Joshua S. 1991. "Reciprocity in Superpower Relations: An Empirical Analysis." *International Studies Quarterly* 35 (2): 195–209.
———. 1992. "A Conflict-Cooperation Scale for WEIS Events Data." *Journal of Conflict Resolution* 36 (2): 369–85.
Goldstein, Joshua S., and John R. Freeman. 1990. *Three-Way Street: Strategic Reciprocity in World Politics.* Chicago: University of Chicago Press.
———. 1991. "U.S.-Soviet-Chinese Relations: Routine, Reciprocity, or Rational Expectations?" *American Political Science Review* 85 (1): 17–35.
Goldstein, Joshua S., and Jon C. Pevehouse. 1997. "Reciprocity, Bullying, and International Cooperation: Time-series Analysis of the Bosnia Conflict." *American Political Science Review* 91 (3): 515–29.
Gourevitch, Peter. 2002. "Domestic Politics and International Relations." In *Handbook of International Relations,* ed. Walter Carlsnaes, Thomas Risse, and Beth A. Simmons. Thousand Oaks, CA: Sage Publications.
Hao, Yufan, and Lin Su, eds. 2005. *China's Foreign Policy Making: Societal Force and Chinese American Policy.* Ashgate, UK: Ashgate Publishing.
Harding, Harry. 1992. *A Fragile Relationship: The United States and China since 1972.* Washington, DC: The Brookings Institution.

———. 1997. "U.S.-China Relations, 1995–97: From Crisis to Hope to Uncertainty." In *The Political Economy of Sino-American Relations: A Greater China Perspective*, ed. Y. Y. Kueh and Brian Bridges. Hong Kong: Hong Kong University Press.

Johnston, Alastair Iain Johnston. 2003. "Is China a Status Quo Power?" *International Security* 27 (4): 57–85.

King, Gary, and Will Lowe. 2003. "10 Million International Dyadic Events." Murray Research Archive.

Kueh, Y. Y., and Brian Bridges. 2001. *The Political Economy of Sino-American Relations: A Greater China Perspective*. Hong Kong: Hong Kong University Press.

Lampton, David M. 2001. *The Making of Chinese Foreign and Security Policy in the Era of Reform, 1978–2000*. Stanford, CA: Stanford University Press.

Lebo, Matthew J., and Will H. Moore. 2003. "Dynamic Foreign Policy Behavior." *Journal of Conflict Resolution* 47 (1): 13–32.

Luetkepohl, Helmut, ed. 2004. *Applied Time Series Econometrics*. West Nyack, NY: Cambridge University Press.

McGinnis, Michael D., and John T. Williams. 1989. "Change and Stability in Superpower Rivalry." *American Political Science Review* 83 (4): 1101–23.

Mearsheimer, John. 2001. *The Tragedy of Great Power Politics*. New York: W. W. Norton.

Moore, Will H. 1995. "Action-Reaction or Rational Expectations?: Reciprocity and the Domestic-International Conflict Nexus During the 'Rhodesia Problem.'" *Journal of Conflict Resolution* 39 (1): 129–67.

Myers, Ramon H., Michel C. Oksenberg, and David Shambaugh. 2001. *Making China Policy: Lessons from the Bush and Clinton Administrations*. Lanham, MD: Rowman & Littlefield.

Organski, A. F. K., and Jacek Kugler. 1980. *The War Ledger*. Chicago: University of Chicago Press.

Putnam, Robert. 1998. "Diplomacy and Domestic Politics: The Logic of Two-Level Games." *International Organization* 42 (3): 427–60.

Rajmaira, Sheen, and Michael D. Ward. 1990. "Evolving Foreign Policy Norms: Reciprocity in the Superpower Triad." *International Studies Quarterly* 34:457–75.

Ross, Robert S. 1997. "Beijing as a Conservative Power." *Foreign Affairs* 76 (2): 33–44.

———. 1998. *After the Cold War: Domestic Factors and U.S.-China Relations*. Armonk, NY: M. E. Sharpe.

Roy, Denny. 1994. "Hegemon on the Horizon? China's Threat to East Asian Security." *International Security* 19 (1): 149–68.

———. 1998. *China's Foreign Relations*. Lanham, MD: Rowman & Littlefield.

Schrodt, Philip A. 1994. "Event Data in Foreign Policy Analysis." In *Foreign Policy Analysis: Continuity and Change*, ed. Laura Neack, Jeanne A. K. Hey, and Patrick J. Haney. New York: Prentice-Hall.

Shirk, Susan L. 1993. *The Political Economy of Economic Reform in China*. Berkeley: University of California Press.

Tammen, Ronald, Jacek Kugler, Douglas Lemke, Allan Stam, Mark Abdollahian, Carole Alsharabati, Brian Efird, and A. F. K. Organski. 2000. *Power Transitions*. New York: Chatham House.

U.S. Census Bureau. 2008. "Trade in Goods (Imports, Exports and Trade Balance) with China." Foreign Trade Division, Data Dissemination Branch, Washington, DC. www.census.gov/foreign-trade/balance/c5700.html. Accessed March 23, 2008.

Wang, Jisi, and Wang Yong. 2001. "A Chinese Account: the Interaction of Policies." In *Making China Policy: Lessons from the Bush and Clinton Administrations*, ed. Ramon H. Myers, Michel C. Oksenberg, and David Shambaugh. Lanham, MD: Rowman & Littlefield.

Ward, Michael D. 1981. "Seasonality, Reaction, Expectation, Adaptation, and Memory in Cooperative and Conflictual Foreign Policy Behavior: A Research Note." *International Interactions* 8:229–45.

———. 1982. "Cooperation and Conflict in Foreign Policy Behavior." *International Studies Quarterly* 26:87–126.

Ward, Michael D., and Sheen Rajmaira. 1992. "Reciprocity and Norms in U.S.-Soviet Foreign Policy." *Journal of Conflict Resolution* 36 (2): 342–68.

Williams, John T., and Michael D. McGinnis. 1988. "Sophisticated Reaction in the U.S.-Soviet Arms Race: Evidence of Rational Expectations." *American Journal of Political Science* 32 (4): 968–95.

Index

Acemoglu, Daron, xiii–xiv, 7–10, 17, 18–20, 23–24
Ackerly, Brooke, 78
Action-Reaction Model. *See* Reciprocity Model
Adsera, Alicia, 154
Ainsworth, Scott, xiii, xvii–xviii
American Bar Association, 108
American Civil Liberties Union, 113
American Medical Association, 148–49
Ames, Roger, 74, 76, 86–89

Bao Jia system, 51
Becker, Gary, xvii
Bell, Daniel, 78
Berry, Jeffrey M., 158n4
Boix, Carles, 10, 20, 28n24, 154
bureaucracy, 138, 152–53. *See also* information
Bureaucratic Politics Approach, 200–201
Bureaucratic Routine Model. *See* Policy Inertia Model
Bush, George W., 184, 194

Cai, Yongshun, 152–53
Capitalism and Freedom. See Friedman, Milton

Chen, Xingbo, xviii
Chiang, Kai-shek, 100, 101
China: accession to World Intellectual Property Organization, 124, 125; administration by law, 38–39, 48; administrative decision making, 39–40; administrative oversight, 41–42; administrative reform and other countries, 48–49; agricultural rents, 6; American political thought and, xv; American values and, xv; bureaucracy in, 6; civil service, 44, 46; commune system, 51, 53, 56, 58, 149–50; Confucian thought, xv, 74–75, 77–78, 99–100, 114; constitution of, 52, 57, 97, 103–4, 106; courts, 106; *dadui*, 53; Daoism in, xv, 74–75; democracy and liberal democracy, 74; democratization in, xiv, 14; dual price system, 153; economic liberalization in, 14; elections in, xii, 16; environmental problems, 163–64; environmental protection in, xviii, 156–57, 166–67; foreign policy, 49–50; freedom of speech in, 112–13; *gong jia*, 149, 150; *guanxi*, xvii, 141, 156; *hukou*, 114;

and human rights, 98; inequality in, 18; intellectual property protection, xvi; intellectuals and democracy in, 3; and interest groups, xvii–xviii, 25; internal migration, 155; Internet in, 18, 48, 114–15, 156; invasions of, 4; judges in, 110–12; judicial independence in, 106; *kuai*, xvii, 141; Kuomintang, 101; labor rights, 113–14; landowners in, 6; land tenancy, 5; law, 14–15; Legalism, xv, 75; legislation, 105; Marxist thought, xv, 145; middle class, 29n33; ministries, 38; participatory versus representative democracy, 64–65; peasant fertility decisions, 6; peasants in, 6; philosophy, xv; political legitimacy, 157; property rights in, 14; protests in, xiii; public finance, 43–44; public management, 42–43; public security, 19; public service history, 180–81; *qingshi*, 110, 111; reform and opening, 35, 122, 179; residents' assemblies, 60–61; residents' committees, xii, xiv; residents' committees and the state, 62, 68n7; revolts in, 7; rule of law and, xv–xvi; service orientation, xiv; State Council, xiv, 35–36, 115; state-owned enterprises, 15; and Taiwan, 50, 193, 200, 212; and the Three Changes, 163; and the Three Represents, 21, 104; *tiao*, xvii, 141; and the United Nations, 50, 166, 171–72; and the United States, ix–x, xii, xiv, xvii, 25–26; and the United States and intellectual property protection, 126–28; and United States environmental cooperation, 172–74, 176–77; versus United States environmental policy, 175–76; versus United States funding of public service, 185–87; versus United States public service, 184–85; and the U.S.S.R., 28n17, 101; village committees, xii, xiv;

villagers' assemblies, 60; water pollution, 161–62; and western philosophy, xv
China Law Society, 149
China threat theory, 200
Chinese Communist Party, 98, 101
Chow, David C. K., 100
Clinton, Bill, 131, 198
Cultural Revolution, 12, 13, 28n15, 55, 97, 101–2, 103

Dahl, Robert, 158nn6–7
danwei system, 51, 54, 55, 56, 58
DeLay, Tom, 107
democracy: American founders' analysis, 4; and famine, 27n13; values-based explanations for, 4, 10–11, 27n3, 74
democratic peace theory, 199
democratization, 9–10, 18; and economic growth, 29n35; and income, 17–18; and industrialization, 20; and inequality, 19, 28n24; and middle class, 20–23; redistribution in, 9–10
Deng, Xiaoping, xvi, 14, 50, 97, 104
dictatorships, and commitment, 8–9
domestic politics approach, 201–2
Dworkin, Ronald, 75–76

Ecological Functions Districts, 162
Economic Origins of Dictatorship and Democracy. See Acemoglu, Daron
elections, 138

Fan, Wen, xi, xiv
freedom, 81–82
Freeman, John R., 204
freerider problem, 146–48, 150
Friedman, Milton, xii

Gil, Ricard, 25, 157
Gilley, Bruce, 23
Goldstein, Joshua, 196, 204, 214nn3–4
Goldstein Cooperation Scale, 196, 207
Goldstein Score. *See* Goldstein Cooperation Scale

government-organized nongovernmental organizations, 149
Grafstein, Robert, xi, xii–xiii, xiv, 26
Granger causality, 206, 207
Great Leap Forward, 12–13, 14, 27n12, 55, 103, 145, 149–50

Hall, David, 74, 76, 86–89
Hamilton, Alexander, 106–7
Hammer, Michael, 187
Hand, Keith J., 114
Hardin, Russell, 27n11
Helms, Jesse, 108
Hobbes, Thomas, 76
Hsun, Tzu, 157
Hu, Jintao, 24, 50
Hughes, Charles Evans, 112

IDEA. *See* International Dyadic Event
information: bureaucracies and, 152; elections and public opinion and, 154; groups and, 152–53; markets and, 153–54
information aggregation, 138, 151–55
International Dyadic Event, 195–96

Jiang, Zemin, 14, 21, 50, 104, 194, 198

Kapust, Daniel J., xv
Kissinger, Henry, 193
Kong, Qingtang, xvi

law, 84–85
Lee, Teng-hui, 193
Li, Ruoxi, xiii, xvii–xviii, 26
Li, Xiaojun, xix
Li, Zhaoxing, 193
Light, Paul, 187
Lucas, Robert E., 5
Lysenko, Trofim, 144–45

Maltese, John, xv
Mao, Zedong, 12, 13, 49–50, 97, 101, 102, 144–45; Hundred Flowers Campaign, 101, 144
Marbury v. Madison, 105

Martin v. Hunter's Lessee, 105
Marx, Karl, 22
Mencius, 157
Mertha, Andrew, 157
minben, 77
Moore, Barrington, 5
Moore, Will H., 205
Mulligan, Casey B., 25, 26, 157

Nationalist Revolution, 12
National People's Congress, xvi, 52, 105, 106, 115, 164
National People's Congress Standing Committee, 115
National School of Public Administration, x, xiv
NATO. *See* North Atlantic Treaty Organization
Natural Law, 100
Naughton, Barry, 5
Near v. Minnesota, 112
New York Times, 196
Nixon, Richard, 209, 213
nongovernmental organizations, 149, 169
North Atlantic Treaty Organization, 194

O'Connor, Sandra Day, 108
Olson, Mancur, 12, 146–48
Organic Law of Urban Residents' Committee, 59
Organic Law of Villagers' Committees, 58–59, 60
Organization for Economic Cooperation and Development, 170–71
Organski, A. F. K., 198–99

Paine, Thomas, 103–4
Payne, Mark, 154
Peerenboom, Randall, 109–10
People's Daily, 196
Pie, Lucian, 74
pluralism, 139–43; criticism of, 143–44
Policy Inertia Model, 202–6, 208
Power Transition Theory, 198

private goods, 146–47, 150
Przeworski, Adam, 10–11, 17, 27n10
public goods, 146–48, 150

Qin Dynasty, 11
Qing Dynasty, 7, 12, 100

Randt, Clark, 131
Rational Expectations Model, 202–6
rationalism, 74
Rawls, John, 76, 79
Reciprocity Model, 202–6, 208
revolution, 8
Roberts, John, 108
Robinson, James A., xiii–xiv, 7–10, 17, 18–20, 23–24
Roosevelt, Franklin, 108, 182

Sala-i-Martin, Xavier, 25, 26, 157
Schattschneider, E. E., 143–44, 158n8
selectorate, 21, 23, 201
Shan, Ningzhen, xviii
Shapiro, Martin, 98
shared attitudes, 140–41
Shirk, Susan L., 28n17
Sino-U.S. relations, xix
social security, 26
spontaneous order, 82–84
Sun, Zhigang, 114–15

Taiwan Strait Crisis, 193–94
tax incidence, 6
Third Plenum of the Eleventh Party Congress, 103
Tiananmen Square, 194
Tocqueville, Alexis de, 75

Truman, David B., 139–40, 146, 158n3

United States: Constitution, 101, 112; export-competing industries in, 210–11; federalism in, xvii; import-competing industries in, 210–11; judicial independence, 106–8; judicial review, 105; labor and trade groups, 148; lobbying groups, 201–2; president, 175, 201, 209; public service in, 182–84; Reinventing Government, 187–88; Social Security, 188
U.S. Environmental Protection Agency, 175–76

VAR. *See* Vector Autoregression
Vector Autoregression, 195, 205–7, 211, 214n7
Virtual Research Associates, 195–96, 214n4
VRA. *See* Virtual Research Associates

Walker, Jack L., 158n9
Wang, Jianfeng, xi, xiv–xv
Weingast, Barry, 27n11
Wen, Jiabao, 40, 117n16, 163
Wong, David, 77
World Trade Organization, xii, 98
wuwei, 73, 87, 90
wuyu, 87

Yuan, Shikai, 12

Zhou, Shengxian, 163, 167

About the Contributors

Scott H. Ainsworth is an associate professor of political science at the University of Georgia. He received his Ph.D. from Washington University in St. Louis and specializes in the study of lobbying and special interest politics. He is the author of *Analyzing Interest Groups* (Norton) and has published in numerous journals including *American Journal of Political Science, Journal of Politics*, and *Legislative Studies Quarterly*.

Chen Xingbo graduated with a Ph.D. in sociology from Tsinghua University. He is now an assistant professor in China's National School of Administration. He is in charge of training the leading civil servants of the government. His research covers public policy-making and social development.

Fan Wen received his Ph.D. from Beijing University and is currently a professor of politics and philosophy at China's National School of Administration. He is the author of several books about political philosophy and coauthor of *Deng Xiaoping* and *Modern China & World*.

Robert Grafstein is a professor in the Department of Political Science at the University of Georgia where he directs the university's China Study Abroad Program. He received his Ph.D. from the University of Chicago and specializes in political economy. He is the author of *Institutional Realism* and *Choice-Free Rationality*. Grafstein has published numerous articles in journals such as *American Political Science Review, American Journal of Political Science*, and *Journal of Politics*. He has lectured widely, including in China and Japan.

Daniel Kapust is an assistant professor of political science at the University of Georgia. He received his Ph.D. from the University of Wisconsin and specializes in the study of political philosophy, publishing several articles concerning the history of political thought.

Qingtang Kong received a master's degree in political science at Beijing Administrative College, directs the law office at Beijing City Construction Company, and is a research fellow at the School of Law at Beijing University. He is the author of numerous publications on legal issues surrounding property development.

Ruoxi Li is a graduate student in political science at the University of Georgia. She is specializing in the study of American politics with a minor in Asian politics.

Xiaojun Li is a doctoral student at Stanford University specializing in Chinese politics and international relations. He also holds master's degrees in political science and statistics.

John Anthony Maltese is the Albert Berry Saye Professor of Political Science at the University of Georgia and specializes in the study of law and constitutions. He received his Ph.D. from Johns Hopkins University.

Shan Ningzhen is a master's student at Beijing Administrative College and served as the assistant director of the Daning Environmental Protection Bureau in Shanxi, China. She has written on the construction of an environment-friendly society and eco-politics.

Jianfeng Wang is the director of the China Governance and Development Program at the University of Georgia. He received his Ph.D. in political science at the University of Eastern Michigan and specializes in the study of local and community government, focusing particularly on China.